Women and Politics in the Third World

Women and Politics in the Third World provides a feminist analytical perspective on the specific forms of resistance, organisation and negotiation by women in Third World states.

Using case studies the book focuses on difference as a theoretical basis for investigating feminine political activism. Arguing that Western analysts have attributed weakness to terms such as motherhood, marriage and domesticity as choices made by non-Western women, they show that such strategies are used by women to pursue particular goals such as seeking resources, welfare or freedom from oppression for their children. These strategies, the book suggests, should not be classified as unimportant or temporary; they can be highly effective even within such discourses as Islamic fundamentalism.

The contributors to this volume have embarked on an innovative path which highlights differing political approaches in regions as diverse as Latin America, South East Asia, China and the Middle East. It will provide a real insight for students wishing to understand the diversities and complexities of women's political participation in these areas.

Haleh Afshar teaches Politics and Women's Studies at the University of York and Islamic Law at the Faculté Internationale de Droit Comparé at Strasbourg. She was born and raised in Iran where she worked as a journalist and a civil servant before the revolution. She remains active in feminist Iranian politics and has written extensively on the subject.

Women and Politics
Edited by Haleh Afshar and Mary Maynard
University of York, UK

Series advisers:
Kum-Kum Bhavnani, *University of California, Santa Barbara*
Haideh Moghissi, *Queen's University, Kingston, Canada*
Afsaneh Najmabadi, *Harvard University*
Pippa Norris, *Harvard University*

This new series will present exciting and accessible books covering both the formal public domain of politics and the informal and practical strategies and organisations that women throughout the world use to obtain rights, to meet their needs and to improve their situation in life. The series will combine theoretical and empirical work, revealing how and why the political experience of women has been neglected, and contributing to the ongoing reconceptualisation of the political.

Also in this series:

No More Heroines? Russia, Women and the Market
Sue Bridger, Rebecca Kay and Kathryn Pinnick

Women and Politics in the Third World

Edited by Haleh Afshar

London and New York

First published 1996
by Routledge
11 New Fetter Lane, London EC4P 4EE

Simultaneously published in the USA and Canada
by Routledge
29 West 35th Street, New York, NY 10001

Typeset in Baskerville by
Florencetype Ltd, Stoodleigh, Devon
Printed and Bound in Great Britain by
Clay Ltd, St Ives plc

British Library Cataloguing in Publication Data
A catalogue record for this book is available from the British
Library

Library of Congress Cataloguing in Publication Data
Women and politics in the Third World / edited by Haleh Afshar.
     p. cm. – (Women in politics)
   Includes bibliographical references and index.
     1. Women in politics – Developing countries. I. Afshar, Haleh,
1944– . II. Series.
HO1236.5.D44W665   1996
305.42′09172′4 – dc20
                                                              95–34526
                                                              CIP

ISBN   0–415–13853–1 (hbk)
ISBN   0–415–13861–2 (pbk)

Contents

Notes on contributors

Haleh Afshar teaches Politics and Women's Studies at the University of York and Islamic Law at the Faculté Internationale de Droit Comparé at Strasbourg. She was born and raised in Iran where she worked as a journalist and a civil servant before the revolution. She is the joint convenor of the Development Studies Association's Women and Development Study Group and has edited several books produced by this group; the most recent include *Women in the Middle East* (Basingstoke: Macmillan, 1994); and, jointly edited with Mary Maynard, *The Dynamics of Race and Gender* (London: Taylor & Francis, 1994). Haleh Afshar is also the convenor of the Political Studies Association's Women's group. She remains active in feminist Iranian politics and has written extensively on the subject.

Delia Davin teaches Chinese Studies in the Department of East Asian Studies at the University of Leeds. She lived in China for several years and is still a frequent visitor to the country. She has written extensively on women, gender issues and population policy in China. Her books include *Woman-work: Women and the Party in Revolutionary China* (Oxford: Clarendon, 1976), *China's One-Child Family Policy*, edited with Elizabeth Croll and Penny Kane (London: Macmillan, 1985) and *Chinese Lives: An Oral History of Contemporary China*, edited with W. J. F. Jenner (Harmondsworth: Penguin, 1989).

Kathy Glavanis-Grantham teaches Sociology at University College Cork in Ireland. She previously taught in the Department of Sociology and Anthropology at Birzeit University, Palestine, from 1982 to 1991. During this time she participated in several development and research projects in both the West Bank and the Gaza Strip, a number of which involved working with Palestinian women's groups. She has also carried out research on the small peasant household in Egypt. Her research interests focus on issues of agrarian change and gender-related topics, in particular women's role in national liberation movements, with special reference to the Middle East. Her publications include a co-edited volume *The Rural Middle East* (London: Zed, 1990).

Rohini Hensman is a researcher and writer who has been active in the women's movement and trade union movement. Although now settled in Bombay, she is originally from Sri Lanka, where she spent her childhood. She has written several articles, especially on women and work, and co-authored two books, *My Life is One Long Struggle: Women, Work, Organisation and Struggle* (Belgaum, India: Prathishabd, 1982) and *Beyond Multinationalism: Management Policy and Bargaining Relationships in International Companies* (New Delhi: Sage, 1990). Her most recent publications are *To do Something Beautiful* (London: Sheba, 1990) and *Journey Without a Destination: Is There a Solution to the Problem of Sri Lankan Refugees?* (London: Refugee Council, 1993).

Maria Holt has a BA in Political Science and Middle East and Islamic Studies from the University of Toronto, and an MA in Middle East Politics from the University of Exeter. Her main areas of interest are in Islam, the Palestinian–Israeli conflict, Middle Eastern women and the situation in Lebanon. She has written many articles and book reviews for a variety of periodicals specialising in the Middle East. She has been working for the Council for the Advancement of Arab–British Understanding since 1991.

Ziba Mir-Hosseini obtained her first degree in Sociology from Tehran University and her PhD in Social Anthropology from the University of Cambridge, where she is a research associate. She also works as a freelance consultant on gender and development. She has done extensive fieldwork in rural and urban Iran as well as in urban Morocco, and is the author of *Marriage on Trial: A Study of Islamic Family Law in Iran and Morocco* (London: Tauris, 1993) and a forthcoming monograph on the Ahl-e Haqq sect of Kurdistan.

Aiping Mu is a researcher in the School of Humanities and Social Sciences, University of Glamorgan. Her previous education includes a Bachelor degree in Medicine (Third Army Medical University of China), a Diploma in Chinese (Beijing Open University) and a Master's degree in Population Policies and Programmes (Sir David Owen Population Centre, University of Cardiff). Born and raised in Beijing, she worked as an agricultural worker, Peking opera singer, medical orderly and later as an obstetrician and gynaecologist in China. From 1984 to 1988, she was a national Co-ordinator of Family Planning Education Programme for the State Family Planning Commission in Beijing. Her recent research has involved women's fertility behaviour in the context of social policies in China.

Donna Pankhurst is a lecturer in the Department of Peace Studies at Bradford University. She has researched in Southern and Eastern Africa on issues of gender, the politics of land and the transition to democracy.

Jenny Pearce is a lecturer in the Department of Peace Studies, University of Bradford. She is the author of *Under the Eagle: US Intervention in Central America and the Caribbean* (London: Latin America Bureau, 1982), *Promised Land, Peasant Rebellion in Chalatenango, El Salvador* (London: Latin America Bureau, 1990) and various other co-authored books on issues of politics, development and social change in Latin America.

Jasbir K. Puar completed her MA in Women's Studies at the University of York in 1993 and is working on her doctorate in Ethnic Studies at the University of California at Berkeley. Her publications appear in diatribes and Socialist Reviews and include 'Resituating Discourses of "Whiteness" and "Asianness" in Northern England: Second Generation Sikh Women and Construction of Identity' (*Socialist Review*, Winter 1995) and '"Writing my Way Home": Travelling South Asian Bodies and Journey Stories' (*Socialist Review*, Summer 1995).

Shirin Rai is a lecturer in Politics at the University of Warwick. She is the author of *Resistance and Reaction: University Politics in Post-Mao China* (Hemel Hempstead: Harvester-Wheatsheaf, 1991) and the co-editor of *Women in the Face of Change: Soviet Union, Eastern Europe and China* (London: Routledge, 1992) and *Stirring It: Challenges for Feminism* (London: Taylor & Francis, 1994) and several articles on issues of gender in China and India. She is currently working on a project on 'Women, Public Power and the State' funded by the Nuffield Foundation.

Georgina Waylen is a lecturer in Politics at the University of Sheffield. Prior to this, she was lecturer in Politics and Contemporary History at the University of Salford and lecturer in Politics at the School of Development Studies, University of East Anglia. Her main areas of interest are gender and Third World politics, particularly Latin America. She has conducted research on women and structural adjustment and democratisation, particularly in Chile. She has also published articles on women's political participation, women's movements in Latin America and she is the author of *Gender in Third World Politics* (Buckingham: Open University Press, 1986).

Series preface

Difference, equality, identity, politics, nationhood, sexuality and the state. As I write this preface, in the aftermath of the Conferences on Women held in and near Beijing, it is evident that it is these terms that set the boundaries of many of the enthusiastic and spirited debates. And it is also evident that it is precisely these terms that provide the frames for contemporary debates within academic Women's Studies. As new Women's Studies courses and writings continue to appear, placing these issues at their core, it is fast becoming apparent that there is still, however, a lack of books that address issues of women and politics *specifically*. It is that gap that this new series, *Women and Politics*, edited by Haleh Afshar and Mary Maynard, seeks to redress.

The *Women and Politics* series focuses on activities and struggles that fuel the dynamic of change in the formal/public domains, as well as in the informal/ personal domains. Thus, politics for this series is persuasively defined within a feminist context – to include the range of public and personal activities that women across the world engage with in order to obtain their public and domestic rights.

Women's relationship to formal, organised politics has often been one that highlights the tensions and contradictions in the workings of those politics. So, the lack of women in formal political structures demonstrates not only the institutional sexism generated by such politics, but also forces us to examine, and to decide when, and wether, those political structures are worth fighting, indeed dying, for. In a similar vein, women's involvement in domestic and community-based politics shows us that women's activities are often institutionally devalued. Or, if not devalued, then used to keep 'women in their place', as in the case of women's fertility and motherhood. Women's resistances, whether expressed as formal politics or as struggles within communities, have often not been seen for what they are – that is, as challenges to the state, or to nationhood, or to patriarchal formations, or, indeed, as challenges to all three. It is as challenges to all three – through formal politics, through political theory and through the informal and practical strategies built and used by women – that women's resistances are explored in this series.

Women's resistances in the Third World – to authoritarianism, to the hegemonic authority of First World writings and practices, plus their/our involvement in political struggles at both macro and micro levels – are sometimes not seen. However, in this stimulating and timely volume, these involvements and resistances are explicitly placed at centre stage. The analysts who have contributed their chapters to this collection represent a broad range of geographical locations, historical periods and methodologies. The emphasis in the book is to bring into focus the activities that women involve themselves with – in both the formal and informal spheres – in the Third World. The common thread running through all of the chapters is that presently accepted notions of key issues – such as the state, war, fertility, motherhood and religious practices – must all be revised in the light of this woman-centred approach. At the same time, this collection argues that women are not a universal category; but that it is necessary, as Haleh Afshar says in her Intro- duction, 'to disaggregate women's activities'. In other words, it is necessary to realise that not only do national boundaries create difference, but so also is difference manifest within nation-states, whether along the lines of gender, religion, class community or relationship to the state. This edited collection thus provides a map for current discussions on what could, and does, consti- tute women's political activities.

This collection of clearly argued chapters, all written specially for the book, thus creates an essential volume for all those graduate and undergraduate students, teachers and researchers whose interests lie within the field of women and politics – be it through Women's Studies courses, Political Theory and Political Science courses, Sociology and History courses, or indeed, through Third World and Development Studies.

All of the volumes in this series engage with theoretical debates and empir- ical analyses that impinge upon the study of women and politics. In so doing, they demonstrate that women's contributions cannot simply be added in to politics, rather, that politics is forced to transform itself through the contri- butions of women.

Kum-Kum Bhavnani
Santa Barbara, California
September 1995

Acknowledgements

I would like to thank the Development Studies' Association (DSA) for funding and supporting the Women and Development Study Group and the Political Studies' Association (PSA) for funding and supporting the Women's Group. I would also like to thank members of these groups for participating in the meeting held at York in May 1994 where earlier drafts of these chapters were discussed. Thanks are similarly due to the University of York's Centre for Women's Studies and its members for hosting the PSA and DSA's women's groups' annual meeting and offering kind hospitality to many of the participants.

In particular I would like to thank the contributors to this volume who have given much of their time generously to this book; they have come to meetings to present their papers, to discuss the drafts of the chapters and to comment on and contribute to one another's work. For me it has been a most enriching experience and I thank them all for so cheerfully putting up with the exacting editorial demands showered on them. Those who met their deadlines patiently waited for the stragglers; the pervasive good humour and supportive and sisterly responses were invaluable.

Last but not least I'd like to thank Molly and Ali for giving me the time and even giving up their beds to accommodate contributors and Maurice Dodson for holding the fort.

Haleh Afshar

Introduction

Since the early 1960s women's roles in the processes of development have been increasingly recognised and their contributions documented and analysed. But political scientists, particularly in the West, have been less willing to acknowledge women's extensive participation in political processes. This volume is a contribution to the growing body of feminist literature which is seeking to redress this imbalance.

Women's political activities have, for far too long, been seen as marginal or non-existent. This view is reinforced by the relatively small numbers of women in positions of power and leadership, particularly in the West. As a result, the Western-centred academic analysis of politics that has evolved ignores women and places them at the peripheries of the political processes. Third World women activists have been made invisible through a male-dominated discipline of political theory as well as an earlier phase of feminism which had serious misconceptions about femininity, motherhood and the family.[1] Western feminisms negated Third World women's choices of paths of political activism which used the local prevalent ideologies and were often located within religious or maternal discourses.

The contributors to this volume bring Third World women to the centre of the political analysis and highlight the different forms of feminine political activism that has been ignored and undervalued by orthodox academicians. They discard the undertones of weakness and subservience that have generally been attributed to terms such as motherhood, marriage and domesticity and respect the choices made by non-Western women. Their analyses demonstrate clearly that political theories of state, democratisation and activism must be revised to encompass women's activities, undertaken within such contexts as devotion to religion, even within discourses such as Islamic fundamentalism. Then it will be easy to see that women use concepts like 'motherhood', or 'complementarity' rather than 'equality', to pursue particular goals such as seeking resources, welfare and/or freedom from oppression for their children. Their forms of negotiation with the state must not be equated with weakness nor should their strategies be classified as either temporary or unimportant.

This collection of essays seeks to disaggregate women's activities in the framework of the political formation of post-colonial states. Though often seen as a single united bureaucratic formation, the contributors to this volume argue that it is essential to recognise that, where the nation-state is concerned, the parts often do not result in a coherent whole. Women are frequently at their most effective when they find a way of utilising the diverging interests of the bureaucracy and the administration or interpolating their demands in the contradictory intentions of different arms of the state and the nation's stated ideologies.

In Chapter 1 Georgina Waylen maps out a framework with which to study women in Third World politics. She posits three basic premises: first, that women should be put back into the study of formal politics; second, that the fundamentally gendered nature of ostensibly neutral concepts such as nationalism, citizenship and the state be demonstrated; third that a conventional definition of 'the political' be widened so that many of the activities undertaken by women be incorporated. Waylen's chapter seeks to engender the analysis on these bases. The part played by different groups of women in the conventional political arena is examined, focusing for example on the role of women leaders. Women's political activity outside the conventional arena is also analysed, both oppositional activity and that in favour of the status quo.

Shirin Rai's chapter focuses on the debates on the state within the feminist literature. It makes a claim for bringing the state back in to the discussion of women's lives in the Third World. Rai argues that the current debate on the state is entirely West centred, and does not take into account the particular features of the post-colonial states that affect the lives of Third World women. It urges a fresh approach to this question which must have as its starting-point the lived realities of women's existence, negotiations and struggles.

Donna Pankhurst and Jenny Pearce continue the debate by looking at democratisation. They argue that an analysis of the subject that merely seeks to add women in is both inadequate and inappropriate. A feminist perspective on democratisation must engage in a serious analysis of the nature of political change taking place in many Third World countries. Such an analysis must include an understanding of political marginalisation and democratisation as well as the interactions between class, gender and ethnicity. Feminist analytical perspectives cannot view democratisation as an unproblematic concept and must take into account the variety of ways in which politics in the Third World works through, or in reaction against, the exclusion or marginalisation of socially diverse sections of the population, including, but not limited to, women.

Rohini Hensman's chapter shows that far from being marginal, particularly in the context of authoritarian governments, women's activities are amongst the most important components of political processes. Taking a wide perspective across four Latin American and four South Asian countries, Rohini Hensman illustrates the way in which women have organised outside formal political structures to resist authoritarianism. Although the situations are diverse, in each of these cases women have organised autonomously, in defence of what they perceive to be their own interests and concerns, and this activity has brought them into direct conflict with authoritarian regimes or movements. Their goals, as well as their methods of organisation and struggle, have been distinct from that of more orthodox male-dominated movements, and in some cases they have continued to struggle when other forms of political opposition have been drastically weakened or silenced.

The role played by these women is traced to two main sources. First, where they are fighting for their own rights, they are opposing male authoritarianism, which both reinforces and is reinforced by state authoritarianism to varying degrees. Thus to the extent that any functional definition of democracy has to include the equal rights of women to control their own lives and participation in social decisions, their struggle forms an essential component of democracy. Since women in particular are put at a disadvantage by lack of this component, they have a special interest in fighting for it – except in the case of those strata of women whose privileges within an authoritarian system outweigh the disabilities they suffer.

Second, where women have organised themselves and fought to defend the lives and welfare of their children, this has involved a politicisation of the traditionally 'feminine' role of motherhood. These women have found themselves pitted against repressive, totalitarian movements and regimes, and have fought back with amazing courage and resourcefulness. Their ability to turn their maternal role (traditionally perceived as a source of weakness by most Western feminists) into a reservoir of immense strength makes it imperative to look more closely at the values being affirmed by these mothers, and to recognise them as universal human values which ought to have a central place in any progressive movement for social change.

A different perspective is provided by Jasbir K. Puar, a non-white US aid worker whose interactions with Nicaraguan women recipients were affected by the complex politics of race and gender. Her chapter outlines her experiences and highlights the interdependence of often helpless, and frequently hapless, young, enthusiastic, but not so well informed, aid workers and the more experienced, but needy, local women. Their opportunities and priorities are often entirely different from those of donors. For these women the politics of aid, like national politics, has had to be negotiated in terms of needs and possible scenarios of successful access to extremely scarce resources. They sought tangible goods rather than good advice.

In the chapters that follow, the strategies used by women to obtain what welfare, health care and opportunities they can from more or less powerful states is examined. Using specific case studies from post-revolutionary or embattled states, the authors discuss the problems faced by women who have been active in resistance movements or have had to come to terms with the contradictory demands made of them by ideological and practical needs. Women in China, Nicaragua, Iran and Palestine have sought to endorse much of the revolutionary ardour that led to the emergence of the state, or the resistance movement and its politics, while seeking to extract policies that would enable them to meet their own economic and strategic needs.[2] These chapters consider the use made of the media and local literature; the prevalent discourses of femininity, motherhood, domesticity, and the demands made by women. Using the conservative prevalent political language, these women often pursue goals that bear remarkable similarities to feminist demands in the West.

The political participation of women both at the formal and informal levels and the articulation of the prevalent ideologies with policies that have often proved detrimental to women is discussed. These chapters illustrate the varied and complex ways that different women in different countries have engaged both with the content and the context of the laws that affect their lives. They have made effective use of creeds and stated government principles to curb, alter or reverse some political trends. All too often women are caught at the centre of the state's contradictory economic and political programmes. Chinese women are required to have only one child, while the economic changes make children valuable resources for peasant families; the state and the family make diametrically opposed demands on women. In Iran the stated policy of separation of the public and private spheres and the ideological wish to restrain women within the household clash with the economic needs of families to have at least two full-time breadwinners. Nevertheless, far from being helpless victims, women can and do negotiate a variety of more or less effective solutions to carve out a space for themselves in the political domain.

Delia Davin and Aiping Mu analyse some of the issues discussed by Rohini Hensman in terms of their articulation with state policy in China. Davin looks at the wider political questions and the way that they have been reflected in the Chinese literature on women's issues since 1980. She highlights the problems that have gained importance and the policies that have been pursued; demands for equality and the efforts to establish it, concerns about employment and education and attempts at integrating women into the formal political process, as well as writings concerned with population policy. Davin argues that both the recent economic reforms and the long-running population policy had some adverse effect for women. These in turn have encouraged more serious efforts, both academic and official, to investigate and analyse the position of women in China. The slightly greater freedom to write and publish has also promoted greater variety in writing about women. However, women's issues and population policy remain very sensitive topics in China, not least because of the potential impact on China's international prestige, very much in evidence with the UN Conference for Women held in Beijing in September 1995.

Aiping Mu's chapter concentrates on the implementation of social policies that have had controversial impacts on fertility behaviour among rural women in China. The government's requirement that each family should have only one child has entailed measures such as delaying marriage and practising contraception. At the same time the implementation of rural economic reform policies has resulted in more demand for family labour; the introduction of a market economy created more employment opportunities and more mobility for rural women.

Mu argues that the rural industrialisation that followed the economic reforms transformed the occupational pattern of rural women from agriculture to non-agricultural. This in turn facilitated the implementation of the one-child policy which was more vigorously enforced in the collective economy based rural industrial units. Although the fertility rates declined, there was a gap between individual preferences and the goals of the national population policy. Rural families have found it difficult to accept the concept of a one-child policy. Thus conflict over fertility between rural couples and the state authorities is likely to continue for a long time.

The chapters on Iran include an analysis of the use of the Persian media and women's journals by Iranian elite women to highlight the tensions that exist between women and the state on the delineation of an appropriate place for women in the public domain as well as the implementation of appropriate population planning. Ziba Mir-Hosseini's chapter continues this theme by concentrating on similarities and differences of the 'modernist' and the 'Islamist' feminist discourses in Iran. Mir-Hosseini argues that a remarkable and unexpected result of the Islamic revolution has been to raise the nation's gender consciousness and place women at the centre stage of politics in Iran. Haleh Afshar's chapter analyses the use made by Iranian women of the Islamic discourse to demand practical solutions for child care, employment opportunities and political participation. In the bargain that they have struck, elite Iranian women have accepted the veil as the non-negotiable emblem of Islamification in the country.[3] Like some Latin American women, they have placed motherhood at the centre of political negotiations.[4] Using the Islamic terminology and defending their rights as mothers and providers of domestic havens, they have demanded that the state fulfils its obligations towards them. It must enable them to become good mothers, by providing them with easy admission to education; help them to become good citizens, by providing effective child care for working mothers. Iranian women have accepted a divided labour market, which denies them access to certain jobs. In return they have demanded more flexible working hours and specific periods set aside to enable them to fulfil their 'mothering duties'.

The chapters on Palestine by Maria Holt and Kathy Glavanis-Grantham demonstrate the problems faced by women involved in the resistance movement and caught in the rising tide of Islamism. Palestinian women, like their Iranian counterparts, have had to formulate demands that are compatible with the formal Islamic dictum. At the same time they have sought to alleviate the more draconian chauvinist measures and inject their interpretations into the political arena.

Holt's chapter explores the contradictions between Western perceptions of Palestinian women and the rather more complex reality of their lives. Holt reviews recent Palestinian history, including events such as the 'catastrophe' of 1948 when the majority of Palestinians were forcibly uprooted from their land, the 1967 war which resulted in the Israeli occupation of the West Bank and Gaza Strip, the Palestinian Intifada and, most recently, the September 1993 Declaration of Principles which brought limited self-rule to parts of the occupied territories. Throughout, Palestinian women have remained active and have developed their involvement – both practical and political – in the national struggle. They have created a multiplicity of organisations and have participated in the conflicting currents of nationalism, Islamism and feminism in their society.

The contributors to this volume demonstrate that if the experiences of women the world over is to be understood and included in the study of politics, then the mainstream must be broadened to take on the range of political activities of women. It is not possible to add gender on to the orthodox political theories and expect them to make sense. Women are not an additional extra in the discipline of politics; they play an integral part in the processes that shape the destinies of nations. Women's demands and priorities are often different from those of male politicians who set the agendas. What is interesting is the different and effective ways that women living in different countries, and under different political systems, succeed in negotiating a way forwards towards their strategic goals. Political science would indeed be much the poorer if it did not develop to encompass the complex and significant role played by women in the political arenas.

ACKNOWLEDGEMENTS

I am most grateful to all the contributors of this volume for assisting in the writing of this introduction. In particular I would like to thank Delia Davin, Rohini Hensman, Aiping Mu and especially Donna Pankhurst for their extensive and meticulous comments on an earlier draft of this introduction.

NOTES

1 See for example M. Barrett and M. McIntosh (1982) *The Anti-Social Family*, London: Verso and S. de Beauvoir (1959) *Memories of a Dutiful Daughter*, Harmondsworth: Penguin. For the reassessment see K. Grieve 'Rethinking Feminist Attitudes towards Motherhood', *Feminist Review* 25(March): 38–45.
2 For detailed discussions see M. Molyneux (1985) 'Mobilization without Emancipation? Women's Interests, the State, and Revolution in Nicaragua', *Feminist Studies* 11(2) and S. A. Radcliffe and S. Westwood (eds) (1993) *'Viva': Women and Popular Protest in Latin America* (London: Routledge).
3 For detailed discussion see D. Kandiyoti (1988) 'Bargaining with Patriarchy', *Gender and Society* 2(3): 271–90.
4 See Rohini Hensman, Chapter 4 in this volume, and S. Westwood and S. A. Radcliffe, 'Gender Racism and the Politics of Identities' and J. Schirmer, 'The Seeking of Truth and the Gendering of Consciousness: The Co Madres of El Salvador and the CONAVIGUA Widows of Guatemala', both in S. A. Radcliffe and S. Westwood (eds) (1993) *'Viva': Women and Popular Protest in Latin America*, London: Routledge.

Chapter 1

Analysing women in the politics of the Third World

Georgina Waylen

This chapter aims to outline some of the issues involved in the analysis of women in Third World politics. It would be impossible for a piece of this type to be comprehensive in its coverage or to outline a definitive approach to the study of women in Third World politics but it does aim to provide some guidelines. Some of the themes covered will be specific to the study of women and politics in the Third World, while others will also be relevant to the study of women and politics more generally. This is based on three important assumptions. First, 'politics' does not have the same impact on women as it does on men as is often assumed and therefore this needs to be investigated. Second, the political process often alters gender relations, i.e. relations between men and women, and this needs to be explored. Third, women often participate as political subjects in political activity in different ways from men, which raises questions about the distinctiveness of 'women's political activity' – should it be classified and analysed as a separate entity? Addressing these questions has important implications for the study of politics as it has been conventionally constructed.[1]

When looking for guidance in this endeavour, problems emerge with the conventional literature. Compared to some other social sciences such as sociology and anthropology and the humanities such as literary studies and history, orthodox political science has been slow to incorporate a gendered perspective into its approach (Silverberg 1990). The discipline of politics finds this hard to do. The traditional subject matter of the discipline – 'high politics' – treaties, wars, power politics as it is played out in the top echelons of the public sphere, not to mention the institutional politics of parties, executives and legislatures, is typically male dominated.

In any discussion of gender relations and politics, the public/private split is a crucial notion which has both informed orthodox accounts and inspired feminist critiques. While much of this literature has been written in a Western context, and despite its often universal tone, about the First World, the influence that many of the ideas and concepts have had on political activity and its analysis in the Third World means that it is important to consider them here. Stretching back to contract theorists of the seventeenth and eighteenth centuries and beyond, most of the political theory which underlies Western liberal democracy and liberal democratic theory has at its roots the separation of the public and the private. Beginning with Locke, the private domestic sphere was seen as lying outside of the proper realms of investigation and interference by the state or others. The public sphere was seen as the arena where everyone was incorporated as an individual citizen in the political world. Few links were made between the two spheres and theoretical attention was focused on the public arena, as domestic life and the private sphere was assumed to be irrelevant to social and political theory. Of huge significance to the study of gender relations were the assumptions underlying this – implicitly individual citizens active in the public sphere were assumed to be male heads of household, and women were relegated analytically to the private sphere, subsumed within the household headed by the individual male. This ignores both the links between the two spheres, and varying role played by the state in constructing the boundary between them. While appearing gender neutral, maintaining a division between private and political life as central to liberal democracy is maintaining a division between men and women, where only men can be abstract individuals (Pateman 1983; 1989). The political is therefore defined as masculine in a very profound sense which makes it hard to incorporate women on the same terms as men and excludes many of those activities that women are involved in as not political. This is combined with an approach which sets up frameworks and theories which, while appearing gender neutral, work to exclude women. It is not enough then just to get a better understanding of the role of women in formal politics: a wider analysis, using broader definitions of the political, is needed.

Developments in feminist analyses in the 1980s have provided new theoretical insights relevant to this endeavour. Before this the notion of 'woman' as a unitary and a historical category had often been taken for granted. Some feminists had treated women as one homogeneous group, making the assumption that it was both possible and unproblematic to generalise about all women and their interests. This often meant that the experience of white, middle-class and Western women was generalised to black, working-class and Third World women. As part of a sea-change in theoretical debates, the different ways in which the category 'woman' has been constructed historically have been explored (Riley 1988). The notion of a 'women's interest' shared by all women regardless of race, class and sexuality has become highly contested.

Three major elements have contributed to the breakdown of this kind of universal theorising (Barrett and Phillips 1992). First, black women have provided a powerful challenge to much of the work of white feminists, arguing that their analyses were imbued with racist and ethnocentric assumptions, again generalising the experience of white feminists to black women (b hooks 1984; Moraga and Anzaldua 1983). Second, the re-emergence of the 'equality versus difference' debate broke down the confident distinctions between sex and gender, and in some quarters sexual difference came to be celebrated rather than denied (Scott 1988). Debates moved on to ask how to deal with embodiment, arguing that it is not difference that is the problem, but how it is constructed and dealt with (Bock and James 1992). Third, the feminist challenge to mainstream theorising has been paralleled by the post-structuralist and post-modern critiques of the universal grand frameworks which characterised enlightenment thought and has heralded the end of the meta-narrative (Nicholson 1990). There has been a shift from 'things', i.e. an emphasis on structures so favoured by a social science approach, to 'words', an emphasis on language and discourse derived from literary and critical theory (Barrett 1992). Form and representation become important as language is no longer seen as transparently and directly reflecting 'reality'. This has been accompanied by the fracturing of the 'cartesian' unitary human subject and the self so beloved of rationalist enlightenment thought to be replaced by notions of difference, plurality and multiplicity.

Interest has increased in the construction of the subject and the notion of identity. Identity is seen as complex and a combination of different elements such as class, race, gender and sexuality, not simply one factor (Butler and Scott 1992). There exists therefore the plurality of identities in the single subject. At the same time, there is also a greater recognition of diversity and difference between women. It therefore becomes impossible to say, in any uncomplicated way, that all women are oppressed by all men. The need to forge commonality across difference through alliances and coalitions becomes a key issue within feminism.

The use of enlightenment categories and grand universal frameworks had particular implications for analyses of Third World women made by First World feminists and academics (Spivak 1987). First, many analyses were informed by notions, paralleling ideas about the common oppression of women, that 'sisterhood is global', i.e. that there was more uniting women of different races, classes and sexualities than dividing them. This was often expressed in various cross-cultural analyses of patriarchy. Second, when difference was actually acknowledged it was often done by turning all Third World women into a non-Western 'other'. The 'Women in Development' literature, in particular, is often marked out for displaying these characteristics – treating all Third World women as the same, whether they were, for example, upper-class urban educated professionals or lower-class rural peasant women and advocating general 'solutions' to various perceived problems which affected them from the framework of a universal homogenising feminism. This had the effect of removing agency from Third World women, often seeing them as passive victims of barbaric and primitive practices (Lazreg 1988; Mohanty 1988; 1991; Ong 1988).

Where does this leave the study of women in Third World politics? The inadequacy of the conventional politics literature indicates that several things have to be done. First, women have to be put back into the study of formal politics. But as Donna Pankhurst and Jenny Pearce point out in Chapter 3 of this volume in the context of the debates about democratisation, women should not be 'added in' to the analysis of political processes at the expense of other forms of social relations such as class and ethnicity. Second, it is necessary to make clear how ostensibly neutral political processes and concepts, such as nationalism, citizenship and the state, are fundamentally gendered. Third, it is not enough simply to reintegrate women as actors in the study of conventional politics but those activities women are typically involved in outside the male-dominated institutional sphere must also be included in such analyses. This challenge to the conventional construction of the political is crucially important, as without it much of women's political activity can be dismissed or marginalised as it does not fit easily into conventional categories and, as a result, the important role it plays in the political process will be ignored. New developments in feminist theorising have meant that if universalistic discourses of patriarchy and women's oppression can no longer be used uncritically by a white Western and predominantly middle-class feminism as they have been in the past, there is a need to find ways of examining, first, the role played by different groups of women in conventional politics, and the part played by different groups of women in political activity outside of conventional politics, which can accommodate specificity, diversity and heterogeneity. This means an approach which can look at the complexity of women in the Third World from a perspective of the multiplicity of difference rather than 'otherness'.

CONVENTIONAL POLITICS

While conventional politics is largely seen as synonymous with electoral politics in the First World, this correlation doesn't hold so clearly in the Third World where authoritarian and military regimes and even the revolutionary overthrow of the state have been more commonplace. It is now well documented that men and women participate differently in all forms of formal politics in both the First and Third Worlds: in both getting issues on the political agendas and in policy making and implementation (Ackelsberg 1992). In the past men's political behaviour has been seen as the norm by political scientists, and women's analysed in terms of its deviation from this male norm. As part of this, many myths and stereotypes about women's political participation have grown up, e.g. that women are passive, apolitical and conservative, which feminist political scientists have endeavoured to puncture (Randall 1987). It has been widely observed, that initially on gaining the vote, women do not vote with the same frequency as men in both the developed and developing world. However, this gap closes rapidly and once voting rates are controlled for age, class, education, etc., these differences disappear. It is clear that women's tendency to vote less is not inherent but transient and contingent, e.g. it declines with increasing urbanisation. In the Chilean election of 1989 women had a higher propensity to vote than men.

There is, however, a marked tendency for women to participate less than men in formal politics the higher up the echelons of power you look (Peterson and Runyan 1993). At the grassroots level women on the whole make up a smaller percentage of the members of political parties than men. In the late 1960s women made up between only 15 and 20 per cent of party members in Chile and Peru. There was no greater number in the socialist block: in 1980 women formed only 19 per cent of ordinary Cuban communist party members. Women have often been marginalised in women's sections. Many one-party states in the Third World, particularly in Africa, created women's organisations or co-opted already existing ones which became part of the dominant political party. These have been more vehicles for the state to control women's participation, mobilising them on its terms and providing the regime with a base, rather than ways for women to gain representation within the system (Staudt 1986: 208). In Zimbabwe, for example, the ZANU women's organisation was headed by Sally Mugabe, the president's wife. However, with democratisation in parts of Latin America, many women activists have set up more autonomous women's sections in parties of the centre and centre left with distinctly feminist agendas (Waylen 1994).

Inevitably, given the low numbers of women members of political parties, the numbers elected to representative bodies are also low. While women tend to participate in greater numbers in local level politics, the average percentage of women in national legislatures globally in 1987 was 10. This hides wide diversity. In 1987 the proportion of women legislators in sub-Saharan Africa was approximately 7.5 per cent; Latin America 7 per cent; South Asia 5 per cent and South East Asia 12 per cent. But the proportions had increased in all regions since 1975 (United Nations 1991: 32). It appears that women fare better in systems with proportional representation. In Chile the return to electoral politics saw fewer women elected than there had been in the early 1970s before the military took power.

There tend to be even fewer women found in the executives of governments whether they are authoritarian, elected, state socialist or revolutionary. Often, a very small number of women are appointed to posts which reflect the role that women so often play in the private sphere, e.g. women are often given responsibility for health, education, welfare and women's affairs (where this portfolio exists). In 1987–8 an average of only 3.5 per cent of the world's cabinet ministers were women and ninety-three countries, comprising thirty-one from Africa, twenty-four from Latin America and the Caribbean and thirty from Asia and the Pacific, had no women ministers at all. Women are largely excluded from key areas such as economic policy, defence and political affairs. Even in the 'social' areas, women formed only 9 per cent of the ministers in Africa and 6 per cent or less in the rest of the Third World (United Nations 1991: 31).

There are several explanations for this pattern of participation in conventional politics. Many women are constrained by their roles in the private sphere, which prevent them from participating in the public sphere on the same terms as men and gaining the experience deemed necessary for a career in politics. However, it has been suggested that this affects middle and upper-class women to a lesser extent in much of the Third World, because they can utilise the labour of female servants to free them from their domestic respon-sibilities (Richter 1990–1: 530). Almost universally middle-class women, because of factors such as economic resources and employment, levels of education and confidence, find it easier to participate than poorer women in the upper echelons of conventional politics. However, it is not only the nature of many women's lives which prevents them from participating, but also the structures of formal politics. This ranges from the timing of meetings, the combative style and machismo (often commented on in left-wing parties), and more widespread discrimination against women, for example in selection pro-cedures, which prevents them from rising in political parties (Caldeira 1986).

One phenomenon, which has been noted particularly in Asia and appears to go against these trends, is the relatively high number of women leaders in the Third World, such as Indira Gandhi, Benazir Bhutto, Corazon Aquino and Violetta Chamorro (Genovese 1993). There are particular explanations for this which do not contradict the basic pattern. Mary Fainsod Katzenstein (1978) has claimed that in India there is a link between the degree to which politics is institutionalised and the participation of women, as the permeability of institutions allows women to achieve political prominence. Also in the Asian context, Linda Richter (1990–1) has argued that, among the factors which enable women to reach leadership positions are elite status, high levels of female participation in the movements struggling for independence, and crucially important, links to politically prominent male relatives, often accom-panied by their martyrdom, e.g. their assassination. Richter also claims that women leaders suffer important disadvantages over their male counterparts: they do not generally have an institutional base, a regional constituency, an administrative track record or a military niche, often being seen as temporary leaders, making them vulnerable to coup attempts. In Latin America, the 'supermadre' is seen as important. Elsa Chaney (1979) has argued that women in politics have often played the role of mother of the people. Eva Peron's social welfare activities, seen as dispensing help to the poor and sick, are often cited as an example of this.

While women are on the whole under-represented in formal politics, this does not mean of course that the policies made and implemented in the polit-ical process do not have a huge impact on the lives of different groups of women and on gender relations in general, as Aiping Mu demonstrates in her examination of China's fertility policy in Chapter 7 in this volume. When examining policy making and its outcomes, the gendered nature of the state becomes an important focus. There are often large numbers of women employed in state bureaucracies, but few are found at the top of the state hierarchies in all types of political system whether electoral, authoritarian or state socialist (Staudt 1989). In the 1980s the highest proportion of female public sector administrative and managerial workers was found in Latin America at 20 per cent, with 13 per cent in Africa and 10 per cent in Asia. While these figures had increased significantly in all areas since 1970, women are found only rarely in positions in central banks, economics ministries or foreign trade (United Nations 1991: 35). The state therefore is a gendered hierarchy, with women having an uneven representation in the bureaucracy (Franzway *et al.* 1989: 30). Some analysts have gone on to focus, not simply on the lack of women but also on the embedded masculine style and organisation of state bureaucracies, epitomised for example by the Weberian rational model (Ferguson 1984). It has been suggested, however, that in some Third World states, middle-class educated women are in a good position to play a strategic role in the bureaucracy. (Charlton *et al.* 1989: 13). Indeed Alvarez, after examining Brazil, has suggested that state-led development increases employment opportunities for female professionals and technocrats within the state (Alvarez 1990: 261).

When examining links between state action and gender relations, policies and their impact can be divided into three major categories (Charlton *et al.* 1989). The first set is policies which are aimed particularly at women. These often focus around so-called protective legislation and reproduction, e.g. abortion and laws surrounding childbirth such as the provision of maternity leave. A second subdivision is those policies which deal with relations between men and women, particularly property rights, sexuality, family relations, areas where power relations between men and women and therefore sets of gender relations are often institutionalised. The laws and regulations surrounding these issues frequently become an area of contestation when attempts are made to alter the existing pattern of power relations, as occurred with the enforcement of colonial rule in Africa when marriage, divorce and women's mobility became highly contested (Barnes 1992; Channock 1982; Manicom 1992).

The third set, general policies, are supposedly sex-neutral but have a different impact on men and women. These can be further subdivided into those policy areas linked to the public sphere and somehow seen as masculine, such as state-defined politics, war, foreign policy, international trade, resources extraction and long-distance communication; and those connected with welfare and reproduction. Women have traditionally been excluded from the so-called masculine areas of policy. The most extreme example of this has been war, where women have, until very recently, participated on a different basis from men. While national liberation struggles and revolutionary mobilisations have incorporated women as fighters, this, too, has often happened in gender-specific ways, i.e. the image of the woman fighter as mother with a rifle in one arm and a baby in the other (Reif 1986). Those policy areas more intimately connected to the private sphere and reproduction, for example, housing, health and education, fall under the general rubric of welfare and the welfare state. In contrast to the 'masculine' policies of the public sphere, welfare states have, for some time, been the subject of feminist analyses, particularly in the First World, looking at how they were established assuming particular patterns of gender relations or with the effect of creating or maintaining particular gender roles, and emphasising issues of control and empowerment for women (Wilson 1977).

Even in much of the Third World where welfare states are far less developed and comprehensive, women are, on the whole, a large proportion of providers of state welfare services. The state sector therefore provides employment opportunities for different groups of women. Middle-class professional women are more likely to be employed by the state than the private sector, e.g. as teachers, social workers, nurses in sex-segregated employment (Seager and Olson 1986). Women also form the majority of consumers of welfare services. This is because of the role traditionally ascribed to many women in the domestic sphere as mothers and household managers, i.e. it is women within the household who often liaise with welfare services on behalf of other members of the household, e.g. the young and old. It is women who often make up the majority of the poor and are the major recipients of whatever welfare services exist. Any cuts in welfare services have particular implications for many women, both as providers and consumers of state welfare services, as has been seen in the impact of adjustment policies in the Third World (Afshar and Dennis 1992). Welfare states therefore have a differential impact on particular groups of women. Poor women, as the recipients of welfare services whether chosen or imposed, experience the welfare state very differently from the middle-class professional women who are employed to provide these services. This brings us to consider the gendered nature of the state, citizenship and nationalism.

CITIZENSHIP, NATIONALISM AND THE STATE

These three categories are linked together. Citizenship is an important way in which the relationship between the individual and the nation-state has been theorised. It is not gender neutral. Men and women have been incorporated into citizenship in Western states in very different ways. Initially citizenship was restricted to men (for long periods excluding working-class men and men of different races such as black slaves in America) and incorporated them as soldiers and wage-earners, i.e. through activities in the public sphere; only later were women incorporated, often as mothers, through their activities in the private sphere. So despite current formal equality as voters, men and women have been differentially incorporated as citizens by the state.

This raises the question of links to the nation and nationalism as citizens are citizens of a nation-state. Clearly in the study of Third World politics, an analysis of nationalism and the processes surrounding the creation of ethnic identities and the nation-state is crucially important. Nationalism also is not constructed in a gender neutral fashion (McClintock 1993; Parker *et al.* 1992).

While recognising the lack of a unitary category woman, Nira Yuval-Davis and Floya Anthias (1989) have located five major ways in which women have tended to participate in ethnic and national processes and state practices on different terms to men. These are:

- as biological reproducers of members of ethnic collectivities, as 'mothers of the nation'
- as reproducers of the boundaries of ethnic/national groups
- as participating centrally in the ideological reproduction of the collectivity and transmitters of its culture
- as signifiers of ethnic/national differences – as a focus and symbol in ideological discourses used in the construction, reproduction and transformation of ethnic/national categories
- as participants in national, economic, political and military struggles

(Yuval-Davis and Anthias 1989: 7).

The control of women and their sexuality is therefore central to these processes. Kandiyoti (1991) has argued that this identification of women as bearers of cultural identity will have a negative effect on their emergence as full-fledged citizens. In the post-colonial context, while many nationalist movements and nationalist projects equated the emancipation of women with 'modernity', some successor states have then appeared to reverse reforms when the previous secularist projects appear to break down (Kandiyoti 1991).

It is clear that a gendered analysis of the nation-state is necessary here. There were, for a long time, few feminist analyses which went beyond seeing the state as either somehow essentially good or essentially bad for women in general. These views of the state are too simplistic, because it is not fixed whether the state is essentially good or bad. Indeed, the state has no necessary relationship to gender relations; it is evolving, dialectic and dynamic. It is far better to see the state as a site of struggle, not lying outside of society and social processes, but having, on the one hand, a degree of autonomy from these which varies under particular circumstances, and on the other, being permeated by them. Gender (and racial and class) inequalities are therefore buried within the state, but through part of the same dynamic process, gender relations are also partly constituted through the state (Pringle and Watson 1992). The state therefore partly reflects and partly helps to create particular forms of gender relations and gender inequality. Feminist analyses therefore have advanced from looking at the way the state treats women unequally in relation to men, to examining the ways in which, for example, the project of the welfare state has constituted a 'state subject' in a gendered way. Gendered identities are in part constructed by the law and public discourses which emanate from the state (Showstack-Sassoon 1987).

As Shirin Rai argues in a much longer analysis in this volume, because the relationship between the state and gender relations is not fixed and immutable, battles can be fought out in the arena of the state. Consequently, while the state has for the most part acted to reinforce female subordination, the space can exist within the state to act to change gender relations (Alvarez 1989; Charlton *et al.* 1989). At different times and within different regimes, opportunity spaces can be used to alter the existing pattern of gender relations. Women's relationship to the state, particularly its welfare element, can also be seen as a site of contestation which provides the context for mobilisation, and the welfare state can function as a locus of resistance. The actions of the state can also become a focus for political activity by groups outside the state, e.g. poor women campaigning for an extension of services. Alvarez, for example, has argued that the extension of the remit of the state into the realm of the private has the effect of politicising the private, e.g. through issues such as abortion, rape and domestic violence. This politicisation then gives women's movements a handle to campaign around and influence the political agenda. Shifting the boundary between the public and the private then becomes an important point of influence (Alvarez 1990).

Different groups of women therefore interact with the state in different ways, and can have some influence over the way in which the state acts. It is important to analyse under what conditions and with what strategies women's movements can influence the state and policy agendas. Debate has centred around whether women's movements should attempt to work with the state and political parties. 'State feminism' has emerged as an important issue in the context of democratisation with the return to civilian governments in some Latin American countries. Can feminist movements be successfully incorporated into the state and achieve their own agendas or do they simply get co-opted (Waylen 1993)? This brings us to look at 'women's political activity'.

WOMEN'S POLITICAL ACTIVITY

Why do women undertake political activity under certain circumstances, what form does this activity take and how can women's movements be analysed in the Third World context? If identities are complex, comprising multiple intersections of class, race, gender and sexuality, causing individuals to react in different ways at different times, women will act politically, not simply on the basis of gender, but race, class and sexuality as well, in a complex interaction. In the same way as it is difficult to talk of a unitary category 'woman' and women's interests, it is impossible to talk of a women's movement. There is not one movement, but a diversity of different movements of which feminist movements are one part. Broad generalisations are therefore not possible.

It is important not to fall into the trap of essentialism here. Some scholars, for example, have analysed women's activities in terms of an 'ethic of care' and maternal thinking, arguing, in positive and perhaps rather romantic terms, that women bring to activities in the public sphere supposedly 'female' values of caring, mothering and peacefulness (Gilligan 1983; Ruddick 1989). They have been criticised for both essentialism and universalism: looking at gender to the exclusion of other forms of difference such as race and class, and trying to create grand universal frameworks.

Recently attention has also focused on the form that women's political activities take, including whether women find new ways of 'doing politics' (Waylen 1992). Using approaches influenced by post-modernism and post-structuralism, political action is seen, in part, as a struggle over dominant meanings, including dominant ideas of woman, and aiming to change those meanings. Using the ideas of Foucault amongst others, knowledge and the ability to construct knowledge equals power. Much greater emphasis is therefore put on the form of political protests: on their use of the body and symbols and metaphors and how far they subvert dominant discourses of womanhood. One of the most powerful symbolic and subversive acts carried out by women protesting at the disappearance of their relatives has been the takeover of public space not normally seen as part of their domain for their protests. This has been accompanied by other metaphorical and symbolic devices, leading some to highlight the importance of staging and performance in political action, e.g. contrary to an essentialist interpretation, that the Madres are performing as mothers (Franco 1994). In Chile women protesting about human rights abuses danced the Cueca (the Chilean national dance always danced by a man and woman) alone to emphasise powerfully that their men were missing.

What is needed, therefore, is some exploration of the bases on which women come together as women. This would also focus on, for example, the ways in which women use their socially prescribed roles to act politically, and explore the relationship between gendered identities and political activity without ignoring class and racial identities and the form that this activity takes. Increasingly, the politicisation of women's social roles has been analysed, for example the ways in which women have used their roles as mothers or household managers as the basis of protests or to make demands, for example as Rohini Hensman does in Chapter 4 in this volume (Kaplan 1982). Most of the activities involve entering the public sphere and either making demands or acting collectively, whether on a national, local or community-based level. This kind of action therefore entails the politicisation of the private sphere and entry into the public sphere on that basis. The participant's gender therefore becomes a fundamental part of this type of political activity, as the fact of their being women is a central part of the action. This can involve using 'traditional' social roles for oppositional purposes and also challenging and subverting these roles. Often women involved in 'the politics of everyday life' do not see their activities as political (Caldeira 1990). However, in some contexts, for example, under authoritarian rule, such activities are defined by the regime as oppositional, subversive and therefore come to be seen by both protagonists and others as political.

Women's movements organise in a variety of different ways around a variety of different issues. One fundamental division which can be made is between those activities which are in defence of the status quo, i.e. trying to preserve the existing social order; and those which are attempting to change the status quo, i.e. can be broadly defined as oppositional.

Looking first at those activities which seek to defend the status quo, these have sometimes caused anxiety to feminists. Often this has been framed in the following terms – why should groups of women mobilise in defence of something which is not seen as being in their long-term interests (defined as some kind of a feminist project of emancipation and liberation) and organise to uphold and continue a system which is seen as oppressing them? In the past, this has been explained as being due to women's naivety, and by political scientists as due to women's inherently reactionary political beliefs. Debates have also centred around how far women have been either complicit with or victims of certain regimes. None of these approaches is terribly helpful. The examples of women mobilised by the right show that the women involved often found their activities empowering, enabling them to be active and mobilised in the public sphere, often doing things in the name of motherhood and womanhood using very 'unfeminine methods' (Waylen 1992).

Deniz Kandiyoti (1988) has supplied a potentially more useful way of explaining and analysing the apparently contradictory reasons for and strategies behind women's political activities in defence of the status quo, in the form of the patriarchal bargain. According to Kandiyoti, 'different systems may represent different kinds of "patriarchal bargain" for women with different rules of the game and differing strategies for maximising security and optimising their life options' (Kandiyoti 1988: 277). Kandiyoti believes that this formulation helps to explain why women act in certain ways which may superficially seem to be in conflict with their long-term interests. Women pay the price of a particular bargain and in return get a degree of protection. If a particular bargain looks as if it might be breaking down, women may mobilise to hold on to rules which appear to worsen their situation, because it is part of a strategy of maximising security by gaining and keeping the protection of men. This is likely to occur in the absence of other more empowering alternatives for women. Kandiyoti cites the case of the United States where one response to some men opting out from the breadwinner role has been attempts to bolster the family in order to reinstate the patriarchal bargain in a society which has very little to offer women on their own. Other examples might be female support for arranged marriages and women binding the feet of their daughters. This notion of the patriarchal bargain can provide a framework with which to analyse, for example, the activities of middle-class women on behalf of the right against Popular Unity in Chile in the face of their elevation of women's 'traditional' roles and the apparent attempts of the left to undermine them (Waylen 1992).

The most documented form of activity undertaken by women's movements is oppositional. There is great diversity in those movements and activities which can be seen as oppositional and which attempt to alter the status quo.

First, there are those activities which attempt to influence the state and political parties, and therefore interact with the conventional political arena. This can be through protest or lobbying, e.g. the human rights campaigns of the Madres of the Plaza de Mayo. The demands made can either be specifically concerning women, e.g. abortion, or more general demands relevant to their roles as household managers, e.g. food subsidies and prices. Second, there are autonomous activities which do not attempt to pressurise the state, e.g. autonomous women's organisations and community organisations organising around economic survival.

Important questions therefore arise: first, how can they be disaggregated, e.g. in terms of the sorts of women involved and the aims and objectives of the movements; second, what are the links between different types of women's movement, particularly between feminist and other women's movements; and third, the relationship of these movements to other oppositional movements. One way of disaggregating these questions is to use Maxine Molyneux's (1985) notion of practical and strategic gender interests. According to Molyneux, 'women's interests' do not exist in any general sense, but she argues for a notion of 'gender interests', which can be divided into practical and strategic gender interests.

Practical gender interests arise from actual situations and are formulated by the women in those situations, and will vary from situation to situation. A number of analyses have used this notion to explain female collective action arising in response to an immediate perceived need, e.g. the leading role often played by women in food riots, and the examples of miners' wives mobilising to defend the jobs and interests of their male partners. Practical gender interests therefore are generally expressed as social and economic demands. These sorts of activities correspond to the category 'the politics of everyday life'. They can take the form of spontaneous protests, the most obvious being food riots of the sort which occurred in many Third World countries in the 1980s sparked off by the imposition of harsh structural adjustment packages. They can also take the form of more organised campaigns and activities (Radcliffe and Westwood 1993). These are often not exclusively women-only but women often make up the majority of the members. Movements organising around practical gender interests frequently focus around consumption issues, often organising in a particular location or community. Some activities which can be characterised in this way involve the pressurising of the state or political parties, for example campaigns in poor areas to get the state, whether on a local or national level, to provide services such as water, electricity and improved health care. Other activities operate more autonomously, often focusing around collective survival strategies, for example communal kitchens providing food on a collective basis, setting up workshops to produce goods for sale as part of income-generating schemes, e.g. bakeries, craft workshops, credit unions such as SEWA in India (Everett 1989). Other examples include women's centres which offer crèches, advice and meeting rooms. While these sorts of activities are often based in poor urban areas, there are examples of women's movements operating in rural areas, particularly peasant and landless women (Fisher 1993: 75–102).

It is clear from the examples of women organising often to protect the livelihoods of their families that class and gender are closely linked in this case. The majority of these movements can be categorised as 'popular' or working class. This is not always the case: Argentina's housewives movement can be seen as an exception, because it was middle- and lower-middle-class based but the middle-class had been very badly hit by economic crisis (Fisher 1993: 145–50). This kind of activity typically involves the politicisation of women's social roles, as their roles as mothers and household managers form the basis of their political activities and entry into the public sphere. According to Molyneux (1985), movements operating around practical gender interests do not necessarily act to reduce gender inequality, nor are they often intended to.

In contrast, strategic gender interests are those interests which can be derived deductively from an analysis of women's subordination and from the formulation of a more satisfactory set of arrangements (Molyneux 1985). It is these strategic gender interests which are often called 'feminist' or women's 'real' interests, and, according to Molyneux, require a feminist level of consciousness to struggle for them. Feminist movements can therefore be seen as movements of women coming together autonomously and self-consciously as women, pressing gender-based demands. They do not, on the whole, rely on the politicisation of women's social roles. Different types of feminist movements have appeared in the Third World as well as in the First World. Some middle-class based feminist movements emerged at the same time as nationalist movements campaigning for independence from colonial powers for example in India, and middle-class based movements campaigning for female suffrage appeared in Latin America in the early part of the twentieth century (Jayawardena 1986; Miller 1991). A variety of feminist movements have (re)emerged since the early 1970s (Saporta *et al.* 1992).

However, it is clear that there is a need to explore the links between 'feminism' and popular women's movements. Many studies have shown that groups of women, involved in campaigns around practical gender interests, have become increasingly focused on issues around women's subordination and come to see themselves as increasingly feminist (Fisher 1993: 177–200). However, they often see this as a form of 'popular feminism', i.e. it is not the same as either feminism from the First World, nor often the feminist movements active within the Third World countries themselves. The difference is often expressed in terms of movements which do not prioritise gender issues over and above the issues which surround class and imperialism. As Mohanty argues 'feminist movements have been challenged on the grounds of cultural imperialism, and of short-sightedness in defining the meaning of gender in middle-class, white experiences, and in terms of internal racism, classism and homophobia' (Mohanty 1991: 7). Some contemporary feminist movements,

for example, in many parts of Latin America, are seen by many as predominantly middle-class movements, and for example in Brazil, as predominantly
white. A rigid analytical dichotomy between movements active around practical and strategic gender interests is overly simplistic as there is considerable
overlap between the two.

CONCLUSION

It is clear when looking at women in Third World politics that Third World
women do not constitute an 'automatic unitary group', but that the term
'Third World women' can be used as it designates a political constituency
(Mohanty 1992: 7). Mohanty believes what constitutes Third World women
as an oppositional alliance is a common context of struggle. She wants to get
away from analyses which see Third World women as victims, focusing instead
on a dynamic oppositional agency of women. Mohanty uses Benedict
Anderson's (1983) notion of 'imagined communities' to move away from essentialist notions of potential alliances, substituting 'imagined communities of
women with divergent histories and social locations, woven together by the
political threads of opposition to forms of domination that are not only
pervasive but systemic' (Mohanty 1992: 4). Mohanty therefore believes that it
is possible to 'retain the idea of multiple fluid structures of domination which
intersect to locate women differently at particular historical conjunctures, while
at the same time insisting on the dynamic oppositional agency of individuals
and their engagement in "daily life"' (1992: 13). The notion of an imagined
community of struggle can be extended to Third World oppositional
struggles in general. It therefore becomes difficult to see women's oppositional
activities as discrete entities somehow separate from other struggles, for
example against colonialism, imperialism and for national liberation.

However, it is crucially important that the analysis of the political activities
of women's movements does not occur separately from the analysis of formal
politics. The use of wider definitions of the political means that the two must
be integrated. In particular, there is a need to explore the interaction between
the two in terms of the state and political parties. This will allow for more
sophisticated understandings of concepts such as citizenship which play such
an important role in the analysis of political processes.

NOTE

1 For a longer discussion of many of the issues raised in this article see Waylen (1996).

REFERENCES

Ackelsberg, M. (1992) 'Feminist Analyses of Public Policy', *Comparative Politics*, 24(4):
    477–93.

Afshar, H. and Dennis, C. (eds) (1992) *Women and Adjustment Policies in the Third World*, London: Macmillan.

Alvarez, S. (1989) 'Contradictions of a "Women's Space" in a Male-Dominant State: The Political Role of the Commissions on the Status of Women in Postauthoritarian Brazil', in K. Staudt (ed.) *Women, International Development and Politics*, Philadelphia, PA: Temple University Press.

Alvarez, S. (1990) *Engendering Democracy in Brazil: Women's Movements in Transition Politics*, Princeton, NJ: Princeton University Press.

Anderson, B. (1983) *Imagined Communities*, London: Verso.

Barnes, T. (1992) 'The Fight for the Control of African Women's Mobility in Colonial Zimbabwe', *Signs* 17(3): 586–608.

Barrett, M. (1992) 'Words and Things: Materialism and Method in Contemporary Feminist Analysis', in M. Barrett and A. Phillips (eds) *Destabilising Theory: Contemporary Feminist Debates*, Cambridge: Polity.

Barrett, M. and Phillips, A. (eds) (1992) *Destabilising Theory: Contemporary Feminist Debates*, Cambridge: Polity.

Bock, G. and James, S. (eds) (1992) *Beyond Equality and Difference: Citizenship, Feminist Politics and Female Subjectivity*, London: Routledge.

Butler J. and Scott J. (eds) (1992) *Feminists Theorize the Political*, London: Routledge.

Caldeira, T. (1986) 'Electoral Struggles in a Neighbourhood in the Periphery of São Paulo', *Politics and Society* 15(1): 43–66.

Caldeira, T. (1990) 'Women, Daily Life and Politics', in E. Jelin (ed.) *Women and Social Change in Latin America*, London: Zed.

Chaney, E. (1979) *Supermadre: Women in Politics in Latin America*, Austin, TX: University of Texas Press.

Channock, M. (1982) 'Making Customary Law: Men, Women and Courts in Colonial Northern Rhodesia', in M. Hay and M. Wright (eds) *African Women and the Law: Historical Perspectives*, Boston University Papers on Africa, 7, Boston, MA.

Charlton, S. Everett, J. and Staudt, K. (eds) (1989) *Women, State and Development*, Albany, NY: SUNY Press.

Everett, J. (1989) 'Incorporation versus Conflict', in S. Charlton, J. Everett and K. Staudt (eds) *Women, State and Development*, Albany, NY: SUNY Press.

Ferguson, K. (1984) *The Feminist Case Against Bureaucracy*, Philadelphia, PA: Temple University Press.

Fisher, J. (1993) *Out of the Shadows: Women, Resistance and Politics in South America*, London: Latin American Bureau.

Franco, J. (1994) 'Crossed Wires: Gender Theory North and South', Paper presented to Conference on Latin American Cross Currents in Gender Theory, Portsmouth, UK, July.

Franzway, S., Court, D. and Connell, R. W. (1989) *Staking a Claim: Feminism, Bureaucracy and the State*, Cambridge: Polity.

Genovese, M. (ed.) (1993) *Women as National Leaders*, London: Sage.

Gilligan, C. (1983) *In a Different Voice*, Cambridge, MA: Harvard University Press.

hooks, b (1984) *Feminist Theory: From Margin to Center*, Boston, MA: South End Press.

Jayawardena, K. (1986) *Feminism and Nationalism in the Third World*, London: Zed.

Kandiyoti, D. (1988) 'Bargaining with Patriarchy', *Gender and Society* 2(3): 271–90.

Kandiyoti, D. (1991) 'Identity and its Discontents: Women and the Nation', *Millennium: Journal of International Studies* 20(3): 429–43.

Kaplan, T. (1982) 'Female Consciousness and Collective Action: The Case of Barcelona 1910–1918', *Signs* 7: 546–66.

Katzenstein, M. F. (1978) 'Towards Equality: Cause and Consequence of the Political Prominence of Women in India', *Asian Survey* 18(5): 473–86.

Lazreg, M. (1988) 'Feminism and Difference: The Perils of Writing as a Woman on Women in Algeria', *Feminist Studies* 14(1): 81–107.

McClintock, A. (1993) 'Family Feuds: Gender, Nationalism and the Family', *Feminist Review* 44 (summer): 61–80.

Manicom, L. (1992) 'Ruling Relations: Rethinking State and Gender in South African History', *Journal of African History* 33: 441–65.

Miller, F. (1991) *Latin American Women and the Search for Social Justice*, Hanover, NH: University Press of New England.

Mohanty, C. (1988) 'Under Western Eyes: Feminist Scholarship and Colonial Discourses', *Feminist Review* 30: 61–88.

Mohanty, C. (1991) 'Introduction. Cartographies of Struggle: Third World Women and the Politics of Feminism', in C. Mohanty, A. Russo and L. Torres (eds) *Third World Women and the Politics of Feminism*, Bloomington, IN: Indiana University Press.

Molyneux, M. (1985) 'Mobilization without Emancipation? Women's Interest, the State and Revolution in Nicaragua', *Feminist Studies* 11(2): 227–54.

Moraga, C. and Anzaldua, G. (eds) (1983) *This Bridge Called my Back: Writings by Radical Women of Color*, New York: Kitchen Table Press.

Nicholson, L. (ed.) (1990) *Feminism/Postmodernism*, London: Routledge.

Ong, A. (1988) 'Colonialism and Modernity: Feminist Representations of Women in Non-Western Societies', *Inscriptions* 3/4: 79–93.

Parker, A., Russo, M., Sommer D. and Yaeger P. (eds) (1992) 'Introduction', in *Nationalisms and Sexualities*, London: Routledge.

Pateman, C. (1983) 'Feminism and Democracy', in G. Duncan (ed.) *Democratic Theory and Practice*, Cambridge: Cambridge University Press.

Pateman, C. (1989) *The Disorder of Women: Democracy, Feminism and Political Theory*, Cambridge: Polity.

Peterson V. S. and Runyan, A. (1993) *Global Gender Issues*, Boulder, CO: Westview.

Pringle, R. and Watson, S. 'Women's Interests and the Post-Structuralist State', in M. Barrett and A. Phillips (eds) *Destabilising Theory: Contemporary Feminist Debates*, Cambridge: Polity.

Radcliffe S. and Westwood S. (eds) (1993) *Viva: Women and Popular Protest in Latin America*, London: Routledge.

Randall, V. (1987) *Women and Politics*, 2nd edn, London: Macmillan.

Reif, L. (1986) 'Women in Latin American Guerilla Movements: A Comparative Perspective', *Comparative Politics* 18(2): 147–69.

Richter, L. (1990–1) 'Exploring Theories of Female Leadership in South and South East Asia', *Pacific Affairs* 63(4): 524–40.

Riley, D. (1988) *Am I That Name: Feminism and the Category of 'Women' in History*, London: Macmillan.

Ruddick, S. (1989) *Maternal Thinking: Towards a Politics of Peace*, London: The Women's Press.

Saporta, N., Navarro, M., Chuckryk P. and S. Alvarez, (1992) 'Feminisms in Latin America: From Bogotá to San Bernardo', *Signs* 17(2): 393–434.

Scott, J. (1988) 'Deconstructing Equality versus Difference', *Feminist Studies* 14(1): 33–50.

Seager, J. and Olson, A. (1986) *Women in the World: An International Atlas*, London: Pan.

Showstack-Sassoon, A. (ed.) (1987) *Women and the State*, London: Hutchinson.

Silverberg, H. (1990) 'What Happened to the Feminist Revolution in Political Science?', *Western Political Quarterly* 43(4): 887–903.

Spivak, G. C. (1987) *In Other Worlds: Essays in Cultural Politics*, London: Routledge.

Staudt, K. (1986) 'Stratification: Implications for Women's Politics', in I. Berger and C. Robertson (eds) *Women and Class in Africa*, New York: Holmes & Meier.

Staudt, K. (1989) 'Gender Politics in the Bureaucracy: Theoretical Issues in

Comparative Perspective', in K. Staudt (ed.) *Women, International Development and Politics*, Philadelphia, PA: Temple University Press.

United Nations (1991) *The World's Women 1970–90: Trends and Statistics*, Social Statistics and Indicators, series K no. 8, New York: UN.

Waylen, G. (1992) 'Rethinking Women's Political Participation and Protest: Chile 1970–90', *Political Studies* 40(2): 299–314.

Waylen, G. (1993) 'Women's Movements and Democratisation in Latin America', *Third World Quarterly* 14(3): 573–88.

Waylen, G. (1994) 'Women and Democratization: Conceptualising Gender Relations in Transition Politics', *World Politics* 46(3): 327–54.

Waylen, G. (1996) *Gender in Third World Politics*, Buckingham: Open University Press.

Wilson, E. (1977) *Women and the Welfare State*, London: Tavistock.

Yuval-Davis N. and Anthias F. (1989) (eds) *Women-Nation-State*, London: Macmillan.

FURTHER READING

For a discussion of the general issues involved in the study of women and politics see Vicky Randall's (1987) *Women in Politics*. Georgina Waylen's (1996) *Gender in Third World Politics* takes up in far more detail many of the issues raised in this chapter and examines particular political formations such as revolution and authoritarianism in the Third World. Barbara Nelson and Najma Chowdhury's (1994) edited collection *Women and Politics Worldwide* (New Haven, CT: Yale University Press) has a number of Third World country case studies. For some recent developments in feminist analysis see Michele Barrett and Anne Phillips (1992) *Destabilising Theory*. For different approaches to the analysis of women's political activity see 'Mobilization without Emancipation?' by Maxine Molyneux (1985); 'Bargaining with Patriarchy' by Deniz Kandiyoti (1988) and Chandhra Mohanty's (1988) 'Under Western Eyes: Feminist Scholarship and Colonial Discourses', as well as C. Mohanty, A. Russo and L. Torres (eds) (1991) *Third World Women and the Politics of Feminism*.

Chapter 2

Women and the state in the Third World

Shirin Rai

This chapter examines the debates on the state within the feminist literature. It makes a claim for 'bringing the state back' in to any discussion of women's lives in the Third World. It argues that the current debate on the state is largely West-centred, and does not take into account particular features of the post-colonial states that affect the lives of Third World women. It urges a fresh approach to this question which must have as its starting-point the lived realities of women's existence, negotiations and struggles.

IN OR AGAINST STATE?

Much of Western feminist state theory has largely ignored the experience of Third World women under the post-colonial state. Often the assumptions made are Western-centred but the theorising takes on a universalising language. Similarly, some of the theories of the 'developmental state' (as opposed to 'theories of development' in general) have developed in gender-blind and sometimes Orientalist ways (Joseph 1993: 26), and therefore ignore the particular relationship that women in the Third World find themselves in *vis-à-vis* the post-colonial state. They tend to overlook the processes of state and class formations in the Third World, and therefore the relations of exploitation operating in the economic and the socio-political terrain. This further leads to assumptions about the nature of struggle and the strategies that can be included or are to be excluded from the ambit of struggle. There is now a growing literature on women and the state in the Third World, which seeks to challenge the universalising language of the Western feminist and developmental state discourses about women, the state and struggle. I shall argue that what we need is a continuing and more focused debate about women and the post-colonial state as Third World women come to experience not only national but also international economic and political power in the era of 'restructuring and democratisation'. Such a focus will also allow us to examine the growing and diverse areas of women's political activities which include not only opposition, but also negotiation, not only struggle, but also strategic bargaining in spaces that are intersections of the private and the public spheres (see also Waylen and Hensman, chapters 1 and 4 in this volume).

Feminists and hostile territories

Both political science and development studies were in the early days hostile territories to women. While in political science issues of gender were ignored, and even now are only patchily introduced, in development studies the case has been different. While feminist interventions in development studies ensured that issues of gender were present (especially in the form of critique) in its discourse as early as the 1970s, the policies and politics of development that arose from debates within development studies show less gender awareness (see also Waylen in this volume). Feminists have had anxieties about the ways in which women have been 'added on' to the projects and discourses of politics and development rather than any reformulation of the central issues addressed by these disciplines in the light of feminist contributions and debates (see Pankhurst and Pearce, Chapter 3 in this volume). In particular these have centred around the question of the state, a key concept in political science that evokes deep suspicion, anger, fear, and hostility among feminists.

Similarly, in development studies, while feminists have engaged vigorously in a critique of its primary concerns, there too we find that the central question – this time of the developmental state – has remained largely unaddressed. This suspicion of the state has more recently been buttressed by the development of post-structuralist explanations of power. Indeed, since the 1970s, the concept of the state has been so reduced in status that its very existence has been brought into question. 'Where the concept remains in everyday use, it is used descriptively, mostly by the "practitioners" of social policy and social welfare' (Pringle and Watson 1992: 54–5). However, during the 1970s and 1980s there was also a growing sense of the power of the state as the welfare state became more important in the lives of individuals – regulating, defining, providing and monitoring. Women began to enter the arena of local politics and legal dispute in order to represent their own interests (Pringle and Watson 1992).

There have developed over a period of time two very different approaches to the question of the state. Historically, both have roots in the experience of women's movements in different contexts. In countries with strong class affiliations and a tradition of class-based political action like Britain, feminist writing was dominated by the Marxist analysis of the state as an oppressive instrument of the ruling (capitalist) class. Marxist feminists added the 'women question' to the class question in capitalist societies by emphasising the role of the state as a mediator between the two different but complementary systems of patriarchy and capitalism (Eisenstein 1978; Wilson 1977). In countries with a strong tradition of welfare state politics, there has been less resistance to dealing with the state. In Australia and Scandinavia for example, a positive value has been placed on state intervention, and the state has been more clearly seen as an arena for bargaining among interests (see Hernes 1984). Women's interests have been regarded as one among others, and feminists have insisted that they must be articulated within that space. Not only the question of interest articulation, but also that of participation in state functioning has been seen in a positive light. The 'femocrat' is the creature of this strategy of influencing the state in the interests of women by infiltrating it (see Franzway *et al.* 1989). Though the Marxist feminist and femocrat approaches took very different views of the state, both acknowledged the state as a reference point in feminist politics. Both also spoke of the state in institutional and functionalist terms. In sum, both took the state seriously.

The other feminist approach towards the state has been inspired by post-structuralism. Within this category too there are differences. Some would regard politics as a 'set of debates and struggles over meaning' and the state as 'erratic and disconnected rather than contradictory'. They would point out that what 'intentionality there is comes from the success with which various groupings are able to articulate their interests and hegemonise their claims: it is always likely to be partial and temporary' (Franzway *et al.* 1989: 61, 63). Further, post-structuralist feminists would argue the focus of our analysis of public power should not be an impossible unity of the state, but micro-level organisations and institutions that affect individual lives daily. Unlike the Marxist feminists, they do not see the state, in its dispersed sense, as simply reflecting and bolstering gender inequalities, but 'through its practices, plays an important part in constituting them; simultaneously, gender practices become institutionalised in historically specific state forms. It is a two way street' (Franzway *et al.* 1989: 64). A more radical version of this post-structuralist critique of feminist theories of the state asks the question, 'whether the state is a specifically problematic instrument or arena of *feminist* political change' (Brown 1992: 8). This poses the dilemma that the post-structuralist feminists discussed above have not acknowledged in full. 'If the institutions, practices, and discourses of the state are as inextricably, however differently, bound up with the prerogatives of manhood in a male-dominated society . . . what are the implications for feminist politics?' (Brown 1992: 8). The answer given to this question by post-modern feminists would to suggest that for women to 'be "protected" by the very power whose violation one fears perpetuates the specific modality of dependence and powerlessness marking much of women's experience across widely diverse cultures and epochs' (Brown 1992: 9). The state in this analysis is a regulating, constraining, structuring network of power, and interaction with it can only have one outcome – the production of 'regulated, subordinated, and disciplined *state* subjects' (Brown 1992: 8; Allen 1990; Smart 1989; 1992).

These debates among feminists are ongoing. Indeed, increasingly women are coming to view this debate as critically important to their understanding of their own lives. What is particular about this debate, and unsurprising, is that it has focused almost exclusively on the Western state formations and processes. While some post-modern feminists do point to how the 'process of decentering and diversifying politics helped increase the visibility of historically marginalised interests and perspectives, for example, feminist, post-colonial and "Third World" interests' (Weedon 1993), questions such as whether the post-colonial state poses any particular problems for women, whether Third World women can relate such a Western-centred debate to their own lives, and whether an analysis of Third World states by feminists might throw up questions for feminists theorising and debating the state, have not been asked. Are there any particular features of the post-colonial state that need to be taken into account by Third World women when they consider their own relationship with the state? In the next section I discuss the post-colonial state from this perspective.

The post-colonial state

One of the most interesting developments in state theory since the Second World War has been the theorising of the post-colonial states and the developmental states. The latter, primarily Japan and the East Asian economies, were first theorised by Chalmers Johnson (1982). The case studied by Johnson were all characterised as 'strong' states. This description fed into and from the already existing work of Gunnar Myrdal (1968; 1970) where he distinguished between the 'strong' state – in this case his native Sweden - and the 'weak' or 'soft' state – India. The defining features of the 'strong' state in this literature have been 'state capacity' to 'implement logistically political decisions throughout the realm' (Mann 1984: 189). Further, strong states are characterised by a high degree of bureaucratic autonomy from institutions and groups in civil society. They are also seen as corporatist – whether democratic or authoritarian – and as such there is 'a significant degree of institutionalised interaction and dialogue between the state elites and autonomous centres of power within civil society' (Onis 1991: 123). In the soft states, on the other hand, was the 'general inclination of people to resist public controls and their implementation' (Myrdal 1970: 209). The focus was therefore on the levels of successful implementation of decisions achieved by particular states. A discussion therefore arose about factors that would enhance or reduce this capacity (see Charlton and Donald 1992). Michael Mann (1984) contributed to this debate by distinguishing between 'despotic' and 'infrastructural' power. Despotic power in Mann's scheme 'denotes power by the state elite itself over civil society' within 'routine, institutionalised negotiation with civil society groups' (Mann 1984: 188). Infrastructural power 'denotes the power of the state to penetrate and centrally co-ordinate the activities of civil society through its own infrastructure' and is therefore better able to implement state policy (Mann 1984: 190). This distinction is important to emphasise that there exists no direct, linear co-relation between 'state autonomy' and 'state capacity' (Onis 1991: 123). The first will not automatically lead to the other.

Another distinction made between the 'strong' and 'weak' states was the clearly defined relationship between the executive and the bureaucracy on the one hand ('the politicians reign, the bureaucrats rule') and a close co-operation between the state and the 'peak interest groups' in civil society on the other. In the 'weak' states these linkages were weak too. The bureaucracy is of particular interest in this debate as in the 'strong' states its size is kept to the minimum, thus making it more focused, and efficient, and also more disciplined and accountable. In 'weak' states the bureaucracy is generally too 'flabby' to be effective and to huge to be controlled. As a result corruption becomes an independent variable in the functioning of 'weak' states further subverting the implementation of state policy. This can be partly explained by institutional factors such as the size of the bureaucracy, or the effectiveness of controls put in place by the political executive, and partly by the particularity of what has been termed the state's 'embeddedness' in civil society in such states.

The concept of 'embeddedness' has been imported into the developmental state debate from the work of Karl Polanyi in which he argues that 'The human economy, then, is embedded and enmeshed in institutions, economic and non-economic' (Polanyi, cited in Lie 1991: 220). Johnson used this concept to emphasise the 'embeddedness' of the Japanese *state* (a 'strong' state) in civil society resulting in 'an apparently contradictory combination of Weberian bureaucratic insulation with intense immersion in the surrounding social structure', laying the basis of that state-society (read 'peak interest group') co-operation so needed for pursuing the single goal of economic development. This use of the concept of 'embeddedness' implicitly challenges the Weberian wisdom of the need for a 'rational bureaucracy' as a prerequisite of a modern state. It does not, however, ask the question about the level of 'embeddedness' of the 'weak' state in its civil society and to what effect. While a 'strong' state is able to harness the energies of the civil society through dialogue and co-operation of elite groups, in the 'weak' states the fragility of their infrastructure may lead to its infiltration by the dominant interests of civil society. Compromise here is not based on recognition of mutual strength but on the weakness of the state's ability to enforce its decisions.

A final point needs to be made here. What has been emerging from various studies of the East Asian experience is that the state formation in these countries was unique and historically rooted. The unusual degree of external threat faced by all these nation-states, together with their experience of redistribution of economic resources (land reforms for example) gave them a unity of purpose that was not achieved by most other post-colonial states. However, it is important to note here that other states did have their own social and economic agenda of transformation and nation-building. They did not have, however, the infrastructural power to put that agenda into effect. This might have been due to the lack of an immediate external threat, the introduction of pluralist political systems that could not sustain a developmental programme, the complex heterogeneity of their populations divided on the basis of language, ethnicity, religion, or race, or the incapacity of the state to encourage the citizens to develop a stake in the country. In India for example,

> Reality of the liberal democratic process combined with authoritarian trends, promotion of capitalist economy and controls over it, centralization of state authority and the steady growth of regional forces, an increasingly coercive state apparatus and administration of programmes of a welfare state, an emerging techno-managerial system pursuing non-secular policies, and at the international level being independent and dependent at the same time . . . [indicate the complexity of its] state process.
>
> (Mohanty 1990: 151)

While traditional elites were being co-opted into the new state networks, with the 'weakness' of the post-colonial state towards these elites ensuring political stability, tensions also emerged from the clash of expectations released by the rhetoric of change and the reality of compromise. One of these tensions has emerged from the clash of the rhetoric of gender equality and the reality of a patriarchal political power system. 'Weak' state, without adequate infrastructural power, could only look to the exercise of 'despotic power' which further put back the goal of rapid, focused economic development. What we have then in most countries of the Third world is a complex state situation.

While it is clear from the above discussion that some of the Western feminist debates do not take into account the different types of state formation, it is also obvious that much of the literature on the developmental and post-colonial state is at best gender-blind (see Elson 1992). A serious problem with the developmental model of state formation – the distinction between 'strong' and 'weak' state – is that it does not allow for an uncovering of the patriarchal power that is an essential part of both types of states. So, for example, it cannot explain the compromise of a 'strong' state like the People's Republic of China with patriarchal forces in the interests of political stability and economic growth (see Evans 1992; Rai 1992). There is, however, a growing literature by Third World feminists challenging both these perspectives.

Third World feminist perspectives

In the writings of Third World feminists, however, we find a different approach to the question of the state. The state (especially the post-colonial state) is regarded as of critical importance in women's lives both public and private. Mernissi (1991), for example, even speaks of the 'feminisation' of the male in the post-colonial state (her own being Morocco) as the traditional role of the economic provider is no longer the exclusive concern of the man in the family, and as the modernising state draws women into the public arena through both law and public provision such as education. Similarly, in India we find a considerable emphasis placed upon the power (or lack) of the state to formulate men and women (see e.g. Kapur and Cossman 1993). Many women's groups have, for example, been involved in the drawing up of the *National Perspective Plan for Women 1988–2000* (Ministry of Human Resource Development 1988) 'recommends certain special interventions for women as transitory measures to ensure that they catch up with the mainstream by 2000 A.D.' (ibid.: ii). There is thus an implicit setting up of a binary opposition between the state and patriarchal forces in society (Mehdid 1993: 9).

Other women writers in this area point conversely to the symbiosis between the state and patriarchy: 'Whereas the traditional exercises of patriarchal authority tended to rest with particular men – fathers, husbands and other male kin – the communalisation of politics, particularly when backed by state-sponsored religious fundamentalism, shifts the right of control to all men' (Kandiyoti 1991: 14). However, neither group argues for an abandonment of the state either as a concept or as an arena for struggle. Furthermore, emphasis is laid by all on questions of women's access to the public sphere both in the economic and political fields (see Kandiyoti 1991; Mehdid 1993). Secularisation, democratisation and modernisation of the state and of the political sphere are regarded as relevant to the lives of women while at the same time there is an acknowledgement of the state's penetration by the community. As Alvarez (1990) argues in the context of South America,

> feminists should neither dismiss the State as the ultimate mechanism of male social control nor embrace it as the ultimate vehicle for gender-based social change. Rather, under different political regimes and at distinct historical conjunctures, the State is potentially a mechanism either for social change or social control in women's lives.
>
> (Alvarez 1990: 273).

See also Chhachhi (1991) and Mehdid (1993).

Finally, in the writing of feminists like El-Sadawi (1980), the presence of international capitalism looms large. She argues, together with others, that the penetration of international capitalism in Third World states brings about a general social crisis that leads to the impoverishment of whole communities and that women suffer most in this context of exploitation (see also Longrigg 1991; Rosa 1987). Kandiyoti, however, points out that the impact of capitalism on women's lives is not entirely negative. Capitalism, while exploitative, also leads an attack upon traditional patriarchy in the countries of the Third World creating new opportunities for women in the public sphere. This ongoing work on Third World states is an important alternative perspective that the universalising debates among Western feminists neglect to take into account.

In the light of the discussion about the writing on the state within feminist theory, and the particularities of the developmental state that affect women in the Third World in ways that are different from those in Western societies, can we begin to construct explanations of state practice and the complex strategies that women create, and continue to employ in their interactions with the states in the Third World?

Negotiating the state

For the women in the Third World the state and civil society are both complex terrains: fractured, oppressive, threatening and also providing spaces for struggle and negotiation. Both the state and the civil society form the boundaries within which women act and are acted upon. To ignore these boundaries can only be foolhardy for women due to the capacity of the state for violence. Transgression of these boundaries is a different question, however. Transgression involves knowing the boundaries that are to be pushed. The knowledge of these boundaries comes in different ways to people of different classes, races and cultures. At times boundaries become visible only in the process of transgressing them, whether the transgressors saw their actions as transgression or not forming a critical part of the story. Transgression of boundaries also involves countering strategies that are many layered. Acquiescence and opposition, humility and pride, anger and conciliation, idealism and pragmatism are all interwoven into a complex pattern of interaction with the state.

What we must also acknowledge is the unfolding character of the state. From local government officials to social services, from the police to the judges, women experience the power of the state differently as their demands and struggles develop. But it is important to note that this power of the state is not a focused power bolstering a structure that we can point to. In order to understand the unfolding character of the state we have to approach the state as a hierarchically arranged multiplicity of power relations. It is only then that we can follow the different roles played by different organisations of the state, at different times, for different reasons. So, for example, since the 1980s the Supreme Court in India has often taken a social interventionist position in its judgments. The Court has increasingly taken a stand that 'in a developing society judicial activism is essential for participative justice. . . . Justices are the constitutional invigilators and reformers [who] bring the rule of law closer to the rule of life' (P. N. Singh 1981–2, cited in Cooper 1993: 6). In this spirit the Indian Supreme Court, through a group of radical judges, has taken the view that 'constitutional interpretation fundamentally differs, almost mystically, from statutory interpretation' (Cooper 1993: 8). In a landmark case *People's Union for Democratic Rights* v *Union of India* the Supreme Court allowed the petitioners to charge the Government of India for failing to uphold the fundamental rights of its citizens. The judgment, in the favour of the petitioners who had argued that the Indian Government had failed to enforce Article 23 of the constitution which prohibits 'traffic in human beings and forced labour', established a precedent of interpreting the fundamental rights of Indian citizens in a more flexible way. The Court judged that 'in a country like India, where there is so much poverty and unemployment and there is no equality of bargaining power, a contract of service may appear on the face of it voluntary, but it may in reality be involuntary' (Cooper 1993: 10). A leading exponent of this view, Justice Bhagwati urged that the constitution 'must be interpreted creatively and imaginatively with a view to advancing the constitutional values and spelling out and strengthening the basic human rights of the large masses of people in the country' (ibid.)

As we have seen in our discussion of the various feminist approaches to the state, strong cases have been made by those who argue for working in and through the state, and those who are furiously opposed to this. We have also seen that the state in developing societies, whatever its welfare rhetoric, cannot be equated with the welfare states of the Western liberal societies. However, what I want to explore now is whether the different nature of the developmental state allows us to form a judgement about the various possibilities and strategies of action available to women in the context of such a state.

Three features of the post-colonial state that we discussed earlier are of relevance at this point. First, the fact that most post-colonial states saw themselves as agents of social and economic transformation. Through their constitutions, laws and legislation, these states created a framework within which they sought to change and develop societies marked by the experience of colonial exploitation. Whether on the basis of liberal secularism, as in India, or one of religious identity as in Pakistan, these states tried to significantly refashion and remodel their societies. Indeed, much of the writing about the 'woman question' in India, as in many other Third world countries, acknowledges this transformative role of the state. Indian Supreme Court's interventionist approach can be understood in the context of the evolution of a liberal welfare state that had social justice as a prominent part of its political rhetoric.

Second, we need to take into account the ability of a state to enforce its laws and regulations. As we saw in our discussion of the developmental state, that has been made the yardstick by which states can be categorised into 'strong' and 'weak' states. Where the 'infrastructural power' of the state is weak, the implementation of directives can become hostage to random factors outside the control of the state. Thus, the implementation of directives, however radical, could be contingent upon the personal attributes of enforcers rather than the capacity of the state to ensure the implementation of its laws. 'Good judges/bureaucrats' thus become important as independent factors in the lives of people, but as such do not fit into the structural network of the state. Corruption, the third feature that I want to discuss here, then becomes an important variable particularly in the functioning of a 'weak' state, affecting the lives of different people differently. Women, of course, are affected in different ways from men; the 'favours' asked for not only are financial, but also can be sexual. As implementation of rules is undermined by endemic corruption working with(in) the state is not always possible. Protest has to replace petition, and support mobilised outside the institutions and corridors of state power. This can bring women into confrontation with the state. At this stage the rules of the political game can change significantly as the state no longer feels able to contain the demands of groups. The strength of the opposition as well as the mobilisation of state power against the opposition will be important factors in the political struggle at this point. Visibility in confrontation is one thing that states try to avoid; gaining visibility is important for oppositional (women's) groups. By becoming visible they force the coercive arm of the state – the police – to become visible too, thus exposing it to public scrutiny and media interest. Here, of course, the spaces provided (or not) by the civil society to organise is an important variable.

What we begin to piece together from our study of the women and the state is that it is a highly complex picture, and one that is radically different from the reality faced by Western women. In the next section I want to explore some of these differences and themes.

IN AND AGAINST THE STATE?

It seems to me that there are two different standpoints that we have to keep in mind when we discuss the question of the state *vis-à-vis* women. The first is that of the daily lived realities of women's lives. Here we have to consider both the nature of the state formation under which particular groups of women live, as well as different social and political variables that affect their dealings with the state. The second is the standpoint of the feminist response to the state. Whether as strategy or as critique the options before feminists have to be distinguished from those before the first group quite deliberately in order that we might be in a better position to understand both. The relationship between theory and practice has to be foregrounded once again to be able to address the question of the political role that women can and need to play in the arena of public power. I shall come back to this later.

One of the most startling differences between the women in Western liberal states and those in the Third World is the extent to which they are directly 'touched' by the regulatory power of the state. Women in Third World countries are more removed from the state in all its manifestations than are Western women. This is because the state in the Third World is unable to provide the kind of safety network that the Western liberal state does with its welfare provision. Both the upper-class women and those of the lower classes do not fall within the ambit of state functioning. In health, education, child care and employment the upper-class women have traditionally depended on the private sector, and so too the poorest women: the first group because of the access to private, non-state resources, the second, because the state can provide them with very little support.

Second, as most Third World states can be categorised as 'weak' states, women in these states do not become aware of many areas of state legislation and action. The dissemination of information about new legislation is extremely varied and patchy. Illiteracy and exclusionary social practices further exacerbate this isolation from the processes of the state. The lack of political will to disturb traditional family values is one manifestation of the 'weak' patriarchal state. Political expediency overrules the rhetoric of social justice fairly easily when the state perceives the threat to its continuance. Further, the lack of the infrasrtuctural power of the state means that its laws are altogether ignored in many parts of the country. So even though Indian women have constitutional rights of inheritance, divorce and maintenance for example, the enforcement of these rights is at best patchy.

However, another feature of the Third World states is that these states are much less internally regulated. I would like to make clear here that the category 'Third World' does not, for the purposes of this discussion, include state socialist countries like China which do not conform to the state–civil society relationship model that is critical to the understanding of the 'state capacity' argument.

We have already spoken of the high level of corruption among the Indian bureaucracy. The state is also largely unchecked at the local levels in the scale of violence it operates against the people. The women's movement in India, for example, is rooted in women's opposition to police brutality (Spivak 1987) in the 1970s. Rape, murder and beatings in police custody continue to be a common feature of state operation especially in rural areas. At the time, depending upon their race, class and caste situation, most Third World women have fewer resources to withstand violations of the state. The lack of education, economic vulnerability, weak infrastructural social support and inavailability of information leave women in these states more dependent upon their own resources which in themselves are meagre. These also determine to a large extent the options that women have, and think that they have, available to them in their dealings with the state.

Finally, because of the deep 'embeddedness' of most Third World states in the civil society, Third World women experience pressures from and in both areas of their lives. The civil society is not an uncomplicated 'space of uncoerced human association and . . . of relational networks – formed for the sake of family, faith, interest and ideology – that fill this space' (Walzer 1992: 89). The civil society is a deeply fraught space with hidden and explicit dangers that lurk there in the garb of national, religious and ethnic identities as fashioned by male-directed movements of various kinds. In this context, the 'embeddedness' of the state in the civil society cannot be regarded in the positive light that many developmental economists do: 'This idea that "bureaucratic capacity and social connectedness may be mutually reinforcing rather than in opposition" in turn becomes "the key to the developmental state's effectiveness"' (Chalton and Donald 1992: 7). For women the reinforcing of bureaucratic capacity by social norms can be a terrifying combination threatening any attempt to change their lived reality. In this context, however, the fracturing of the state becomes important.

One of the most significant contributions of post-structuralist argument to
the theorising of the state has been its insistence that there is no unity that
we can point to as the state. What we have been used to calling the state can
be regarded only as a network of power relations existing in co-operation and
also in tension. The study of the functioning of the various agencies of power
in operation in the case that we discussed above illustrates the validity of the
post-structuralist approach to the state. However, precisely because of this
fluidity and dispersal of power we cannot regard the 'touch' of the state as
universally polluting as many post-modern feminists would have us believe.
We cannot simply argue, as Wendy Brown does, that an appeal to the state
for protection 'involves seeking protection *against* men *from* masculinist institutions' (Brown 1992: 9). This is not only because one of the implications of
the post-structuralist arguments about the dispersal of power is the acknowledgement of the varied forms that power takes and the uses to which it is
and can be put. If we add to this reading of power relations our understanding
of the complexity of the civil society as it approaches women, taking simply
an 'against the state' position becomes positively dangerous. The civil society
is as deeply masculinist as is the infrastructure of state relations. Third world
women (and for that matter Western women too) cannot look to one to oppose
the other. Both spaces – of informal and formalised networks of power – are
imbued with masculinist discourses; neither is 'uncoerced', however different
the forms and mechanisms of coercion.

This takes me back to the question of theory and practice that I raised at
the beginning of this section. For most women in the Third World the state
figures only marginally in their lives. It looms large only when women trans-
gress the boundaries set by the state in various areas of public and private life
that it has jurisdiction over. Therefore, for the majority of women the question
is not whether or not to approach the state. *It is they that are approached by the state,*
in many instances in a brutal and violent way (see Spivak 1987). In that context, can one argue that 'to be "protected" by the very power whose violation
one fears perpetuates the specific modality of dependence and powerlessness
marking much of women's experience across widely diverse cultures and
epochs' (Brown 1992: 9)? In the face of exercise of violent state power, the
'protection' given by a court order prohibiting that violence can make the
difference between life and death to individual women (see Williams 1991).

Second, the question surely is not one of simply 'seeking protection', but
of *fighting* state violence. The forms that this struggle might take may vary
from country to country, state formation to state formation. But to focus simply
on the regulating, structuring, constraining power of the state and to overlook
the struggle against all these is to sell short the daily lives of millions of women.
Worse, it is the road to inaction and nihilism. Women's struggles are routinely
made aware of the limitation of the protection offered by legislation and court
orders. As a result they do wage their struggles on many different fronts in
order to *create* a protection for themselves that could not be ensured simply

by administrative or judicial directives. This they do through many different strategies, for example, by making themselves heard in the public arena, both directly in their own voices and also in others' words. Thus, when Brown (1992) writes,

> Just as microelectronics assembly plants in Third World 'Free Trade Zones' do not simply employ women workers but produce them – their bodies, social relations, sexualities, life conditions, genders, psyches, consciousnesses – the state does not simply handle clients or employ staff but produces state subjects, *inter alia*, bureaucratized, dependent, disciplined and gendered ones

she completely ignores the tremendous struggle that Third World women carry on daily in the 'Free Trade Zones' to resist the multinationals and their own states taking over all meaning in their lives (see Rosa 1987). Brown also, of course, portrays women in an entirely passive light.

Finally, I would argue that the question of 'in and against' the state has to be looked at afresh. Ehrenreich and Piven (1983) make a case for increasing women's involvement with the state by pointing to the radical potential of such a project for women both as individuals and as a growing collective. The London Edinburgh Weekend Return Group (1980) in their influential book *In and Against the State* make a different point: 'The state, then is not "our" state. It is "their" state, an alien, oppressive state' (1980: 53). However, they remind us that 'we have made positive gains [under this hostile state] not by "winning power" in any formal sense but by taking a degree of control, counter-posing our forms of organisations to theirs' (ibid.: 147). I would argue, not in opposition but from a different standpoint, that if we do not regard the state as a unity we cannot look upon struggle as a unified strategy either. My concern in this chapter has been to point to the lack of intentionality of a unified state structure, and also to point to the spaces that are available, and can be created for and through struggle for retrieving, reconstructing and regaining control over the meanings and signifiers in women's lives. They do this in different ways taking into account their own experience, needs, situations, and they approach the various forms of state differently: in opposition, in co-operation, through subversion not simply of rules but of articulated intentions of state forms, and through negotiations. And they do all this actively, if not always with a coherence and intentionality of their own: 'It is because subjects do not, strictly speaking, know what they are doing that what they do has more meaning that they know' (Bourdieu, quoted in Risseeuw 1991: 154). It is on this struggle – in all its myriad forms – that we must focus to understand the relationship that women construct with the state in which they live.

REFERENCES

Allen, J. (1990) 'Does Feminism Need a Theory of the State?', in S. Watson (ed.) *Playing the State*, London: Verso.

Alvarez, S. (1990) *Engendering Democracy in Brazil: Women's Movements in Transition Politics*, Princeton, NJ: Princeton University Press.

Barrett, M. and Phillips, A. (eds) (1992) *Destabilising Theory: Contemporary Feminist Debates*, Cambridge: Polity.

Brown, W. (1992) 'Finding the Man in the State', *Feminist Studies* 18(1): 7–34.

Charlton, R. and Donald, D. (1992) 'Bringing the Economy Back In: Reconsidering the Autonomy of the Developmental State', Paper presented at Political Science Association, Annual Conference, Belfast, April.

Chhachhi, A. (1991) 'Forced Identities: The State, Communalism, Fundamentalism and Women in India', *Women, Islam and the State*, Philadelphia, PA: Temple University Press.

Cooper, J. (1993) 'Poverty and Constitutional Justice: The Indian Experience', *Mercer Law Review* 44: 1–25.

Davis, K., Leijenaar, M. and Oldersma, J. (eds) (1991) *The Gender of Power*, London: Sage.

Davis, M. (ed.) (1987) *Third World, Second Sex* London: Zed.

Eisenstein, Z. R. (ed.) (1979) *Capitalist Patriarchy and the Case for Socialist Feminism*, New York: Monthly Review Press.

Elson, D. (1992) 'Gender Analysis and Development Economics', Paper presented at ESRC Development Economics Study Group, Annual Conference, March.

Ehrenreich, B. and Piven, F. F. (1983) 'Women and the Welfare State', in I. Howe (ed.) *Alternatives: Proposals for America from the Democratic Left*, New York: Pantheon.

El-Sadawi, N. (1980) *The Hidden Face of Eve*, London: Zed.

Evans, H. (1992) 'Monogamy and Female Sexuality in the People's Republic of China', in S. Rai, H. Pilkington and A. Phizacklea (eds) *Women in the Face of Change: The Soviet Union, Eastern Europe and China*, London: Routledge.

Franzway, S., Court, D. and Connell, R. W. (1989) *Staking a Claim: Feminism, Bureaucracy, and the State*, Cambridge: Polity.

Guha, R. (1982–7) *Subaltern Studies: Writings on South Asian History and Society*, Delhi: Oxford University Press.

Hernes, H. M. (1984) 'Women and Welfare State: The Transition from Private to Public Dependence', in H. Holter (ed.) *Patriarchy in a Welfare Society*, Oslo: Universitetsforlaget.

Howe, I. (ed.) (1983) *Alternatives: Proposals for America from the Democratic Left*, New York: Pantheon.

Johnson, C. (1982) *MITI and Japanese Miracle*, Stanford, Calif: Stanford University Press.

Joseph, S. (1993) ;Gender and Civil Society', *Middle East Report* 183 (July–August): 22–7.

Kandiyoti, D. (ed.) (1991) *Women, Islam and the State*, Philadelphia, PA: Temple University Press.

Kapur, R. and Cossman, B. (1993) 'On Women, Equality and the Constitution: Through the Looking Glass of Feminism', *National Law School Journal* (special issue on Feminism and Law) I: 1–61.

Lie, J. (1991) 'Embedding Polanyi's Market Society', *Sociological Perspectives* 34(2): 219–35.

Longrigg, C. (1991) 'Blood Money', *Amnesty* February/March: 16–17.

Mann, M. (1984) 'The Autonomous Power of the State', *Archives Européennes de Sociologie* 25(2): 185–212.

Mehdid, M. (1993) 'Feminist Debate on Women and the State in the Middle East', Paper presented at the Conference of Socialist Feminists, London, July.

Mernissi, F. (1991) *Women and Islam: An Historical and Theological Enquiry*, Oxford: Blackwell.

Ministry of Human Resource Development (1988) *National Perspective Plan for Women 1988–2000*, New Delhi: Government of India.

Mohanty, M. (1990) 'Duality of the State Process in India', in *Capitalist Development: Critical Essays*, Bombay: Popular Prakashan.

Mouffe, C. (1992) *Dimensions of Radical Democracy: Pluralism, Citizenship, Community*, London: Verso.

Myrdal, G. (1968) *Asian Drama*, London: Allen Lane.

Myrdal, G. (1970) *The Challenge of World Poverty*, London: Allen Lane.

Onis, Z. (1991) 'The Logic of the Developmental State', *Comparative Politics*, 24(1): 109–26.

Pringle, R. and Watson, S. (1992) 'Women's Interests and the Post-Structuralist State', in M. Barrett and A. Phillips (eds) *Destabilising Theory: Contemporary Feminist Debates*, Cambridge: Polity.

Rai, S. (1992) 'Watering Another Man's Garden', in S. Rai, H. Pilkington and A. Phizacklea (eds) *Women in the Face of Change: The Soviet Union, Eastern Europe and China*, London: Routledge.

Risseeuw, C. (1991) 'Bourdieu, Power and Resistance: Gender Transformation in Sri Lanka', in M. Davis, M. Leijenaar and J. Oldersma (eds) *The Gender of Power*, London: Sage.

Rosa, K. (1987) 'Organising Women Workers in the Free Trade Zone, Sri Lanka', in M. Davis (ed.) *Third World, Second Sex*, London: Zed.

Said, E. (1979) *Orientalism*, New York: Vintage.

Smart, C. (1989) *Feminism and the Power of the Law*, London: Routledge.

Smart, C. (1992) 'The Woman of Legal Discourse', *Social and Legal Studies* 1(1).

Spivak, G. C. (1987) 'Draupadi', in Spivak, *In Other Worlds: Essays in Cultural Politics*, London: Methuen.

Walzer, M. (1992) 'The Civil Society Argument', in C. Mouffe (ed.) *Dimensions of Radical Democracy*, London: Verso.

Watson, S. (ed.) (1990) *Playing the State*, London: Verso.

Weedon, C. (1993) 'Feminism and Postmodernism', Paper presented at the Women's Studies Network (UK) Conference, Northampton, July.

Williams, P. (1991) *The Alchemy of Race and Rights*, London: Harvard University Press.

Wilson, E. (1977) *Women and the Welfare State*, London: Tavistock.

FURTHER READING

R. Charlton and D. Donald's (1992) 'Bringing the Economy Back In: Reconsidering the Autonomy of the Developmental State' is a good and easy text to refer to on the debates about state autonomy and capacity. It provides a critical assessment of relevant literature that is up to date, in an accessible fashion. It does not, however, address gender issues at all. The state capacity literature is also very well covered by Ziya Onis (1991) in 'The Logic of the Developmental State'.

R. Pringle and S. Watson's (1992) 'Women's Interests and the Post-Structuralist State', in M. Barrett and A. Phillips (eds) *Destabilising Theory* is an accessible and sophisticated analysis of the post-structuralist and gendered analysis of the state debate. They argue for a view of the state that destabilises its intentionality in favour of a focus on its constituting institutions and discourses in order to analyse strategic possibilities available to women at a given point in time.

Chapter 3

Feminist perspectives on democratisation in the South
Engendering or adding women in?

Donna Pankhurst and Jenny Pearce

This chapter is concerned with the danger of over-prioritising *gender* as a social category by which women are politically marginalised in the political transformations taking place in Latin America (LA) and sub-Saharan Africa (SSA). Recent academic attention to the role of women in Third World politics is an important correction to past neglect. This chapter argues, however, that women cannot simply be 'added in' to analyses of contemporary political change. The risk exists where the nature of democratisation is oversimplified and where otherwise useful analyses of the limits of democracy in Western Europe are imposed.[1]

A concern for women in the Third World by feminist analysts has generated a body of literature on the role women have played in bringing about the transitions from military to civilian government in the Third World, and in newly democratic Third World polities, particularly in Latin America and Africa, with which we are particularly concerned (e.g. Abdullah 1993; Alvarez 1990; Jaquette 1989; Liatto-Katundo 1993). This important literature draws attention to the neglect of the role of gender in the politics of the Third World, while by contrast gender is now an essential part of development studies (see also Waylen, Chapter 1 in this volume). This literature also contributes to a political lobby which sees an acknowledgement of women's actual political contributions, and their promotion in the public political sphere, as preconditions for obtaining their dues and full consideration in the development process.

In spite of the important contribution of this literature, our chapter originates from a dissatisfaction with some of its underlying assumptions. First, much of this literature works with an analysis of political change which sees emergent democracies as uncontested 'end states'. While there are significant political changes taking place in many Third World countries, there has by no means been an unequivocal, unilinear path to elected civilian government and the rule of law. A feminist perspective on democratisation, cannot, in our view, fail to engage in a serious analysis of the nature of the political changes taking place.[2]

Second, a concern with political marginalisation in the study of democratisation ought to lead to more than the study of women. Feminists who neglect the way social class and ethnicity *as well as* gender also contribute to political exclusion and marginalisation contribute to a distorted understanding of the relationship of the social to the political in the Third World. In this sense, simply 'adding women' into politics is more than merely an inadequate approach to the study of contemporary politics in the Third World, but actually blocks off key areas of analysis, such as the interaction between gender, ethnicity and class.

What, then, might a feminist perspective on democracy and democratisation in the Third World consist of? We are concerned to develop a gender-aware analysis which does not assume that democratisation is an unproblematic process and which also takes into account the variety of ways in which politics in the Third World works through, or in reaction against, the exclusion or marginalisation of socially diverse sectors of the population.

The chapter sets out the parameters of such an analytical project and highlights some potential pitfalls in empirically based research. To set the scene we need to begin by briefly summarising the peculiar nature of democratisation in LA and SSA. We then go on to examine the usefulness of analyses of Western democracy.

DEMOCRACY IN LATIN AMERICA AND AFRICA

A lot of political change towards democratisation has been stimulated in the Third World by international pressures in recent years. The end of the Cold War clearly marked a new era for the kind of political pressure and intervention which the Third World could expect from the 'First World'. With the ending of competition from the communist countries of the 'Second World' in setting political agendas in the Third World, governments of the United States and Western Europe have been able to bring explicitly political demands into foreign policy and aid agreements. Having given support to authoritarian regimes for geopolitical purposes during the Cold War, these powerful countries of the West are now in the business of promoting elected and accountable governments in the Third World.

The World Bank also swiftly broadened its remit from a narrowly defined economic sphere to embrace the setting-out of appropriate political profiles for Southern countries. Political conditions attached to loans are now co-ordinated with the policies of Western governments in order to promote elected governments and systems of 'good governance'. Such an extension of the scope of the Bank's expert advice is justified by the alleged, but unproven, thesis that democracy and good governance are necessary preconditions for sustained economic growth. Many researchers have been concerned to demonstrate empirically that there is at least a correlation between trends in economic growth and either authoritarian or democratic government, but none has been successful.[3] Nonetheless the imposition of conditions to loans and aid continues as though this has been irrefutably proven.

Of course the stimulus for political change has also come from within these countries. Generalisations are often made about the nature of the move away from military rule and one-party-states in LA and SSA towards democratically elected governments. Indeed, elections have been held in both regions between competing political parties for the first time in many years, and broader political changes have taken place in the area of increased human rights, and wider civil rights (such as freedoms of association and of the press).

However, not only are these considerable political changes varied in degree between different countries, but also they are often fragile, as evidenced by the increasing number of partial and full reversals. One of the key research issues for us here is not so much to establish the extent of this variety or fragility, but rather the *meaning* of these enormous political changes. We are witnessing profound transformations in the formal political machinery occurring at the same time as popular struggles to broaden and deepen human and civil rights. Such a combination of moves towards formal democracy and liberal rights is certainly quite different from the way political change occurred in England, where the latter came after the former. In LA and SSA we may then be witnessing a unique historical combination of processes, as the formal structures of democracy settle on very unsteady foundations of recent and, and in many cases, partial liberal rights.

The type of democracy to be promoted through good governance is to include high degrees of representation and government accountability. Moreover, the participation of women is highlighted explicitly, not only in terms of representation, but also in the development process itself, even though the polities of Western countries have inadequate records on both. The measurement of democratisation, in terms of assessment of conditionality fulfilment by the lending agencies, is often quite formal and procedural.

At heart such assessment is mostly concerned with the establishment of appropriate conditions for the transition to private-sector-led rather than state-led development, but such conditions also include a responsive, accountable and legitimate government which respects and guarantees civil and political liberties. The emphasis on civil and political liberties and representative government by international agencies in their notion of good governance also reflects an aspiration of citizens in these countries, but it is not the only aspiration for the vast majority of the impoverished populations of the Third World. For them, these liberties together with broader political representation are valued mostly for the way they guarantee a political space to demand social and economic rights, better living standards and basic services; they are a means to an end.

By contrast, in Western Europe and North America representation is of paramount concern to gender-aware social scientists as an end in itself, for what it conveys about the extent of women's participation in and exclusion from modern Western democracy. This we believe can help us with our discussion of a feminist perspective on democratisation in the Third World, both positively through the questions it raises and by helping us identify the very real differences between political process in the West and the Third World which cannot be ignored.

DISCOURSES FROM WESTERN EUROPE

The discourse on liberal democracy in Western Europe seems seductively universal, and a sophisticated framework into which analysis of the South can easily be slotted. Within this discourse there is a very rich debate taking place about democratising liberal democracy. It acknowledges tensions between liberalism and democracy, between civil/political rights and socio-economic rights, between political equality and social inequality.

On the face of it, these are issues which fit exactly our concerns in the South, and particularly the inability of some sectors of the populations to engage in politics on the same terms as others – because of their social positions, as summarised by David Beetham,

> From a democratic point of view the problem with a representative democracy in practice is not so much that it restricts political activity to the vote, as that the opportunity for a more extensive involvement, and the degree of influence with government which it carries are dependent upon a variety of resources – of time, of money, of learned capacity – that are distributed unevenly between sections of the population. The freedoms of speech and association not only provide a guarantee of a more extensive political activity than the vote; they are also the means whereby the inequalities of civil society are transmitted to the political domain.
>
> (Beetham 1992: 48)

In the West today, such tension between unequal social structures and egalitarian political rights has been reduced by the way liberalism was reconciled with demands from below to democratise the liberal state. The victory of the franchise in the West was often the very last element in the long democratisation process.

Perhaps the most significant critique of liberal democratic theory and practice in the West is that of the, often hidden, *gendered* nature of both. Initially under pressure from feminists, gender is now being pushed onto the mainstream agenda of discourses about democracy in the West.

The demand by women for the franchise nearly always came towards the *end* of the process of democratisation in the West; quite a different chronology of women's experience of democracy from that of the South, as we shall see. Similarly, removing gender bias from the male-dominated structures of Western liberal democracies now seems to many to be a self-evident priority in making democracy meaningful to the majority of citizens, women being seen as the largest, most marginalised group in spite of its heterogeneity. It is

essentially the feminist perspective on the exclusion of women that dominates
the debate and shapes the political agenda, although other forms of exclusion
on the basis of race (the citizenship status of immigrants, for example) and
class, are not completely ignored.

In the wake of feminist debates on the interactions between class and gender,
race and gender, and post-modernist emphasis on multiple identities, other
forms of marginalisation besides gender are certainly achnowledged.
Nonetheless, it seems people are more often marginalised *as women* than as
members of any other group in Western democracies, and so the conceptual
identification of gender as the main impediment to democracy also seems
appropriate. Empirically based analysis of the Third World calls for a somewhat different emphasis, however.

WOMEN AND GENDER IN THIRD WORLD DEMOCRATIC CHANGE

A growing number of studies of the Third World 'add women in' to, or make
women visible in, politics. They usefully reveal the roles played by women in
bringing about democratic change, and highlight the ways in which they have
been excluded from power. In trying to avoid mere 'women-and-ing', we are
concerned about gender relations in political change, but also wish to focus
on their interaction with other kinds of social relations.

Two Western 'frameworks' make this difficult: the discourse on democracy
in the West with its prioritising of the 'women's issue', and issues identified
by official international aid agencies. Political conditionality and aid priorities
both identify women for special consideration before other social groups. Let
us counterpose these priorities against a thumbnail sketch of elections and
voting in LA and SSA.

When the franchise has been introduced in Latin America and sub-Saharan
Africa, on the whole it has been obtained by women on the same basis as
men, although this has often excluded people (men and women) as members
of other groups, such as illiterates or ethnic minorities. Thus although many
women have been excluded from, *and* marginalised in politics, the basis on
which this has occurred has tended to be as members of these other groups,
rather than as women *per se*.

Poor peasants, indigenous peoples, some ethnic groups and poor urban
dwellers often remain marginal to political processes, even where they formally
have the right to vote in elections. Clientelist politics and other kinds of
influence and control affect the ways in which the underprivileged make
use of the political rights available to them. The liberal rights which were
developed over a prolonged period in the West and quite often before demands
for universal suffrage, have been only partially developed in the Third
World. Elected representative government, where it has existed, has often been
grafted on to very unequal social structures and corruption, fraud and blatant

manipulation have rarely been fully uprooted from the political system which has emerged. Newly elected governments have frequently been very fragile, with weak guarantees of civil, political and human rights. These features inhibit any challenge to the stark social inequalities which can then become reflected in, rather than challenged by, election results.

There are of course gendered aspects to all of these processes, and women have different experiences within the marginalised social groups than men, but they are not automatically excluded and marginalised *in the same way as each other*. We want to emphasise, however, not merely that there are people besides women who are marginalised and excluded from politics, or that women experience this exclusion differently from men. The discourse in the West tends to emphasise women's exclusion in such a way that when transplanted to the Third World it can eclipse other mechanisms of exclusion and marginalisation taking place on bases other than those of gender relations. Without a commitment to integrate the analysis of gender relations within the wider context of other social relations, there is a risk of assuming the primacy of gender as a marginalising process, rather than investigating it.

UNRESOLVED CONCEPTUAL PROBLEMS

An issue which emerges from the Western discourse, but which is also highly pertinent in an examination of the political reality in SSA and LA, is the difficulty of measuring and assessing the meaning of political representation or participation. In the liberal democracies of the West, that has resulted in attempts to investigate precisely how social inequalities affect access to representative bodies and even to develop 'indices of democratisation' (e.g. Beetham 1993).

It is evident from this research that liberal democracies in the North reflect the inequalities in their societies as much as as the emerging democracies in the Third World, although the latter come under far greater, more general, criticism for doing so. In highlighting the exclusion and marginalisation of sectors of the population, including women, as failures of the new democracies, we evidently expect more of them than has historically been provided by democracies of the North. Nor is it only 'we' who have these liberating ambitions for political change in the Third World. The political conditionality attached to aid explicitly includes the participation of the poor and of women in elections and public economic life ('the development process').

In a sense both 'radicals' and 'right-wingers' are making judgements about the Third World as if it is once again on that linear path to political development advocated in the 1950s and so discredited. As 'we' bring women on to the agenda, so the Third World is expected to follow our lead, even though our own practice remains very flawed, just as the conception of 'development' of the modernisation theorists was. This is not, of course, to argue that gender should not be a major component of our analysis of Southern politics. It is to suggest that we should begin by reconceptualising our analysis of where gender fits in to the complex social realities of the South and not merely graft it on to categories and approaches which have emerged from contemporary Northern discourses. This is a major conceptual problem which needs to be explored through particular cases.

A general concern about the situation of women in countries of the South undergoing political change means that we have to look beyond the business of democracy and formal political rights. Even where formal political rights increase, social and economic rights can at the same time be removed. For example, trade union rights can be removed by democratically elected governments, facilitating a greater casualisation of employment which certainly affects women. Structural adjustment programmes implemented by democratically elected governments have routinely cut social services and increased the burden of social provisioning on women in many economic positions.

We owe to the recent debate on democracy in the West the idea that social and economic inequalities *do* affect civil and political rights. But the notion that with democratisation, social and economic rights can actually be taken away and seriously affect access to formal political structures and citizenship rights, comes from an understanding about the relationship between democracy and capitalist development in the Third World. This is another unresolved conceptual problem, which challenges the simple identification of political changes in LA and SSA with a linear progress of democratisation. The tension between the imperatives of capitalist development in the periphery and the extension of basis rights is likely to remain high.

Finally, in seeking meaning for all the kinds of political changes that are taking place under democratisation, and particularly for their gendered aspects, it is difficult to avoid a slide into functionalism. It is all too easy to explain the processes taking place in terms of their advantages to capital-in-general, to the countries and governments of the West, and/or for men in general and/or particular. It is difficult to see reasons for the nature of the changes beyond the fact that they have advantages for these powerful forces, and by default it is all to easy to assume that the outcomes are actually the ideal conditions for such forces.

Of course as such an elision occurs, we can also lose any meaningful focus on *agency*. This itself is a danger in the study of many phenomena, but it is particularly acute when we try to grapple with the meaning of recent political shifts in Latin America and Africa. An important conceptual problem, therefore, remains how to relate a rigorous structural analysis of why these political shifts are taking place, with the contingent elements of women emerging as agents of history, through their many movements and struggles. Merely 'adding women in', or simply making them visible, is therefore a necessary but ultimately insufficient step towards intellectually and politically satisfying explanations of political change in the Third World today.

NOTES

1 The terms North and South have now replaced First and Third World respectively to a large extent in the Latin American and sub-Saharan contexts. However, 'North' and 'South' are not used in this book, as the dichotomous terminology is not so commonly used with reference to other parts of the world, and is not helpful when discussing the experience of democracy in Europe, where 'West' and 'East' are more useful.
2 We do not, however, intend to deal in depth with this point in this chapter. It is the subject of a longer research project which we are involved in.
3 The Overseas Development Administration's Chief Economist admitted in 1992 (at a seminar at Manchester University) that he could find no correlations in Southern countries between economic growth and pluralistic political structures, nor conversely between poor economic performance, and authoritarianism. He stated a clear ambition to find one, as he believed 'instinctively there must be something in it'.

REFERENCES

Abdullah, H. (1993) 'The Democratic Process and the Challenge of Gender in Nigeria', *Review of African Political Economy* 56: 27–37.
Alvarez, S. (1990) *Engendering Democracy in Brazil: Women's Movements in Transition Politics*, Princeton, NJ: Princeton University Press.
Beetham, D. (1992) 'Liberal Democracy and the Limits of Democratization', *Political Studies* (special issue) 40: 40–53.
Beetham, D. (1993) *The Democratic Audit of the United Kingdom*, London: Charter 88 Trust.
Jaquette, J. (ed.) (1991) *The Women's Movement in Latin America*, Boulder, CO: Westview.
Liatto-Katundo, B. (1993) 'Women's Lobby and Gender Relations in Zambia', in *Review of African Political Economy* 56: 79–82

FURTHER READING

There are many recent studies of the role women have played in the struggle for democratisation in the South. In Latin America, the literature has focused particularly on the role of women's organisations and protest activity in the transitions from military to civilian rule in the Southern Cone countries of Argentina, Brazil, Uruguay and Chile. A useful edited collection of case studies is J. Jaquette (ed.) (1991) *The Women's Movement in Latin America*. S. Alvarez (1990) *Engendering Democracy in Brazil: Women's Movements in Transition Politics* is a significant book-length study of the women's movement in Brazil and its contribution to democratic transition in that country. A useful critical essay on some of this literature is provided by G. Waylen (1993) 'Women's Movements and Democratisation in Latin America', *Third World Quarterly* 14(3). The Review of African Political Economy (ROAPE) has provided consistent coverage of debates around gender and politics in Africa during the 1980s and 1990s. Two articles referred to in this chapter offer relevant case studies from Southern and West Africa respectfully: H. Abdullah (1993) 'The Democratic Process and the Challenge of Gender in Nigeria', and B. Liatto-Katundo (1993) 'Women's Lobby and Gender Relations in Zambia', both in *Review of African Political Economy* 56. In terms of debates on democracy and democratisation in Western Europe, particularly Britain, the work of David Beetham is theoretically important while also suggesting directions for research on contemporary problems of democracy: D. Beetham (1992) 'Liberal Democracy and the Limits of Democratization', *Political Studies* 40 and D. Beetham (1993) *The Democratic Audit of the United Kingdom*.

Chapter 4

The role of women in the resistance to political authoritarianism in Latin America and South Asia

Rohini Hensman

In the mid-1990s, thanks to the work of feminist historians who have pains-takingly excavated the evidence buried by a male-biased view of history, it would be hard to deny that women have played a significant role in resis-tance struggles and national liberation movements. What I want to argue here, however, is a stronger position: namely, that in the countries considered, women have in specific conjunctures played a crucial or leading role in the resistance to political authoritarianism, an autonomous role independent of male leadership. The purpose is not to make a very detailed examination of the situations under consideration but, rather, to discuss some of the theor-etical questions raised by the nature of women's political intervention.

Politics is about power relationships: about establishing and maintaining them, or contesting those which already exist (which may, but need not neces-sarily, involve establishing new ones). These relationships occur at all levels: between nation-states or even blocs of nation-states at one extreme, between individuals at the other. And the political activity which establishes, maintains or challenges power relations can take a potentially infinite variety of forms, with varying degrees of organisational coherence and stability.

While some of the chapters in this book are concerned with women's par-ticipation in or exclusion from more formal political processes, this chapter concentrates on ways in which women have organised *outside* formal political structures, not in order to gain access to them but in order to challenge and alter existing power relationships between the state and particular classes, between men and women.[1] What this type of activity questions is not simply the exclusion of women from power in the existing structures, but the validity of the structures themselves. In this context, 'democracy' is understood not in a narrow electoral sense, but in the broadest sense of the right of people, in both theory and practice, to control their own bodies, movements and lives, and participate in decisions to the same extent that they are affected by them. Authoritarianism is the opposite – the negation of this kind of democracy – and I have used the qualification 'political' to mean authoritarianism in public, not private, life. Is there any reason to believe that women are more capable of resisting this kind of politics than men? And if so, how can this be explained?

ARGENTINA

The autonomous intervention of women in politics in Argentina, Chile and Brazil became significant precisely at a point when political life as a whole was at its lowest ebb. The best-known case is probably that of the Madres of the Plaza de Mayo in Argentina. After the military coup in March 1976, the generals sets up over 340 secret concentration camps in the country. Around 30,000 victims, including trade union militants, students, intellectuals, pregnant women and even babies, were abducted, taken to these camps, and never seen alive again. A year later, in April 1977, fourteen women gathered in the Plaza de Mayo to draw up a letter demanding information about their missing children, and subsequently began meeting there regularly every Thursday, in defiance of a government ban. They were joined by more and more women whose children and grandchildren had disappeared, and in October published a half-page advertisement in a national newspaper demanding the release of those in illegal detention. In December, fourteen of the mothers, including their leader, were arrested and disappeared; but the campaign continued (Fisher 1993: 104–10).

In a situation where state terrorism had virtually destroyed all forms of organisation within civil society, the Madres succeeded in sustaining a political organisation and agenda through developing 'new forms of mobilization, such as a walk (ronda) around the plaza; giving old symbols a new meaning (e.g. the white handkerchiefs); [and] their capacity to resignify a public space (the plaza)' (Feijoo 1989: 78). While the loss of their children affected both mothers and fathers, it was women who took the courageous decision to organise themselves and give public expression to their private anxiety and grief, thus initiating a process of organised political protest against the dictatorship.

The economic policies of the military, which resulted in widespread unemployment and a disastrous fall in living standards for working-class and even middle-class families, gave rise to a different kind of protest movement. In 1982, women from middle-class households formed the Buenos Aires Housewives' Movement and distributed leaflets saying 'No to fear, No to "don't get involved"' and calling on housewives to protest against the rising cost of living with bread and meat boycotts. They persisted, despite efforts by the military to intimidate them, and the response was massive: by 1983, thousands of women throughout the country had joined, and they changed the name of the organisation to the National Housewives Movement (ACP) with an eighteen-point programme of demands for price controls on basic foodstuffs and urban services, subsidised school meals, cheap housing, and unemployment benefit. The Community Health Workers (ESC) was a more working-class organisation which, beginning in 1981, began taking up health problems including malnutrition and child health, women's health and contraception, lack of clean water and safe sewerage systems. They survived the dictatorship and expanded subsequently, reaching out to more neighbourhoods and in 1989 setting up the Community Organisation Foundation (FOC) which helped them to take up small-scale income-generating projects and child care (Fisher 1993: 158–67).

All these women's organisations started out with very traditional 'feminine' concerns, but the experience of self-organisation inevitably politicised them. Those who joined the Madres learned the value of solidarity, the empowerment which comes from being part of a collective rather than an isolated and helpless individual: 'We were all mothers together, all mothers whose children had been taken away, and we understood each other's pain. It was a tremendous relief and for the first time since my daughter disappeared I felt I could do something' (Fisher 1993: 106). Even though in most cases they did not succeed in getting their children back or punishing those who were guilty of human rights abuses, the whole process made them identify with the cause for which their children had died:

> They were taken because they made a stand against the military and against injustice, whether it was in their factories, schools or universities. We began to realise that 'politics' meant something more than just the political parties. When we began to understand our children's real histories, their concern for social change, we began to make the same demands.
>
> (Fisher 1993: 134–5)

The involvement of women in housewives' organisations led them to take up issues of women's rights, access to family planning, socialisation of housework, combatting the gender division of labour and machismo, and democratising home life. As Jo Fisher remarks, 'The success of grassroots groups such as the ESC suggests that these organisations have an important role to play in democratising a political system that has so often failed working-class men and women' (Fisher 1993: 150, 168–9).

CHILE

In Chile, massive state repression unleashed after the military coup of September 1973 terrorised the population and immobilised political protest for several years. The *poblaciones* (slums) of Santiago were repeatedly raided by the military, thousands of people were arrested, tortured, and in many cases killed. As in Argentina, women played a key role in organising solidarity groups for political prisoners, and were the first to take to the streets, publicly condemning human rights abuses and protesting against the military regime.

They also organised, on a much larger scale than in Argentina, to feed their families in the face of the devastating impact of the regime's economic policies. *Ollas comunes* (community kitchens), organised by women to buy, prepare and serve food collectively, mushroomed in many neighbourhoods. Initially most of the women involved in them did not see their activity as political but as an extension of their domestic role of feeding and caring for their families. The military, however, were more perceptive: any organisation outside their control was seen as an act of defiance, a subversive activity. Kitchens were raided, women who ran them were detained; in order to continue running, the kitchens had to become clandestine, moving from house to house. Women were pushed into resistance to the military regime without originally having intended anything of the sort (Fisher 1993: 29–33).

In 1978, women organised the first large demonstration since the coup and broke the fear psychosis by

> stepping out of the family, leaving the allegedly protected environment of their homes to invade the streets with their presence and demand a return to participatory democracy. They did so many years before men dared manifest themselves publicly against the regime. The formation of the umbrella organisation Mujeres por la Vida (Women for Life) brought together diverse women's organisations, including the Movement of Shanty-Town Women (Movimento de Mujeres Pobladoras), The Women's Union Coordinating Committee (La Coordinatora Sindical Femenina) and the Feminist Movement, with the slogan 'Democracy in the country and at home'.
>
> (Bunster 1988: 211–12)

As this slogan indicates, the experience of political self-organisation led women to question their marginalisation in the public, political sphere, and their relegation to a private sphere where their role was defined purely in terms of their reproductive potential. Their opposition to the dictatorship and participation in the struggle for democracy was the context in which the demands for recognition as equal partners, women's liberation, and democratisation of private life emerged as important issues (Chuchryk 1989: 162). Even among the many Chilean feminists who continued to emphasise the centrality of class struggle, machismo and women's oppression came to be seen as being divisive of the working class, and therefore to be opposed even from a purely class perspective (Chuchryk 1989: 171).

Grassroots women's groups, despite having started off rejecting feminism and continuing to remain suspicious of middle-class feminists, gradually began to put women's rights on the agenda, raising issues such as domestic violence, sexuality, equality in the home and the workplace, contraception and abortion:

> We wanted to play a part in the working-class struggle for democracy, but we also wanted to fight for our needs as women. We wanted a cultural transformation, a society with many changes in values. It wasn't that we wanted democracy, full stop. We didn't want women to go back to their houses when the struggle against the dictatorship ended. We had a couple of meetings with the feminists and we began to realise that we were

something different from the kind of feminism they were talking about –
that ours was a grassroots kind of feminism.

(Fisher 1993: 191–4, 186)

BRAZIL

In Brazil, as in Argentina, women made their appearance on the political
scene at a time when military rule and state terrorism had virtually stamped
out all other forms of political life. The military coup of 1964 installed a
regime which inaugurated policies of political repression and economic liber-
alisation, thus attacking democratic institutions and living standards simultaneously. In the 1970s and 1980s, community-based organisations of poor
women sprang up throughout Brazil, and organised against human rights
abuses and the rising cost of living, demanding adequate schools, day-care
centres, running water, sewers, electrification, and other urban infrastructural
necessities. In 1979, International Women's Day was celebrated in several
Brazilian cities, and the first Paulista Women's Congress drew nearly 1,000
participants: middle-class feminists as well as women from working-class
women's groups. The Congress discussed not only issues such as living conditions, day care and political participation, but also sexuality, the control of
fertility, and power relations between men and women; the demand for the
democratisation of daily life, and not just political society, was raised. The
Congress acted as a spur to the formation of new feminist as well as neighbourhood women's groups, and took their proposals to the First National
Women's Congress in Rio (Alvarez 1989: 21, 38–9).

The survival of women's organisations in such a situation has been explained
by Alvarez in the following terms:

The ingrained belief that women are indifferent to politics may have led the
military rulers of Brazil to believe that anything women do is intrinsically
'apolitical'. Thus, even when women began organizing campaigns against
the rising cost of living or human rights in Brazil, the military seems to have
allowed women's associations greater political leeway than was granted to
militant left, student and labor organizations, which were seen as more
threatening to 'national security'. The 1975 celebrations of International
Women's Day were thus among the first public assemblies permitted since
the mass mobilizations of 1967–1968. The Feminine Amnesty Movement
was allowed to organize in the mid-1970s when a conventional movement
of that sort might have been actively repressed. In short, the institutionalized
separation between the public and private may, in an ironic historical twist,
have helped to propel women to the forefront of the opposition in Brazil.

(Alvarez 1989: 25–6)

The return to electoral politics resulted in some degree of marginalisation of
the women's movement, but some permanent gains remained, not only in

the continued existence of groups like *SOS-Mulher* (to combat violence against women) and *Grupo Acao Lesbica-Feminista* (to combat heterosexism), but also in more institutionalised changes, such as the creation of the *Delegacia da Mulher*, a police precinct staffed entirely by specially trained female officers to deal with cases of rape, sexual abuse and domestic violence (Alvarez 1989: 48, 56).

In all these three countries, women organising to resist political authoritarianism confronted the military authorities with a dilemma: how could they be repressed simply for trying to be good wives, mothers and housewives? The state's own gender ideology thus gave women a small space for manoeuvre: they used 'the "social construction" of femininity, by making legitimate their cultural female resources – "mother power" – in the political arena. They ... consciously used their nurturing role as a powerful political instrument aimed at destabilising' military rule (Bunster 1988: 211).

The reason why women were able to utilise this minimal space to such striking effect was that they adopted innovative forms of organisation which were unfamiliar to the state authorities and therefore more difficult to handle. When the dictatorship banned political parties and trade unions, the traditional male-dominated forms of organisation, most men were paralysed, deprived of their power of organised action. Women, traditionally less organised, were also less bound by the traditional forms of organisation, and could use their imagination and skill to organise not merely nationally but also internationally to combat authoritarian military regimes.

NICARAGUA

The situation in Nicaragua was slightly different, in that the Sandinista National Liberation Front (FSLN), with a significant proportion of its membership consisting of women, was already engaged in struggle when women's groups became active. In 1977, the Association of Nicaraguan Women Confronting the Nation's Problems (AMPRONAC) was formed to publicise atrocities committed by the National Guard and campaign for the release of political prisoners.

> Nearly three-quarters of the people who took to the streets in the popular insurrection were under twenty-five, and supporting them in their clandestine activity, coming to their defence when threatened and tortured by the National Guard, seemed a natural extension of motherhood. ... AMPRONAC actively recruited women around this aspect of their lives. 'We women experience this political crisis as citizens, wives and housewives,' declared its programme. ... The opportunity to take part in politics through development of their normal roles was a significant factor in the extent of women's involvement in the war.
>
> (Harris 1988: 193–4)

In 1979 AMPRONAC was renamed the Luisa Amanda Espinoza Association of Nicaraguan Women (AMNLAE) after the first young woman guerrilla to be killed by the National Guard, and took on the task of fighting inequality and discrimination against women. Although it continued to emphasise the incorporation of women in the struggle to defend liberated Nicaragua, there was also an attempt to insist on the recognition of women's rights. This was not achieved without a struggle, however. In the early 1980s, AMNLAE was criticised for failing to take up issues like domestic violence, abortion and sex education, and the criticisms were brought into the open in a crisis meeting in September 1985. At that point, 'it maintained its credibility by including in its agenda some of the most pressing concerns of Nicaraguan women: discrimination at work, sexual abuse and domestic violence, the need for sex education and an end to the culture of machismo, especially its result – "irresponsible fatherhood"' (i.e. men who took responsibility neither for supporting nor for taking care of their children) (Stead 1991: 60).

These concerns were subsequently taken up by the FSLN in 1987, in a proclamation which condemned machismo and irresponsible fatherhood, calling on men to share domestic tasks and the responsibility for supporting their children. As a result of pressure from AMNLAE, the Sandinista government even passed legislation to this effect; but the strength of the opposition to these laws was demonstrated by the fact that they were neither published nor implemented. (Stead 1991: 60–3). In a sense, the politicisation of motherhood in an earlier phase of acute political repression made it easier for women to gain recognition for the social contribution made by their normal day-to-day activity in maintaining the home, and to question the convention which laid the entire burden of this work on them alone. But the Nicaraguan case also seems to demonstrate the paradox that more extensive participation of women in a male-dominated liberation movement can restrict or delay the development of a genuine grassroots feminism which, without abandoning its commitment to working-class emancipation, is also firm in its commitment to women's rights.

SRI LANKA

A similar politicisation of motherhood occurred in Sri Lanka, where since the late 1970s a civilian dictatorship and civil war resulted in a thoroughgoing militarisation of society. Initially state repression was directed against the Tamil minority, mostly concentrated in the north and east of the island although present in smaller numbers everywhere. In the name of fighting against a 'terrorist' threat posed by armed militant groups which arose in response to the repression, a virtual war against Tamil civilians was declared, aided by the passing of the Prevention of Terrorism Act 1979, which in effect encouraged human rights abuses by the security forces. Subsequently, when a Sinhalese militant group staged an anti-government insurrection beginning in 1987, the same methods were used against it and its alleged Sinhalese supporters. Meanwhile the Tamil militant groups too became increasingly authoritarian, attempting to wipe out rival Tamil groups, dissenters within their own ranks and Tamil civilian critics, as well as carrying out massacres of civilians from other ethnic groups, including women and even children.

In 1985, the Mother's Front in the northern province of Jaffna drafted and sent to the president a letter cataloguing the effects of the emergency regulations and excesses of the security forces, and demanding an end to them. Although the initial spur to their organisation and action might have been fear for the safety of their children, in a situation where young men were arbitrarily being abducted, tortured and killed, they were also protesting against the total disruption of economic and social life in the province which resulted from the imposition of authoritarian state rule.

Nor did women content themselves simply with opposing repression from the 'other' side, but also tackled the difficult task of opposing it within their own ethnic group. For example, in 1986 Tamil women in the eastern province armed themselves with rice pounders – a common but potentially lethal domestic implement – to prevent the dominant Liberation Tigers of Tamil Eelam (LTTE) from massacring unarmed members of a rival Tamil group. Perhaps the most spectacular instance and the one most reminiscent of Latin America was a Mothers' Front rally, consisting mainly of Sinhalese women, in southern Sri Lanka in 1991. Counter-insurgency operations by the Sinhalese government against a Sinhalese militant group, carried out through the military as well as unofficial death squads, had resulted in an estimated 60,000 disappearances and extrajudicial killings, not only of suspected insurgents but also of civilian critics and opponents of the government. The consequence was an almost palpable atmosphere of terror, in which people were afraid even to voice criticisms in private, much less organise in open opposition to the state. The success of the Mothers' Front rally, undertaken in defiance of a government ban, was a crucial element in breaking the terror which had gripped the south and opening the way once again for organised civilian opposition (Hensman 1992: 502–4).

The ability to be critical of authoritarianism within their own ethnic group also enabled Sri Lankan women to oppose the ethnic war as such, seeing it as a power struggle with only negative consequences for most people of all communities. While organised opposition to the war was confined to a few small groups such as Women for Peace, emotional and verbal opposition was far more widespread. For example, the remark by a Tamil woman refugee – greeted with laughing assent by her friends – that 'Since 1958 the old men have been talking and wasting time; now the young men are taking up arms and wasting time' expresses a very common scepticism about the antics of male leaders (Hensman 1993: 42).

INDIA

In India, the emergence of a countrywide women's movement on a mass scale in 1979–80 was sparked off by a case of police rape – a common but no means unique form of police brutality. The massive demonstrations and agitations by women which followed the Supreme Court acquittal of a policeman who had raped a young woman can be seen as a crucial element in the human and civil rights movement to protect citizens from the arbitrary violence of state functionaries. Many of the women's organisations formed in the course of that campaign survived and grew subsequently, extending their concerns to various other forms of violence against women as well as more general social control over and discrimination against women.

A different and more subtle form of state authoritarianism was displayed in the wake of the Bhopal disaster in December 1984, when a gas leak from a Union Carbide pesticides factory left over 10,000 dead and hundreds of thousands injured. The Government of India passed an Ordinance proclaiming itself the sole legal representative of the survivors in their struggle both to obtain compensation and – perhaps even more importantly from their point of view – to prosecute the company for the negligence and recklessness which had caused the disaster. In 1989, the government came to a settlement with Union Carbide which not only accepted a paltry sum as compensation, but also agreed to drop all criminal charges against the company, much to the outrage of the gas victims it was supposed to be representing. Thousands of infuriated survivors, predominantly women, proceeded to make the long journey to the Supreme Court in Delhi in order to demonstrate against the settlement, which was in fact overturned when a new government came to power. It was remarked by many observers that most of the men appeared to have become disheartened and apathetic as a result of the long-drawn-out, frustrating legal proceedings, whereas most of the women never gave up their militancy or their quest for justice.[2]

In India, although the state is defined as a secular one, authoritarian politics has often taken the form of religious fundamentalism or revivalism, especially Hindu chauvinism. Throughout the history of independent India there have been communal riots in which the majority of victims have been Muslims; but in one of the worst, the Delhi riots of 1984, Sikhs were targeted in a pogrom in which politicians from the ruling Congress Party played a prominent role. Another outbreak of violence, this time directed against Muslims, followed the destruction of the Babri Mosque in Ayodhya in December 1992; a horrific pogrom in Bombay the following month left several hundreds dead, thousands homeless, and an immense amount of property destroyed. These activities were organised and carried out by extreme right-wing Hindu chauvinist organisations, but state collusion was also indicated by the failure – as in the case of the Delhi riots – to take appropriate legal measures against the leaders and perpetrators of the atrocities. A more direct indication of the communalisation of the state was its role in Punjab (with a predominantly Sikh population) and Kashmir (with a predominantly Muslim population) where, in the name of fighting terrorism, state security forces waged a virtual war against helpless civilians.

The threat posed by fundamentalist movements to women's rights is so dire that the emergence of women's organisations as their strongest opponents is hardly surprising. However, the threat to women was least obvious in India, where Hindu revivalism very cleverly adopted elements of feminist discourse while in practice affirming the subordinate status of women, and used traditional symbols of female strength to argue that Hindu women did not need liberation because they already had it within traditional Hinduism.

Nonetheless, women's groups have actively opposed Hindu chauvinism. After every round of communal violence, women's organisations have been in the forefront of relief work, peace marches and door-to-door canvassing for communal harmony. While in general this activity has tended to follow rather than forestall the actual violence, it has played a significant role in limiting the damage and minimising feelings of rancour which could lead to further violence. It is notable that all four video films made in Bombay in the wake of the December 1992 to January 1993 anti-Muslim pogroms as part of a movement of resistance to Hindu religious revivalism were produced by women, and a moving account of atrocities committed against the Kashmiri people by Indian paramilitary forces was once again the work of four women (Choudhury *et al.* 1994). These women's initiatives were not just expressions of humanitarian compassion, but also efforts towards formulating a political agenda opposed to the authoritarianism of right-wing forces, whether they were incorporated in the state or not.[3]

PAKISTAN

Pakistan was created as an Islamic state in 1947 – a condition making for overall conservatism and especially disadvantageous to women. Its Islamic character being the *raison d'être* of the nation, it became particularly hard to challenge instances of discrimination which emerged from it, and early women's organisations like the All-Pakistan Women's Association (APWA, founded in 1949) operated to bring about reforms within these constraints. Paradoxically, it was only after a military coup led by General Ayub Khan had put an end to the unstable parliamentary government that a major legal reform in the interests of women (the Family Law Ordinance 1961) was enacted. The law, which was passed only as a result of determined campaigning by APWA and other women's organisations, restricted (but did not abolish) polygamy, gave women more rights on divorce, and raised the legal age of marriage for females from 14 to 16. The implementation of these reforms was even more restricted than the reforms themselves, and the undemocratic character of the regime made it easier for its fundamentalist opponents to gain strength. However, continued pressure from women's groups prevented the Ordinance from being repealed altogether (Jalal 1991: 94–6).

The populist government of Z.A. Bhutto which succeeded the Ayub Khan dictatorship introduced reformist policies in favour of the rural and urban poor as well as women, but once again, these reforms were only very half-heartedly implemented (Jalal 1991: 98–9). Bhutto's overthrow by Zia-ul Haq's fundamentalist military dictatorship inaugurated a period of openly reactionary, anti-women policies. The Hudood Ordinance, enacted in 1979, made it possible for a rape victim who could not prove she had been raped to be sentenced to public flogging for adultery. The requirement for a woman to 'prove' she had been raped was either confession by the rapist or the evidence of four morally upright Muslim men who had witnessed the crime – a condition which made it virtually impossible for a woman to prove rape, since presumably four upright Muslim men would hardly allow the crime to take place in their presence without intervening to prevent it (Jalal 1991: 102).

The Women's Action Forum (WAF) was formed in 1981 when the Hudood Ordinance was used to sentence a man and a woman who had eloped and got married to being stoned to death and 100 lashes respectively. Starting in Karachi, the organisation spread rapidly, indicating that it was responding to a felt need. In 1983, women's organisations took up an even more horrific case where Safia Bibi, a half-blind servant girl who had been raped by her employer and his son, was sentenced to public lashing and a fine while the rapists were acquitted. The publicity and campaign resulted in the sentence being withdrawn, although the Ordinance remained (Mumtaz and Shaheed 1987: 73–4, 103–4).

The Law of Evidence, proposed in 1982, made a female witness equivalent to half a male witness in a court of law. Once again, WAF and other women's organisations spearheaded the protests against it, and in February 1983 a demonstration of about 300 women was tear-gassed and beaten up by the police. Although the law was finally passed in October 1984, the agitation had succeeded in modifying it considerably, so that only in 'all matters pertaining to financial and future obligations providing these are reduced to writing' was the evidence of a woman considered to be half that of a man. In the case of the proposed Law of Qisas and Diyat, which would have reduced the compensation for the killing or injury of a woman to half that for a man, women's opposition succeeded in stalling the law altogether (Mumtaz and Shaheed 1987: 106–14, 139). It was also probably due to the activity of women's groups that fundamentalists failed to push through legislation making it impossible for a woman to become head of state; but Benazir Bhutto, when she did come to power, did not live up to the hopes which many women had that her government would take firm steps to remove all discriminatory legislation.

While these activities of feminist groups undoubtedly counteracted *some* of the worst consequences of the military's policies for women, other effects were not touched. Women's groups like WAF were faced with a number of crucial questions: 'Is there a need for a pure feminist movement, or for a broader-based women's movement to struggle for women's rights? . . . What, if any, is the relationship that such a movement, whether strictly-speaking feminist or not, should or should not have with other political and social forces operating in the country?' (Mumtaz and Shaheed 1987: 149). Some of these issues were posed very concretely in Lahore when the management of a factory employing a large number of women dismissed several workers, including the more out-spoken women, in an attempt to break the union. Even though some of the victimised women workers were members of WAF, the organisation refused to support them on the grounds that they were being victimised not as women but as union activists. However, this distinction did not make sense to the women workers, who felt that the organisation had failed to support them in a struggle for their rights. Some members were critical of this decision, and the Karachi branch in fact decided to work with rural and urban poor women on their issues, and to form closer relationships with trade unions, teachers, students and other interest groups. As in Chile, there were also women's groups for whom the class issue was primary (Mumtaz and Shaheed 1987: 149–53).

BANGLADESH

Most women's groups in Pakistan, while contesting extreme violations of human rights resulting from Islamic fundamentalism, were reluctant to challenge the Islamic character of the state because this would have been equivalent to questioning the basis of the nation itself. Bangladesh, by contrast, although originally a part of Pakistan, was constituted as an independent state in 1971 after a bloody war of liberation from an Islamic state, with an identity which was Bengali rather than Islamic. The Awami League government of Sheikh Mujib which took power after Independence was politically non-aligned and secular; but after his assassination in 1975 and a series of military coups, power was finally taken by Zia-ur Rahman, who embarked on a pro-Islamic course which was continued by General Ershad, who took power after yet another coup in 1981 (Kabeer 1991: 121–4).

Zia-ur Rahman started the process of de-secularising the state in 1977, with Proclamation Order no. 1 which deleted the principle of secularism from the Constitution and replaced it by 'absolute trust and faith in the Almighty Allah'. The process was continued by Ershad, who in 1988 pushed through the Eighth Amendment, which declared the state religion to be Islam (Kabeer 1991: 131–2). 'Significantly, the first demonstrations and rallies in opposition to the government's Eighth Amendment were called by women's groups: as a leading newspaper commented, "This time the women have taken the lead"' (*Holiday*, 19 April 1988). The same article commented that women's opposition to the Amendment drew its moral roots from the humanistic values which had inspired the liberation struggle. In the words of a resolution adopted at the end of one of the rallies called by women's groups, 'The war was supposed to guarantee freedom of speech, freedom of thought, women's rights' (*Holiday*, 29 April 1988). One of the groups, Naripokkho, also called attention to the attack on minority rights represented by Islamisation of the state (Kabeer 1991: 139).

Farida Akhter, president of the Gonotantrik Nari Andolan in Bangladesh, was expressing a widely held view amongst women's groups when she said that, 'For the women of Bangladesh the task becomes a democratic transformation of the state' (Akhter 1992: 77). However, as in the case of Pakistan, the return to some species of parliamentary democracy with Khaleda Zia's government did not mean a reversal of the Islamisation policies, nor a genuine democratisation of women's lives; the struggle against authoritarianism in private and public life continued.

While international organisation among South Asian feminists has not reached anywhere near the impressive level achieved by Latin American feminists, there have been significant attempts at solidarity and networking – especially important in a region where each country has been in a war or near-war situation with at least one of the others. A draft South Asian Feminist Declaration issued by a joint conference in 1989 remarked that

> Feminism as a movement in South Asia has asserted the principle of autonomous organisation for women, while linking with broader movements at the same time. . . . Linking together in concrete actions, formulating and campaigning on a joint charter of women's rights, sharing visions and developing alternatives to existing development models at the South Asian level from a feminist perspective would be an important contribution towards overcoming the tensions, distrust, and political, economic, social and cultural crisis affecting our countries today.

WOMEN IN RIGHT-WING MOVEMENTS

At this point it is important to emphasise that this is not an argument that women are by nature anti-authoritarian, or that they do not play a role in right-wing movements. Women are, of course, divided by class, ethnicity, religion, political orientation, etc., and these other identities may pit them against each other more than gender brings them together.[4] There are many examples which demonstrate this.

In Chile, while Mujeres por la Vida emerged to co-ordinate organisations mobilising women to oppose the Pinochet regime, the military was also busy mobilising other women to turn them into a base of support for the very same regime. And the effort, begun in 1973, was not unsuccessful. By 1987, pro-regime women's community organisations controlled thousands of women and permeated civilian life.

> The two most important organisations, because of their sophisticated structure and management and their massively articulated impact on

women from all social classes [were] Cema-Chile (Chilean Mother's Centres) and the Secretaria National de la Mujer (Women's National Secretariat), or S.N.M. ... By 1983 Cema-Chile had 6,000 volunteers responsible for organising and indocrinating 230,000 members in more than 10,000 mothers' centres; the S.N.M. boasted of having 10,000 volunteers in 321 branch officers; and it is estimated that during the ten-year period, 1973 to 1983, its activities had involved more than two million women.

(Bunster 1988: 213–14)

The president of both organisations was Pinochet's wife, Lucia Hirart de Pinochet: in the case of SNM, appointed by Pinochet himself. Typically, SNM volunteers would be upper-middle and middle-class, middle-aged women whose lives were not in any way threatened by the military regime; most Cema volunteers were wives of officers of the armed forces and police. These organisations offered such women a chance to play a prominent role in public life without challenging power relations at the domestic or national level. (Bunster 1988).

In India, the Rashtriya Swayamsevak Sangh (RSS), a right-wing Hindu organisation formed in 1925, 'is virtually unique among modern Indian socio-political organisations in being exclusively male. It did, however, set up a women's branch, the Rashtrasevika Samiti, the first, in fact, of its affiliates, way back in 1936' (Basu et al. 1993: 41). By 1993 it had a membership of around 100,000 mainly middle-class women, typically with male relatives in the RSS. Although there were sessions (shakhas) providing members with physical and ideological training, there was a greater stress on family work:

Simple daily rituals are prescribed for home use, with even a 'correspondence course' of postal instructions for those who, after marriage, are unable to attend the shakhas. Members make it a point to visit each other's homes, help out in domestic crises and maintain contact even with those who can no longer find time for Samiti work. Ideology is spread through sustained kinship and neighbourhood contact with non-Rashtrasevika women, and there is a system of informal training for unaffiliated wives of RSS members and sympathizers.

(Basu et al. 1993: 42)

The efficacy of this 'molecular' model of ideological mobilisation was borne out by the participation of 20,000 frenzied women activists (kar sevikas) in the demolition of the Babri Mosque, while women activists of the Mahila Aghadi of the Shiv Sena subsequently participated in the gruesome anti-Muslim pogrom in Bombay. As in Chile, these organisations provided an opportunity for mainly middle-class, middle-to-upper-caste Hindu women to play a role in public life and assert themselves at the expense of a defenceless minority community.[5]

The role of women as mothers is highlighted in these cases too; but what distinguishes it from the subversive motherhood of resistance organisations is that it is firmly rooted within an authoritarian patriarchal structure. In Chile,

> The 'patriotic mother' drummed up by the Pinochet regime is ... strictly subordinated to the pater familias and particularly to the pater patrias (father of the nation); the 'patriotic mother' has a derived secondary identity stemming from her unconditional admiration for the 'father of the homeland', Pinochet himself.
>
> (Bunster 1988: 216)

Similarly in India, the RSS model is one of

> faithful motherhood in which the women affiliated to the RSS would con-fine themselves to the proper training of children and spreading the word through quiet domestic and neighbourhood contacts. ... Members pool resources to reduce the burden of dowry, instead of campaigning against it. Sevikas are always told to try persuasion, but never openly revolt against their families, in matters of choice of husband, marital ill-treatment, or even participation in Samiti work. ... They disapprove of divorce and offer no legal counselling to women fighting against their families for their rights.
>
> (Basu et al. 1993: 42)

Although the Rashtrasevika Samiti represents a restricted form of women's empowerment, the organisation 'accepts final commands from an all-male leadership that refuses any debate on Hindu patriarchy' (Sarkar 1993: 43).

A very different example underlines what these women's organisations have in common. In Sri Lanka the LTTE, one of the most ruthless and authori-tarian of the Tamil militant groups, had a significant number of women fighters, known as the 'Freedom Birds'. These women were undoubtedly playing a non-conventional role, and in their case there was no question of motherhood: indeed, it is believed that one of the factors driving young women (many of them victims of gang-rape and other traumatic experiences) to take up arms in the war-ravaged north and east of Sri Lanka was the virtual impossibility of their ever having a normal family life. In the absence of a *pater familias*, the object of their unquestioning devotion was the male leader V. Prabhakaran (who might be called the father of the Tamil nation), for whom they declared themselves unconditionally ready to fight and die.

What these examples show is that women, in large numbers, can be drawn in to support authoritarian regimes or leaderships; the subservient role played by these women contrasts sharply with the independent, autonomous role of women's resistance groups and organisations. The prominent presence of women on opposite sides in these conflicts emphasises the dangers of treating 'women' as a homogeneous category, ignoring differences of class, community and political orientation; it would obviously be wrong to say that all women are opposed to authoritarian politics.

DIVISIONS AMONG FEMINISTS

An even more troubling issue is the question of what influence these divisions have within the women's movement itself. The Chilean working-class women's organisation MOMUPO (Movement of Women Pobladoras) identified themselves as grassroots feminists who 'not only challenged the assertion that trade unions and political parties speak for all the working class but also questioned the idea that "traditional" feminism speaks for all women' (Fisher 1993: 168). Their suspicion of middle-class feminists was based on a perception of these women as being privileged, and even exploitative:

We've tried to work with middle-class feminists but they talk about a different world from ours. For example, they did a workshop where they told us we've got to value ourselves, stop serving the biggest steak to the men. Of course poor women like us aren't very familiar with steaks! . . . We've been to their women's centres because they have the resources to offer legal advice or psychologists for battered women. It's another world, all carpeted, with pictures on the wall, everything brand new. We felt uncomfortable. The only time we'd been in houses like that was as domestic servants. We are the ones these women use as their servants.

(Fisher 1993: 187)

Middle-class feminists don't come here because we almost never invite them. We've got a lot of resentment towards them because they themselves often exploit women. They pay their domestic employees a miserable wage while they're having their chats about equality.

(Fisher 1993: 197)

Similarly, the Buenos Aires Housewives' Movement sharply distinguished itself from the more upper-class League of Housewives:

We were all housewives and that was one of the differences with the League. Some of us worked outside the home but we still did the housework. To us, a housewife isn't a wealthy woman who doesn't work inside or outside the house, but only orders another woman to do it. We are housewives who do the work ourselves. It's a big difference.

(Fisher 1993: 148)

It has been argued that in Pakistan the predominantly middle- and upper-class membership of most women's groups made it convenient for them to come to an accommodation with the Islamic state, within which they had a privileged position due to their class status (Jalal 1991: 78–9). In India, the predominantly upper-class Hindu membership of most women's groups made them oblivious to the danger of calling for a 'Uniform Civil Code', a slogan easily taken over by the Hindu chauvinist right since 'uniform' by itself does not necessarily imply either 'secular' or 'gender-just'; even more seriously, the diverse political and ideological affiliations of women's groups in Bombay prevented them from coming together and making a strong condemnation of the perpetrators of the 1993 pogroms, or campaigning for the punishment of those who were guilty of horrific gang-rapes of Muslim women. It appears, therefore, that the existence of more privileged sections within the women's movement can hinder the emergence of a unified opposition to authoritarian politics.

FEMINISM AND DEMOCRACY

Despite all these counter-examples, however, we still have to explain the fact that women have proved themselves capable of active, autonomous, vehement opposition to authoritarian politics in situations where men of the same class, community and political orientation have been much weaker in their opposition if not virtually silenced.

The reasons seem to fall into two main categories. The first category depends on a definition of women's rights as democratic rights in the broad sense of the capacity to control one's own life and destiny. Seen in this light, feminism is an essential component of democracy while, conversely, 'democracy' which lacks a feminist dimension is essentially flawed: it embodies the contradiction between democracy in some aspects of public life combined with authoritarianism in male–female relationships. As Chilean feminist Julieta Kirkwood pointed out, the 'democracy' they were used to was of this type: 'Now, confronted by [military] authoritarianism, women, in a certain sense, are faced with a phenomenon well known to them: authoritarianism in their daily experiences' (quoted in Chuchryk 1989: 162). For the majority of women, this means that their struggle for democracy can be consistent and whole-hearted, unlike that of the majority of men who would wish to perpetuate some degree of male domination in gender relations.

The essentially political character of male–female relationships is made more explicit in the South Asian context wherever fundamentalist movements have gained strength. Amrita Chhachhi (1991) has argued that 'state-supported fundamentalism reinforces and shifts the right of control over women from kinsmen to any man of the community. The state emerges as the protector and regulator of the community and the family, resulting in a change in forms of patriarchal control over women' (1991: 167). In these circumstances, the struggle for women's rights involves a *direct* confrontation with the state; but even changes like the establishment of the women's police precinct in Brazil reveal the male bias normally present in state institutions, and the social acceptance of violent crimes against women as somehow being compatible with democratic and human rights. A society which tolerates authoritarianism in daily life is likely to pose less resistance to state authoritarianism than one which consciously encourages democratisation in all spheres of life. In this sense, feminism is intrinsic to the democratisation process not only in these countries but also throughout the world.

THE POLITICISATION OF MOTHERHOOD

The other category of reasons for the role of women in resisting authoritarian politics is intimately connected with the traditional feminine role of motherhood. It appears that in conditions of extreme repression, when the simple task of ensuring the survival and welfare of their loved ones is frustrated by widespread torture, disappearances and extrajudicial killing, women in their thousands take to the streets, they organise and resist. However this resistance is rooted not in any notion of their rights as women, but, on the contrary, in a passionate love for their children. This element is very evident in the testimonies of the Madres of the Plaza de Mayo:

* 'It's very difficult to explain how you feel when they take a child away from you and you don't know what's happened to the child. It's like a terrible emptiness, like something's been wrenched away from inside of you and there's nothing you can do about it.'
* 'They'd taken children from all of us so we all felt the same. We were afraid, but as mothers we felt our children needed us more than ever, that we had to do everything possible to find them.'
* 'Of course there was a lot of fear. Everyone felt it. My family said "be careful, something might happen to you", but I said to them, "what can be worse than them taking my child?"'

(Fisher 1993: 105, 107, 110)

In Sri Lanka too, one group of women explained their opposition to the ethnic war and concern for human and democratic rights in terms of their maternal role:

As women we identify with life-giving processes; we can never support death-dealing systems. The killing of other human beings is alien to us as women. We give birth, care for, nurture and protect life. Every human being is the child of a mother. There is something in our very nature that rebels against the taking of human life, the driving of people from their homes and the wanton destruction of people's means of livelihood.

(Women Against Racism and Militarisation 1986)

There is a problem here for major strands of feminism, which have 'explained women's political marginalisation as a result of their confinement to traditional and private roles' (Jaquette 1989: 188). Childcare in particular is seen as a source of oppression; for example, Shulamith Firestone says that 'the heart of woman's oppression is her child bearing and child rearing role', to be superseded entirely by modern genetic technology (Firestone 1970), and Simone de Beauvoir recommends that 'it would be desirable for the child to be left to his parents infinitely less than at present, and for his studies and diversions to be carried on among other children, under the direction of adults whose bonds with him would be impersonal and pure' (de Beauvoir 1953).

This cool and distant attitude towards children could not be more different from the passionate attachment which drove the Madres to struggle for years and risk their lives in the search for their children. What is the source of the difference? Katherine Gieve, in an article on feminist attitudes to motherhood, felt that 'it is essential to look at things in personal terms and try to bridge the gap between experience and theory' (Gieve 1987: 39); and it would probably be a useful exercise to try and do this in a Third World context, looking concretely at experiences of childhood and motherhood.

For most children, early childhood in a country like Sri Lanka is not an isolating experience; you are constantly surrounded by grandparents and other relatives, neighbours and friends, the adults among whom are referred to as 'aunt' and 'uncle', and, to a child, virtually indistinguishable from family. And yet, in my experience, you still feel the need for a special commitment from a few significant adults. My younger brother was born when I was 18 months old, and I was passed on to the care of my father while my mother took charge of the baby. I know my father's care was just as loving and gentle, yet my mother remembered me pleading with her to love me – apparently anxious about being displaced in her affections by the new arrival. A few years later, I remember accusing our child-minder of loving my brother more than she loved me, and being assured that she loved us both equally. Neither my parents nor I can remember any persistent anxiety or rivalry with my brother on my part, so presumably I was convinced by the reassurances I received.

I realise, of course, that I was an exceptionally lucky child, subjected to neither the physical deprivation nor the authoritarian and exclusive family and community relationships which most Third World children suffer; and yet, like all human beings, I started my life in total dependence on the people around me. To this day I am grateful for the unstinting love I was given by the significant adults in my life, a love which I feel has left me with a sense of security based on the knowledge of being valued for my own sake, without the need to prove myself in competition with anyone else. I cannot believe that such love could be harmful to any child, and on the contrary feel sure it must contribute to a stable identity. It must be quite terrifying coming into the world as a small and totally helpless creature, from time to time racked by uncontrollable pain, and I imagine it must take at least one person's total devotion to give you the confidence to develop as an individual. Physical survival too could be at stake: if mothers found it as easy to abandon children as fathers did in many Third World countries, child mortality would sky-rocket.

Most people are not likely to find themselves in a situation of such utter helplessness in later life, but there are exceptions: for example, being a political prisoner, tortured almost beyond human endurance, derided by the taunt that you have already ceased to exist so far as the outside world is concerned – the fate of the *desaparecido*, the 'disappeared'. I have spoken to Sri Lankan ex-detainees (most of them in fact released as a result of tireless effort on the part of their relatives, especially mothers) and I believe that under such circumstances it could be crucial to have someone who would go to any lengths to secure one's release; it could, in fact, make the difference between life and death.

But what affect does this love have on the giver? Here again, it would be useful to try and bridge the gap between experience and theory. In Western individualistic societies, motherhood usually means isolation, exclusion, and immense psychological pressures. In Third World societies where more of a community life survives, it need not mean these things: indeed, the testimonies of these two women, the first from Bombay and the second from São Paulo, suggest that in these societies children can sometimes be the only bright spot in lives which are otherwise unbearably grim:

> I've been married for six years, and my daughter is five years old. . . . My husband works in this same building colony as a sweeper. My parents married me off to him because he has a stable job, but he drinks a great deal and he beats me up . . . he suspects that I have an affair. He and his mother keep asking me, interrogating me, beating me. They also want me to work harder and kill myself. I have only one hope in life: I want to give the best I can to my daughter. I will tolerate anything, so long as my daughter can be happy. There is no one else for me.
>
> (Rohini *et al.* 1982: 84)

> I married when I was 14 years old. . . . I have been living with my husband for thirty years. . . . When the girls were born, I slept with them, after working like a dog all day long. He never helped me, slept in the other room. Then, when the girls were still, he would come and get me. He would fulfill himself and that was it. Me, never. . . . But because of my daughters I put up with everything. I live for them.
>
> (Chuchryk 1989: 37)

Katherine Gieve felt that 'babies have been curiously isolating for women in the women's movement, creating a gulf not only between those who do and do not have children, but also between the women who do have children' (1987: 39), but that was not my experience in India. My babies made plenty of friends in the women's movement, creating an extra bond rather than a gulf between myself and women who had children as well as those who had not. Later, if I hurried home to my children after work or meeting, it was not out of a sense of guilt but with an anticipation of joy, although the problem of allocating adequate time to competing commitments and activities remained unresolved.

In cultures where children are valued and enjoyed, having children need not be a source of isolation. However, other problems associated with caring for children, such as physical exhaustion and financial deprivation, remain. It is not easy to disentangle the activity of caring for children from the social, political and economic relationships – including the patriarchal family – which make it oppressive for women, but it is essential to do so in the interests of clarity. Is the relationship *as such* an oppressive one for the carer?

It is true in one sense that there is a lack of reciprocity in it, but in another sense this is not true. What is true is that there is at the beginning a vast imbalance in the degree of power, of control, which means that the adult has to do *everything* for the child while the child lacks the power even to reward the adult with a smile. But it is not true that the child's responding love is any less intense, passionate or devoted; on this count, the lack of reciprocity is often the other way around, when adults – including women – so tragically abuse the trust and love they are given by children. So the argument cannot be that this is an *inherently* oppressive relationship where the child oppresses the adult.

It seems that the notion of justice as an abstract equality of rights between abstract individuals does not take into account the real differences of needs and capacities between concrete individuals – between, for example, an able-bodied adult and an infant, invalid or disabled person; in order to take account of these differences, Carol Gilligan has argued for the necessity of an 'ethic of care' to complement an 'ethic of justice' (Gilligan 1982). Moreover, the conventional language of rights also proceeds from the standpoint of a 'disembedded' and 'disembodied' self (Benhabib 1992: 166), defined in separation from others, rather than a real self, which is always defined in relationship to others, and may need to defend those others in order to defend itself: the defence of one's own right to love inevitably involves trying to protect those who are loved from harm and injury. Paradoxically, feminists who emphasise an ethic of justice at the expense of an ethic of love and care may be perpetuating the masculine devaluation of the practice of millions of women. What is required instead is the affirmation of the right to equal respect for the dignity of each individual *combined with* the recognition that those who are in greater need are entitled to that care, and the love which provides them with it is an acknowledgement of that right. The personal is political not only in relationships between men and women (or, more generally, between those who demand equal treatment and equal respect for their dignity as human beings), but also in relationships between adults and children (or, more generally, between those who are stronger or more able and those who are weaker or less able); and it is predominantly women who have brought about this crucial extension of the domain of politics.[6]

A FEMINIST ALTERNATIVE TO MASCULINE POLITICS?

There is a strand of feminism which celebrates the *experience* of motherhood as opposed to the ideology and institution (cf. Rich 1976). However, this position is unsatisfactory unless it makes a point of challenging a division of labour which allocates caring work almost entirely to women. The potential of this division as a source of oppression not just for women but for the whole of society becomes evident if we look at the role of *men* in the *upholding* of political authoritarianism. The personnel of military and paramilitary forces and death squads, the torturers and killers, are almost invariably men. The occasional presence of women in these occupations (as in the LTTE) suggests that there is nothing innate or biological which prevents women from partic-ipating in such activities. Nor are *all* men capable of these atrocities; indeed, there have been cases of male political prisoners who have chosen to be tortured to death rather than to be forced into participating in the torture of fellow-inmates. Nonetheless the question arises: why do so many men allow themselves to be drawn into actions which go against all norms of humanity?

I believe the answer lies in the ideology and practice of masculinity, which on the one hand allows men to feel no shame or guilt about the most brutal exercise of power over other human beings, and on the other hand fails to train boys in the skills of caring and nurturing. Like all processes of learning, this involves internalising appropriate responses to specific stimuli to a point where they become second nature – responses which, in this case, are emotional as well as practical. If your normal response to the sight of a baby is a feeling of tenderness, you won't find it easy to throw it in a fire or dash its head against a wall. If your normal response to the sight of a person in pain is an answering pang of sympathy, your muscles will resist the motions of inflicting torture. Political authoritarianism would not find it so easy to recruit males to be its henchmen if they had already built up an internal resistance in this way.

If it is true, therefore, that the fearlessness and tenacity with which ordi-nary mothers have confronted the most fearsome authoritarian regimes are the product of a division of labour which socialises women and girls into being the guardians of life and repositories of love, there is also a negative side to this division. A celebration of the experience of motherhood takes us no further than where we are at present unless its gendered character is questioned. It is not necessary to be a mother in order to learn the skills of caring or the joys of relating to a small child: indeed, most girls in Third World countries do these things quite independently of having babies of their own, and there is no obvious reason why boys should not do the same. If the politics of groups like the Madres of the Plaza de Mayo is 'based on the all-out defence of the most basic principle – the defence of life and of the right to love' (Feijoo 1989: 70), should it be left to women alone to defend these principles?

Perhaps socialist feminist Heidi Hartmann pointed towards an answer when she wrote that 'the sexual division of labour within capitalism has given women a practice in which we have learned to understand what human interdepen-dence and needs are. While men have long struggled *against* capital, women know what to struggle *for*' (Hartmann 1981: 32–3). Instead of seeing caring and nurturing as a source of oppression to be eliminated from the practice of women, wouldn't it make more sense to affirm the value of such relationships as central to the practice of men too? And instead of socialising girls to be less resistant to being trained as torturers and killers, wouldn't it make more sense to socialise boys to defend life and the right to love?

These spontaneous movements of women fighting for the lives of their children therefore raise in a very direct fashion the question of the goals of feminist struggle: the kind of relationships and society which should be created in opposition to authoritarianism in private and public life. Their politics could be the basis of a movement to carry out a more profound transformation of society, bringing traditional 'feminine' concerns – affirmation of life, satisfaction of needs, relationships of love and caring – out of the private, domestic sphere and into a public life currently dominated by life-denying, profit-seeking, power-obsessed competitive relationships.

NOTES

1 Georgina Waylen, in Chapter 1 in this volume, emphasises the importance of examining women's political activities outside the male-dominated institutional sphere and thus challenging the conventional construction of the political. Ridd and Callaway (1986: 23, 215) make a similar distinction between formal and informal spheres of political activity.
2 Both these cases illustrate the complex relationship between Third World women and the state which Shirin Rai describes, in Chapter 2 in this volume, and the diversity of strategies they employ *vis-à-vis* the state.
3 See also Chhachhi (1988) for the opposition of women to communalism and fundamentalism, and women's efforts to find a political alternative to state repression in Punjab.
4 See Donna Pankhurst and Jenny Pearce, Chapter 3 in this volume, for a further expansion of this point.
5 See also Sarkar (1993).
6 I am grateful to Meena Dhanda, Sair Hensman and Shaku Banaji for commenting on an earlier version of this section.

REFERENCES

Akhter, F. (1992) *Depopulating Bangladesh: Essays on the Politics of Fertility*, Bangladesh: Narigrantha Prabartana.
Alvarez, S. (1989) 'Women's Movements and Gender Politics in the Brazilian Transition', in J. S. Jaquette (ed.) *The Women's Movement in Latin America: Feminism and the Transition to Democracy*, New York: Unwin Hyman.
Basu, T., Datta, P., Sarkar, S., Sarkar, T. and Sen S. (1993) *Khaki Shorts, Saffron Flags*, New Delhi: Orient Longman.
Benhabib, S. (1992) *Situating the Self*, Cambridge: Polity.
Bunster, X. (1988) 'The Mobilization and Demobilization of Women in Militarized Chile', in E. Isaksson (ed.) *Women and the Military System*, Hemel Hempstead: Harvester.
Chhachhi, A. (1989) 'The State, Religious Fundamentalism and Women: Trends in South Asia', *Economic and Political Weekly*, 18 March: 567–78.
Chhachhi, A. (1991) 'Forced Identities: The State, Communalism, Fundamentalism and Women in India', in D. Kandiyoti (ed.) *Women, Islam and the State*, Philadelphia, PA: Temple University Press.
Choudhury, G., Dewan, R., Manimala, and Chhachhi, S. (1994) *Women's Testimonies from Kashmir: 'The Green of the Valley is Khaki'*, Bombay: Women's Initiative.

Chuchryk, P. M. (1989) 'Feminist Anti-Authoritarian Politics: The Role of Women's Organisations in the Chilean Transition to Democracy', in J. S. Jaquette (ed.) *The Women's Movement in Latin America: Feminism and the Transition to Democracy*, New York: Unwin Hyman.
De Beauvoir, S. (1953) *The Second Sex*, Harmondsworth: Penguin.
Feijoo, M. del C. (1989) 'The Challenge of Constructing Civilian Peace: Women and Democracy in Argentina', in J. S. Jaquette (ed.) *The Women's Movement in Latin America: Feminism and the Transition to Democracy*, New York: Unwin Hyman.
Firestone, S. (1970) *The Dialectic of Sex*, London: Cape.
Fisher, J. (1993) *Out of the Shadows: Women, Resistance and Politics in South America*, London: Latin American Bureau.
Gieve, K. (1987) 'Rethinking Feminist Attitudes towards Motherhood', *Feminist Review* 25 (March): 38–45.
Gilligan, C. (1982) *In a Different Voice: Psychological Theory and Women's Development*, Cambrige, Mass.: Harvard University Press.
Harris, H. (1988) 'Women and War: The Case of Nicaragua', in E. Isaksson (ed.) *Women and the Military System*, Hemel Hempstead: Harvest.
Hartmann, H. (1981) 'The Unhappy Marriage of Marxism and Feminism: Towards a More Progressive Union', in L. Sargent (ed.) *Women and Revolution*, London: Pluto.
Hensman, R. (1992) 'Women and Ethnic Nationalism in Sri Lanka', *Journal of Gender Studies* November: 500–9.
Hensman, R. (1993) *Journey Without a Destination: Is There a Solution to the Problem of Sri Lankan Refugees?*, The Refugee Council, 3 Bondway, London SW8 1SJ.
Jalal, A. (1991) 'The Convenience of Subservience: Women and the State of Pakistan', in D. Kandiyoti (ed.) *Women, Islam and the State*, Philadelphia, PA: Temple University Press.
Jaquette, J. S. (ed.) (1989) *The Women's Movement in Latin America: Feminism and the Transition to Democracy*, New York: Unwin Hyman.
Kabeer, N. (1991) 'The Quest for National Identity: Women and the State of Pakistan', in D. Kandiyoti (ed.) *Women, Islam and the State*, Philadelphia, PA: Temple University Press.
Mumtaz, K. and Shaheed, F. (eds) (1987) *Women of Pakistan: Two Steps Forward, One Step Back?*, London: Zed Books.
Rich, A. (1976) *Of Women Born*, London: Virgo.
Ridd, R. and Callaway, H. (1986) *Caught Up in Conflict: Women's Responses to Political Strife*, Basingstoke: Macmillan.
Rohini, P. H., Sujata, S. V. and Neelam, C. (1982) *My Life is One Long Struggle: Women, Work, Organisation and Struggle*, Pratishabd, India.
Sarkar, T. (1993) 'Women's Agency Within Authoritarian Communalism: The Rashtrasevika Samiti and Ramjanmabhoomi', in G. Pandey (ed.) *Hindus and Others*, New Delhi: Penguin.
Stead, M. (1991) 'Women, War and Underdevelopment in Nicaragua', in H. Afshar (ed.) *Women, Development and Survival in the Third World*, Harlow: Longman.
Women Against Racism and Militarisation (1986) *Proceedings of Women's Groups Workshop*, Katuwapitiya, Sri Lanka.

FURTHER READING

Essential reading for a broad view of women's political action in Latin America is *The Women's Movement in Latin America: Feminism and the Transition to Democracy*, edited by Jane S. Jaquette (1989), in which Sonia E. Alvarez's essay 'Women's Movements and Gender Politics in the Brazilian Transition', Patricia M. Chuchryk's 'Feminist Anti-

Authoritarian Politics: The Role of Women's Organisations in the Chilean Transition to Democracy' and Maria del Carmen Feijoo's 'The Challenge of Constructing Civilian Peace: Women and Democracy in Argentina' all appear. Jo Fisher's (1993) *Out of the Shadows: Women, Resistance and Politics in South America*, provides added insights by quoting extensively from fascinating interviews with women involved in popular political movements. The special case of Nicaragua, where women were also significantly involved in the armed struggle, is taken up by Mary Stead (1991) 'Women, War and Underdevelopment in Nicaragua', in Halen Afshar (ed.) *Women, Development and Survival in the Third World*, and by Hermione Harris (1986) 'Women and War: The Case of Nicaragua', in Eva Isaksson (ed.) *Women and the Military System*. The latter collection also contains an illuminating account of women's participation in authoritarian politics in Ximena Bunster (1988) 'The Mobilization and Demobilization of Women in Militarized Chile', which raises the issue of class identities dividing women and pitting them against each other.

In South Asia, political authoritarianism seems to have been closely associated with religious communalism. *Women, Islam and the State*, edited by Deniz Kandiyoti (1991), includes chapters analysing the effect of Islamic fundamentalist politics on women in South Asia and their resistance to it, in Amrita Chhachhi's 'Forced Identities: The State, Communalism, Fundamentalism and Women in India', and Naila Kabeer's 'The Quest for National Identity: Women and the State of Pakistan', which shows how the failure of Islam to constitute a coherent national identity led to the break-up of Pakistan and creation of Bangladesh. Ayesha Jalal's 'The Convenience of Subservience: Women and the State of Pakistan' in the same collection demonstrates how the class benefits derived from an authoritarian political order by upper- and middle-class women could ensure their complicity. The complex interaction of class and gender is also touched on in Khawar Mumtaz and Farida Shaheed (eds) (1987) *Women of Pakistan: Two Steps Forward, One Step Back?*, which looks at the issue from within the feminist movement. Tanika Sarkar's perceptive accounts in 'Women's Agency Within Authoritarian Communalism: The Rashtrasevika Samiti and Ramjanmabhoomi', in Gyanendra Pandey (ed.) (1993) *Hindus and Others*, and in Tapan Basu, Pradip Datta, Sumit Sarkar, Tanika Sarkar and Sambuddha Sen (1993) *Khaki Shorts, Saffron Flags*, are a chilling reminder of the significant role played by women in Hindu communal politics. By comparison, there is a dearth of material on the involvement of women in anti-authoritarian as well as right-wing politics in Sri Lanka, and Rohini Hensman's 'Women and Ethnic Nationalism in Sri Lanka', *Journal of Gender Studies* (November), is only a very preliminary attempt in this direction.

For anyone interested in the ethical dimension of women's anti-authoritarian political action, Carol Gilligan's (1982) *In a Different Voice: Psychological Theory and Women's Development* (Cambridge, MA: Harvard University Press) approaches the issue from the standpoint of psychology, while Seyla Benhabib's (1992) *Situating the Self* (Cambridge: Polity) includes an interesting philosophical discussion.

Chapter 5

Nicaraguan women, resistance, and the politics of aid

Jasbir K. Puar

Globally, women's needs have not always been met by development models; Nicaraguan women are no exception. It is not my intention to provide a history of development policies here; however a brief synopsis is useful for the purposes of this chapter.[1] Generally it can be said that until recently, 'Third World' women as producers have been invisible in development studies,[2] reflecting an assumption that men (not women) are first, workers,[3] and second, primarily the heads of households. Divides between the public as male domain and the private as female are therefore created.[4] Trends towards 'integrating women in development' have resulted in efforts such as the United Nations Decade for the Advancement of Women (1975–85). These measures have generally been where women have been 'added-on' while structural problems remain unaddressed. For example the WID (Women in Development) approach assumes that women should not be left to use their time unproductively and that the problem revolves around women's lack of participation in a system of development strategies which is thought to be otherwise beneficial to the poor.[5] These tendencies to isolate women from the larger picture of development issues have had significant repercussions: land reforms have frequently reduced women's control over land, ignoring traditional use rights, and women's workloads in fuel gathering and water collection have tended to increase with development, to name but a few examples (Sen and Grown 1987: 34–5).

The GAD (Gender and Development) approach is less popular because it is more confrontational; it insists that women cannot be viewed in isolation and focuses on the implications of interrelated gender roles. Yet even this attempt at integrative strategies suffers during the process of implementation into practice, particularly as Western models of health care, literacy and urban planning are repeatedly transposed to Third World countries. The expectations of development policies are often shaped by cultural and political, rather than technical, standards dictated by the First World with its histories of colonialism (Moser 1993: 7). Third World women have not just simply been left out, but rather face a double-bind which reflects not only gender but also historical and cultural biases. One example, as Georgina Waylen notes in

Chapter 1 in this volume, is that 'Women in Development' literature tends to homogenise all Third World women as 'victims' and 'backwards' in relation to 'progressive' Western women. The results of this are often that what are understood as problems by development models do not concur with the needs of the Third World women who are supposedly being assisted. Consequently, these women are blamed when development strategies are not effective, and are conceptualised as 'passive victims'.

Examining the situations of rural Nicaraguan women and their responses to developmental aid can assist in exploring the dynamics of this process. Here I use an example of a humanitarian aid project in Nicaragua, undertaken by a group of US 'citizens', as a case study of how differing perceptions of rural Nicaraguan women's roles and needs impact on the overall development process as a whole. It seems apparent that academic, feminist and popular (mis)understandings of Third World women contribute to ideologies of 'development' which continue, despite substantial successes, to marginalise women. Although economic processes are not my direct focus of critique, certainly decisions about these are influenced by historical and cultural issues which de Groot notes 'have had a significant effect on the terms with which development processes are conceived and applied' (de Groot 1991: 107). Following from the argument that development frameworks are products of historical and cultural ideas from the West, it could then also be claimed that notions of development themselves are constructions of (neo)colonial discourses. Certain questions must be asked: what exactly is humanitarian aid and whose definitions are in operation, who should be dispensing it, and how? How are the terms 'empowerment', 'feminism' and 'aid' being defined, and by whom? How do Nicaraguan women resist gender subordination as well as those delivering aid, and where and how does resistance occur? Differing interpretations of these issues revealed themselves via various tensions at 'points of exchange' during our stay in Nicaragua.

THE 'OUTSIDER-WITHIN'

First, I feel that it is important to briefly elaborate on some issues concerning positionality and representation. I do so with the knowledge that my 'position' or 'standpoint' as a middle-class South Asian woman raised in the West (the USA) is complicated by an 'outsider-within' (Collins 1991) status when present in certain locations. My understanding of the competing discourses of 'race' and 'nation' upon myself entails alternative interpretations of certain events, interpretations with which white liberal gazes may not agree. Most importantly, these observations are about two 'sets' of women of colour whose interactions are being mediated by a 'white' 'superpower', namely the United States, as aid-giver. The specificities of my relationship to (an) 'other(s)' dictate that I am not simply an outsider but one qualified in a multitude of shifting terms in the context of my physical presence in Nicaragua: as a 'rich

American', backed by resources and status, desiring to 'assist' in an attempt to make amends for US government support of the Contras; as a person of colour, commonly mistaken for 'indigenous', who confused the blue-eyed blonde American imagery; as a woman of colour often referred to, not by name as were the other volunteers, rather as 'morena' (dark woman). These fractured and contradictory constructions facilitated a wide and unpredictable range of reactions, not the least common of which was being viewed as no different, and thus at times no 'better', than themselves. Upon our arrival on the farming co-operative (a farm which was jointly run by a group of families) where the volunteer work project took place, I did have a sense of being 'the bad apple in the lot' when, upon meeting me, the father of the family with whom I'd be living commented drily, 'You look just like all of the rest of us.' Amidst the excitement of host families meeting volunteers he was clearly disappointed.

These dynamics reflect interactions of self and other which are not and can never be devoid of structures of power. So while this chapter is explicitly about the Nicaraguan women who have been interviewed, it is also implicitly about my representations of the 'other(s)' and my complicated positionality as a 'Westerner'. I have attempted to negotiate these tensions by acknowledging that this positioning enabled certain perspectives and interactions while disabling others. I have also tried to adopt Abu-Lughod's notion of 'writing *against* culture' which recognises generalisations as 'part of a professional discourse of objectivity and expertise, [and] inevitably a language of power' as well as something that 'produc[es] the effects of a homogeneity, coherence, and timelessness, [which] contributes to the creation of "cultures"' (Abu-Lughod 1993: 8–9). The analysis of specificity shifts the focus from 'generalisations' about cultures to contextualised politics of location and the interactions of subject and object positionings, while still attempting to acknowledge the wider connections to the processes of contestation of meaning and power.

The aims and process of interviewing themselves represent a problematic understanding of Third World peoples. A collaborative effort between myself and Mario Mejia, a fellow volunteer born in El Salvador, resulted in the interviews of thirteen individuals living on the co-op, much of which is used in this chapter. Our eventual goal was to have articles published in some format in a mainstream publication, using mostly interviewees' own words. Hence our emphasis was on 'oral histories'. This was to document the traumas and tragedies of these people and thus generate 'interest' in Nicaragua, particularly since the furore about the Contra war and its atrocities had died down. These aims consequently affected the nature of our questions, which had over-riding focuses on poverty and violence; questions about the inadequacies/lack of food, health care, living conditions, and education and incidents of violence, brutality and experiences of combat in the war. This also determined whom we approached to interview; we focused specifically on those people who we heard had 'colourful' histories. We also wanted 'emotional, story-filled accounts'; (I remember Mario and me discussing who to target for a 'good' interview, and also feeling depressed when our interviews had been mundane, boring, 'bad', 'of no use to us'). We also photographed everyone we interviewed and their families as a sign of thanks, but once again this was primarily for our benefit as we planned to use these 'authentic photos of the poor' to help sell our research and initiate interest.

Thus it seems our 'humanitarianism' and politically correct-ness led us to sensationalise and also capitalise on their situations. While this may be inherent to any type of interactive research and fieldwork within the power structure of interviewer to interviewee, the problem here is that this construct is cloaked under the guise of good intent, aid, and humanitarianism. The power of the researcher to re-present the researched is completely unquestioned because the researched are so incredibly 'disadvantaged' (many people came up to us, even those who were not approached to be interviewed, to thank us for under-taking such a 'helpful' project). The emphasis is thus shifted away from how the re-presentation is actually created, detracting from the importance of the 'product'.

Given these problematics of positionality and representation, the following analysis offered is an attempt to illuminate the hegemonic structures which are maintained within these processes.

FEMINIST CONSTRUCTIONS OF THIRD WORLD WOMEN

> (The) average third-world woman leads an essentially truncated life based on her feminine gender (read: sexually constrained) and being 'Third World' (read: ignorant, poor, uneducated, tradition bound, religious, domesticated, victimised, etc.) This, I suggest, is in contrast to the (implicit) self-representation of western women as educated, modern, as having control over their own bodies and sexualities, and the 'freedom' to make their own decisions.
>
> (Mohanty 1988: 16)

The process of 'othering' Third World women in development as well as women's studies is substantially enabled by a universalising of gender relations and of 'feminism'. This effectively ignores Third World feminisms as well as the social, economic and historical contexts in which these feminisms have developed, creating differing and distinct priorities from those of '(white) Western' feminisms. The tensions between differing feminist agendas and definitions become clear within the context of exchange and interface among Western and indigenous populations, such as a humanitarian aid project. The theorised difficulties of contextualising Western and Third World feminisms are played out in the experiential context and hence become 'authentic' realities for those involved in them, reproducing certain binary oppositions and leaving existing paradigms unchallenged.

Certain tensions have repeatedly surfaced in the scholarship on Latin American women:

> One of the basic conflicts between North American and Latin American women is that freedom is defined by the former as the ability to act like men and to gain their rights and prerequisites, while the latter link female power to sex-role differentiation.
>
> (Nash and Safia 1979: 218)

This 'basic conflict' is often understood through the practical versus strategic gender needs debate. According to Molyneux (1985), practical gender needs include improved health care, child care, and food, and

> are given inductively and arise from the concrete conditions of women's positioning within the gender division of labor . . . these are formulated by the women who are themselves within these positions rather than through external interventions. Practical interests are usually a response to an imme- diate perceived need.
>
> (Molyneux 1985: 233)

Strategic gender needs are posited in opposition to practical ones as those which attempt to change the patriarchal structure of society. They include issues dealing with abortion, domestic violence, and equal access to jobs and conceptualise the redefinition of society based on 'equality' between men and women (Molyneux 1985: 233).

Though it seems clear that certain needs can be understood as immediate and urgent, whereas others involve longer-term processes, I question whether defining women's agendas as either one or the other is particularly helpful or realistic. The positioning of Third World women within such oppositional frameworks seems to privilege a middle-class status automatically understood as having a 'higher' or more 'feminist' consciousness revolving around identity politics. Strategic gender needs are thus understood as what 'will ultimately change society' and practical gender needs as the 'best one could hope for from poor women'. Maintaining practical and strategic gender needs as mutually exclusive concepts also discounts possibilities of practical gender needs feeding into, complementing, contradicting, or even challenging the necessity of various strategic gender needs, thus blurring the defined categories themselves. Finally it must be asked that if strategic gender needs are those which will lead to 'equality' between men and women, whose definition of 'equality' is one using? And why the elevation, once again, of 'equality' over sex-differentiation?

Ferguson offers a feminist-materialist theory which provides a slightly more fluid notion of gender relations similar, perhaps, to Deniz Kandiyoti's (1988) notion of 'bargaining with patriarchy':

sexuality and parenting, since they involve material needs, also involve modes of human cooperation and work to satisfy these needs. I call these modes systems of 'sex/affective production.' The social organization of parenting, sexuality and peer bonding (in friendships, kin ties, and work relationships) must be included in the material 'base' of a society's social practices along with its more specifically economic practices.

(Ferguson 1991: 76)

An example of the interdependent nature of the tensions negotiated by women can be seen in a study of certain housing settlements in Managua, Nicaragua (Vance 1987: 139–65). As women were seen to be the primary users of a home/household and occupied the most time within it, the requests of women in terms of designing and building the homes were taken into account. Although this solidified women's roles within the home as producers and reproducers to be their primary tasks, it nonetheless provided women with housing alternatives which created immediate, practical solutions to problems involving community interaction and child care. While in certain arguments this may function solely as a fulfilment of practical gender needs, this arrangement created arenas within which women may exert a considerable amount of influence while also perhaps facilitating women-only space, more involvement in community affairs, and greater leisure time, thus altering gender dynamics within the home.

The words, actions and attitudes of the women I spoke to on the co-op also suggest interdependent relationships of strategies where one may well facilitate circumstances for the other. Thus a picture of the specific *interconnecting* historical, economic, cultural and political constraints which these women negotiate is necessary to illuminate these interactive dynamics.

ONE VIEW OF NICARAGUA

In Nicaragua, the contemporary women's movement developed in response to and side-by-side with a mass political and social revolution which recognised 'emancipation' of women to be one of its main goals. The 'revolution' was a response to the repressive dictatorship of the Somoza family regime which ruled Nicaragua. Many point to the involvement of women in the revolution as evidence of a widespread movement which created better living circumstances for significant numbers of women. The aims of the women's movement were largely shaped by the economic situation which existed before the 1979 overthrow of dictator Somoza. Prior to the Triumph of the FSLN (Sandinista National Liberation Front) on 19 July 1979, unemployment was at 22 per cent, underemployment at 35 per cent, illiteracy was as high as 93 per cent in rural areas, and there was no organised medical care (Randall 1981: v). This harsh economic reality hit women very hard, particularly because many husbands, unable to support their families, often abandoned them. Hence women were usually the sole person responsible for the maintenance, economic and otherwise, of the family and children (Randall 1981: v).

From the start of the revolution the FSLN recognised the goal of women's emancipation as inherently crucial to the construction of a new societal vision. Within the context of the revolution, women were encouraged and expected to become more integrated within economic and political spheres. Legislation was formulated to guarantee equal rights; for example, equal pay for men and women for the same work, mandatory child care provisions, right to maternity leave, etc. However, much of what the FSLN deemed vital to women's emancipation was little more than full participation of women in the workforce (Anon. 1991: 30). (This reflects the common misperception of the West that work equals emancipation and the unilinear thinking regarding development and industrialisation: Brocke-Utne 1989: 498.) Controversial legislation about increasing male responsibility for the housework, payment for children, and equal access to divorce and child custody was passed, but rarely enforced and actually remained unpublished (Stead 1991: 62).

Images of Nicaraguan women as mothers, martyrs and victims of machismo have been reinforced within the FSLN revolutionary movement and political resistance. Machismo is a pervasive Latin American ideology, taking shape in other forms in other societies, which forms the basis of gender relations in Nicaragua. Machismo perpetuates a system whereby men are not legally responsible for the women with whom they have relations and children. One result of machismo is that 50 per cent of women are single parents and men often have more than one family (Skiar 1989: 13). Hence women as mothers have enormous influence over and responsibility towards their children:

> Ironically, the machismo permeating Nicaraguan culture is primarily learned and reinforced at home, as women are the ideological torchbearers in this society. Women are thus key participants in reproducing the system that harms them. This is perhaps most obvious in the socialisation of children. In Nicaragua, the male ideal is a sexually active man with many women (who always goes back to that most important woman, his mother), while the girl children are raised to be 'good'.
>
> (Anon. 1991: 32)

In 1987 the FSLN presented a policy statement to the Third National Assembly of AMNLAE, the national women's organisation in Nicaragua. While maintaining a commitment to women's liberation based on a socialist vision within the context of the revolution, the FSLN broadened its stance to include and further emphasise ideological issues. Recognising the pervasive influence of machismo, it stated:

> Machismo exalts the supposed male superiority. It excludes women from activities and jobs that are considered 'for men only'. It claims the right

of men to abuse women, and establishes prerogatives and rights that women cannot enjoy. What machismo tries to pass off as immutable principles are the result of deformations imposed on our society by the system of exploitation of man by man.

(FSLN Policy Statement 1987)

As part of the cycle of machismo, women are vitally important to the structure of Nicaraguan society, as safeguarders of the family unit, and are elevated as mothers first and foremost. Women were to remain firmly entrenched in their roles as reproducers, strengthening sex-role differentiation through the celebration and elevation of motherhood:

Women have been the fundamental pillar of the Nicaraguan family, defending and sustaining it even in the most difficult circumstances, for which they deserve the highest respect and admiration.

(FSLN Policy Statement 1987)

So on one hand while the ideology of machismo is condemned by the FSLN, its outcome is given respect. Women's identities were also formulated by the fate of their sons, consolidating status not only from motherhood, but also from martyrdom:

As mothers, they became symbols of courage and integrity, representatives of the spirit and dignity of our people. Mothers of political prisoners, mothers of the disappeared, mothers of those tortured, mothers who carried their sorrow with dignity, struggling in the streets, denouncing the genocide committed by the National Guard in the mountains, launching hunger strikes, or sheltering underground fighters as their own children.

(FSLN Policy Statement 1987)

There is no doubt, however, of the effectiveness in Nicaragua of the focus on sex-differentiation as a means to mobilise women. Motherhood and martyrdom as organising points of reference for political action have been very powerful motifs in resistance movements, as noted by other contributors to this volume (Kathy Glavanis-Grantham, Maria Holt and Rohini Hensman), for example in the cases of Palestinian and Sri Lankan women.

Along with their roles as reproducers, Nicaraguan women must cope with two additional duties: those of producer and of community manager. As producers women often provide a secondary, if not the primary income. Their role as community managers is seen as an extension of domestic duties:

It is considered 'natural', that women should perform an important role in community affairs, especially those directly related to consumption, since these matters related to their roles as mothers and wives ... women who belong to these organisations are simply fulfilling their traditional role in society. They are wives, mothers and housewives defending the welfare of the household and the community . . . their participation is justified by their role as mother and wife.

(Aleman 1991: 95)

As community managers, women become politicised around their duties in the home, in organisations dealing with children, health, education, etc. As with their role as reproducers, this third additional responsibility is not recognised as 'work' since there is no exchange value, and is also a by-product of machismo (Moser and Peake 1987: 13). This completes what is often referred to as the 'triple burden' of women's lives in Nicaragua.

The implications of the Policy Statement are that women's roles as reproducers have become politicised and taken on political importance and status (Anon. 1991: 34). While this facilitates a recognised political arena for women, it also means that sex roles are not redefined (as would be the goal of Western notions of 'equality'):

We are going to struggle so that women can fulfill their maternal function and family responsibilities in even better conditions and without these responsibilities becoming insuperable obstacles to their own development and personal fulfillment.

(FSLN Policy Statement 1987)

This approach to women's emancipation was copied to a great extent by AMNLAE, particularly in the early 1980s. Its priorities centred around supporting the FSLN and the revolution and working closely with the Sandinista army. AMNLAE focused on organising women as mothers of potential and actual draftees, and overlooked their roles as workers (Anon. 1991: 34). The Catholic Church and its influence is another arena deemed to contribute to women's construction as victims, particularly in dealing with issues of abortion and contraception. Thus the roles of women as mothers, martyrs and victims were highlighted and influenced the areas of interchange between First and Third Worlds. These constructions were taken and used to solidify the Nicaraguan 'other' which existed in direct opposition to the white, liberated Western women on the humanitarian aid project.

THE RAMÓN GARCÍA FARMING CO-OPERATIVE

I spent approximately one month in the summer of 1992 with a volunteer work brigade in Nicaragua organised by a non-profit, non-government-affiliated organisation. Such brigades were quite commonplace during the revolution (it was estimated that over 100,000 US citizens participated every year towards the late 1980s) but had died out in popularity when the US-backed Chamorro government defeated the Sandinistas in February 1990.[6] Our group consisted of fourteen volunteers primarily from the San Francisco area, all US residents of various ethnic backgrounds; one Latin man (Latino), one Latin woman (Latina), myself (South Asian), and the rest white and of European descent. None of the volunteers had any professional background in development although many had participated in similar volunteer projects in Latin America. We began the process of organisation approximately three months prior to our scheduled trip; this included slide presentations and guest lectures by past volunteers, journalists and others who had spent extended time periods working in Nicaragua.

We spent the majority of the month working on the Ramón García farming co-operative, located near San Ramón town and about twenty miles from Matagalpa, a city with a population of 30,000. The co-op was established in early 1990 through a joint effort by the FSLN and UNAG (a rural agricultural organisation) and was part of the land return scheme which allowed farmers an entitlement to land. As of July 1992, the co-op consisted of twenty-two families, of varying economic and social backgrounds, as fee-paying members and joint owners of the farm. Production mainly revolves around raising cattle but beans and corn are also grown. At present the co-op receives 50 per cent of its expenditure from UNAG, primarily in the form of livestock, with the expectation that the co-op will be self-sufficient soon. The families receive allotments of food and basic supplies, and what little money which comes in from the sale of produce (primarily milk) is used for the general needs of the co-op such as equipment; hence most families do not have access to personal cash. Upon becoming members each family was built a modest home. A few families also raise their own livestock and grow vegetables and herbs; one family runs a small, informal store.

As brigadistas our responsibilities included participating as fully as possible in the activities on the farm as well as within our host families; helping out with the daily chores, fetching water, grinding corn, milking cattle, planting seeds and erecting fence-posts.

PRIORITIES OF HEALTH AND ECONOMICS

Issues about health problems on the co-op were particularly emotive and ones which I felt the group faced the most problematic situations, reflecting a stance which was not well thought out or considered. As a group we brought down basic medications which were to be distributed based on need to families; aspirin, diarrhoea medication, ointments, cough syrup, etc. When word got out about this, the woman in charge became hounded by requests for medicine, as did most of the brigadistas. There was not enough medication to give similar amounts to everyone, thus upsetting families who received nothing or little and potentially creating rivalry. There were no criteria which we had decided upon to distribute the medication, so the process was left as random and family members took to 'befriending the medicine woman' and making requests through the brigadistas they were hosting. I explained to my host mother that I had no control over the distribution of the limited medication. Recognising the ignorance of our decisions, she commented:

> Why bring medicines when you don't have enough for everyone? My baby is no less sick than the others, but the people who know her will get the most. It is worse knowing we could have had some but won't.

In stating this she criticises our methods of distribution while simultaneously desiring the medicines. More importantly, she realises that we had stimulated a need which was originally dormant and was also a need which could not be sustained or satisfied once we left, because lack of money meant most 'Western' medications were inaccessible. Although the co-op had an extensive system of herbal medications in use, they were supposedly considered inferior to pills and shots. Thus our distribution of this medicine reinforced the notions of inadequacy about their own system, once again under the guise of humanitarianism, and created all sorts of other tensions along the way. Yet our inadvertent conveyance of this inadequacy was not necessarily accepted, as the above quote reveals. Additionally, the women of the co-op maintained the contradictory stance of utilising and cultivating herbal medications, while also demanding Western medicines. However they made no attempts to actually *purchase* Western medicines, admittedly because this was prohibitively expensive, but perhaps they also recognised certain powers of self-reliance. Several women mentioned the possibilities of requesting financial assistance from UNAG to set up a women's health centre and a greenhouse to grow herbs. What they did not request was money for Western medicines, reflecting contradictory desires mediated by economics and our inflammatory presence.

However, in terms of economics, the most significant motivating factor in the shorter run was their children's health:

> During the revolution there were also vaccination campaigns against polio and tetanus for children. Before that and now we pay, and if you can't your children go without – it was terrible, so many children died.

The Ramón García women's group was actually the forum during which women discussed the health problems of their children and made herbal medicines, soyabean milk, and soap:

> During the revolution some medicines were free but still the doctor is very far away. Many of the children are undernourished or always sick so I decided to start collecting materials and ideas to make our own remedies. All the women from the co-op come every week and it is a good time for us to talk about our problems.

The women's group is one example of the initiative of these women. The main reasons provided for organising this group was, as mothers, to find solutions to their children's health problems. However the women also used this women-only space and time to discuss other problems, provide one another with support, and leave their familial situations for a while. They also had created networks with other local women's groups to exchange information and arrange informal visits and workshops. Maternal responsibility also extended to the extra activities and skills that some women choose to learn, for example for the resident midwife of the co-op who explained:

> The Frente [FSLN] was training women how to be a midwife and I wanted to learn, not only to help the women but there were so many babies who were dying because the nearest hospital is 30 miles away.

From these skills also, this woman not only was able to assist those who were delivering without the dependency on distant and expensive medical care, but also formed a network of midwives and health educators from other farms to provide information on women's health issues.

Another situation arose where one volunteer realised that the water containers being used within his family as well as throughout the co-op were old toxic waste containers possibly harmful in the long term. The debate began within our group as to whether to notify the families, recognising that the containers were invaluable on the co-op. There was only one water pump, making it necessary to fetch water continuously throughout the day, and replacing the containers was out of the question for the families because of the expense. There was no group consensus on this issue; several members thought that we should provide new containers; others saw no reason to create undue concern by notifying families of potential danger when their day-to-day existence was under threat. One volunteer made the decision, independently of the group, to tell his family; he was amazed with how unconcerned they appeared to be. This volunteer's 'host mother' told him that unless he was prepared to buy every family new containers, he should keep silent:

> Who knows if we will even be alive tomorrow. How can we be concerned about what might happen ten, twenty years from now? It is difficult enough to collect the containers we have.

Similarly, several brigade members were concerned with the fact that the river was being used as a dumping ground; this was the same river in which people bathed and washed clothing. Informing the families of this health hazard was also met with indifference; there were no other viable alternatives for disposing of refuse.

MACHISMO, MOTHERHOOD AND MARTYRDOM

Although machismo is well recognised as a Latin American ideology, when asked about it most women could not specifically qualify it within their own lives. Women claimed the household as their domain, and considered themselves quite powerful because of this. They did not see their husbands as exerting any considerable influence either negatively or positively over household matters; this was entirely (and proudly) the woman's arena:

> My husband has no idea what I struggle with to feed this family, manage everything in the house, keep it all together. I have full control over the house, the kids, everything.

While the volunteers were defining and constructing machismo in terms of notions of 'equality', the women themselves did so in terms of 'difference' and sex-role differentiation.

Although reluctant to discuss the issue, several women admitted the problem of domestic violence was quite a serious one for some women on the co-op:

> a very big problem here on the co-op is when a husband will not let his wife organise or attend any meetings . . . sometimes these men drink, using the co-op money, and then beat their wives.

The unwillingness of many of these women to discuss this issue is in itself a form of resistance; it was almost as if they knew what our impressions and expectations would be. One woman even told me that the men were told by the women to be on their 'best behaviour' during our stay.

Another way the volunteers seemed to qualify consciousness was through the attitudes to abortion, a particularly difficult subject to broach, as markers and indicators of an advanced society:

> Her husband had hung her from the roof with a rope from her torso. Neither had money for an abortion and he wanted her to lose the baby so this is what he did. It didn't happen – she just stayed hanging there until someone came by and let her down. Before her husband came home she had the baby. Her husband killed it.

It was inconceivable for many of the volunteers that the right to an abortion would not be at the foremost of importance; this attitude was probably reinforced by the debates within the US Supreme Court over the issue of abortion. During a meeting with the co-op's women's group, a brigadista asked the following question:

> The Sandinista constitution does not allow abortions – is this a failure of Sandinismo?

To which an angry woman replied:

> We don't want the right to abortion here in Nigaragua. No woman would have one anyway – it's immoral and against the will of God. You should have as many kids as God is going to give you.

While this statement clearly reflects the pervasive influence of the Catholic Church in Nicaragua, many of the brigadistas took this woman's views as merely 'backwards'. (Additionally, what kind of resistance to our Western constructions does this statement suggest?) Noteworthy is how the question of abortion was raised (in a manner which suggested inadequacy) and also why it was raised – primarily to gauge some comparative rating/standard to Western society. This question was raised several times afterwards with varying responses. The group was much more satisfied with a female Sandinista soldier who wanted to legalise abortion and criticised the FSLN and other women who did not support such legislation:

> Yes, women should have control and legal abortion because we're the ones who have to take care of the babies and there are a lot of problems because we can't provide for their education and health. But I understand why a lot of my 'sisters' don't really feel the same way. It was a failure of the Sandinistas not to have the right to an abortion in the Constitution. The Frente should have worked harder to promote the issue.

Her status as a 'progressive' woman was also similar to the ways in which a women's group in the nearby city of Matagalpa which we visited (comprising educated, middle-class women in their twenties) discussed issues about abortion, and domestic violence quite openly, thus facilitating the creation of advanced/backwards binary constructions. The mere fact that abortion was raised in such an inappropriate situation shows a lack of understanding of economic issues, such as cost and availability of facilities, or the status of motherhood in Nicaragua.

Furthermore it was discovered that no woman on the co-op actually used contraception. This was viewed as child-like, irresponsible behaviour; there was little consideration of the responsibilities of men in this situation, the economic situation, the availability and cost of contraceptives, or the ideology of motherhood within the context of Nicaraguan society and the revolution. This attitude did not take into account the status given to women as martyrs, nor an understanding of childbirth as politicised solidarity with the state via raising children, particularly sons, for the revolution:

> Several of my sons were soldiers, for me and my conscience this was not a reason not to vote for Sandinismo. I still support Sandinismo and also the draft. The mother of San Ramon, the boy who died, she feels the same way – she is still a Sandinista. As mothers we were very sad, we knew that our sons could be killed, but no, we never doubted the necessity of our sons to have to go out there, because we knew they were defending the truth. We had a responsibility as mothers to support them.

As mothers of soldiers these women also felt a great responsibility towards the welfare of their sons and the Sandinista movement, thus reinforcing, as well as reinforced by, FSLN ideology. This commitment to motherhood was evident throughout the co-op and for many brigadistas constructed the women as subservient, passive, simplistic.

As mothers they also saw themselves and were also viewed by Nicaraguan society as the sole individuals responsible for the maintenance, distribution, and 'stretching out' of resources within the household. Of primary importance to all of the women we spoke to were the economic changes which they had undergone before, during, and after the Revolution which affected their families. The women felt that the main victory was that they had more economic security and a slightly better standard of living due to ownership of property:

> Where we lived before the revolution we had to give half of our crops to the landowners. If we didn't they would take everything and we wouldn't eat. On the co-op we own the land and we can keep what we grow.

When discussing the benefits of land ownership and economic security the women talked mainly of the ways in which this affected not themselves, but their ability to provide for their families, and specifically their children. However they only theoretically 'owned' a piece of land, as legally their husbands and not themselves were the actual members of the co-operative, something which signalled to many volunteers a lack of 'emancipation' and 'equal rights'. Again, their status as mothers and their organising and politicisation around that position, although devalued by outsiders, allowed them to exert a tremendous amount of power and influence over their children and homes.

WHAT IS 'FEMINIST CONSCIOUSNESS'?

It is only logical that women focus on their immediate needs in order to guarantee survival of their families and communities (Aleman 1991: 101). It also seems, however, that these immediate needs also facilitated other points of resistance: leaving the household situation, creating women-only space, support groups and networks, using organisational skills, and increased desires for knowledge.[7] All of the women we talked to knew about AMNLAE, the national women's organisation, and the programmes they were involved with during the revolution:

> We started to learn about our rights through classes, instruction and pamphlets. We learned about women's 'problems'. Because before the Triumph, the great majority of peasant women did not even know the names of their body parts. That's how AMNLAE started, giving us instruction and pamphlets so we could get to know our bodies.

The revolution provided the chance for these women to organise and AMNLAE was one support system for their 'politicisation':

> I didn't have any political thoughts or ideas before the revolution, because before the revolution we couldn't talk about politics – women weren't

supposed to. But after the Triumph, I had my own ideas about the situation, yes. For the first time that I could tell one could organise and especially as a woman. Before there did not exist any women's organisations, there was no freedom to organise and women were always marginalised by the government.

The same woman recognised the gender dynamics operating in such a situation:

Only the men were able to participate in the meetings, in anything. The woman was very mistreated on the part of the government and also on the part of men. I am not going to let the man marginalise me, because the man and the woman are partners in life and that's what AMNLAE made us see, that we as women have the same rights as men.

In terms of redefining gender roles, shifts may have been with women who fought. One woman who was mobilised in the mountains during the Contra war explained:

The training was exactly the same for men and women. We learned how to disarm, clean the weapons, shoot, march – all this sort of stuff was the same. Everyone there was equal. There wasn't this distinction that you're a woman and this person is a man.

Does this blurring of gender roles necessarily indicate greater power than negotiation and subversion within sex-differentiated arenas? A fixed understanding of 'feminist consciousness' seems to be predicated by the primacy of 'equality' of men and women. The experiences of these women tend to indicate otherwise, and as Jaquette (1976) states:

the feminist sensitivity to sex-role differentiation and the tendency to measure liberation by the degree to which women adopt male roles may skew our perceptions of the real issue: female power. North American experience to the contrary, it may be possible to maximize female power by retaining sex-role differences. The alternative seems to have been to view Latin American women as backward or passive or weak; and that image seems to me to be strongly contradicted by the data we have on the personality traits of the Latin American woman.

(Jaquette 1976: 222)

CONCLUSIONS

The identity politics appropriate in some contexts ... are not necessarily appropriate in others, nor may they be needed by women in different economic and cultural contexts in the Third World.

(Ferguson 1991: 96)

Constructions of resistance may not necessarily 'travel' from one location to another, and consequently what is perceived as 'helpful', 'liberatory' and necessarily in terms of aid from the deliverer may not be so for receivers. The conflicts regarding perceptions of women's roles, feminist consciousness and strategic versus practical needs are indicative of the systemic problems of humanitarian aid projects and development ideologies in general. For Third World peoples, the reception of aid from white/Western populations may not occur without resistance to and subversion of their 'underprivileged' situations. The volunteers on this project were looking for certain indicators of consciousness, of resistance, of desires for empowerment. These Nicaraguan women were concerned about survival. It is difficult to delineate, given these dichotomies, which aspects of their resistance were primarily about their own immediate needs and which were about contesting the ideologies of the volunteer group; it seems that perhaps in many cases there were elements of both. What is clear, however, is that these women did not unthinkingly simply accept our roles as aid-givers nor our suggestions (in contrast to the unthinking manners in which we handled ourselves). They repeatedly contested our notions of humanitarian aid and our roles as deliverers of such (unexpectedly I might add) through clear assertions of what *they* considered vital to *their* lives. Consequently, if contextualised outside Western frameworks, they would also 'be allowed' to emerge and challenge the monolithic Third World woman image.

I have purposefully qualified myself with 'the volunteers' throughout the chapter, recognising that although I was also an 'outsider-within' in relation to our group, we encompassed certain ideological representations as 'Americans'. I often did not know how I felt about most of these scenarios, able only to reflect upon them afterwards. I am not suggesting that there was not dissent among the group members, but any attempts on my part to point out certain racial and cultural constructs were seen as unnecessary. As a woman of colour on this project, I found that my experiences were seen as anomalies, thus legitimising 'white' experiences and maintaining 'politically correct' romantic notions of such experiences.[8]

Given these contexts, it must be stressed that it is not simply enough to say that there were 'misunderstandings' among the participants of this situation. As de Groot points out, 'partial and/or prejudiced analysis of women's situations ... needs to be understood as the expression of power relations rather than as ignorance or bigotry' (de Groot 1991: 116–17). Ultimately we as a group of Americans and as aid-deliverers asserted our status as progressive, wealthy and First World, thus freezing these Nicaraguan women into oppositional categories of backwards, poor and Third World.

ACKNOWLEDGEMENTS

I would like to thank Haleh Afshar for her editorial comments as well as her support and patience during the process of writing this chapter. Thanks also to Anne Akeroyd for her supervision of and engagement with my work during my time at the University of York.

NOTES

1 For this see J. de Groot, (1991).
2 The term 'Third World' is used, with reservations, not to highlight the disparities between the two, but rather to affirm the relationship of exploitation of the Third World by the First. The term is one of empowerment 'in preference to postcolonial or developing countries' and denotes those 'colonized, neo and de-colonised countries whose economic/political structures have been deformed within the colonial process' (Mohanty *et al.* 1991: ix).
3 De Groot notes that this reflects 'the exclusion or marginalisation of women in Western workplaces during both the nineteenth and twentieth centuries' (de Groot 1991: 119).
4 See Georgina Waylen, Chapter 1 in this volume, for elaboration on public/private divide debates.
5 For detailed descriptions see part I of Moser (1993); also Sen and Grown (1987).
6 This in itself suggests the bandwagon-type effect of such projects; ironically, as many Nicaraguan Sandinista supporters told me, the internationalist movement of volunteers lost momentum at the very stage when moral was lowest and support desperately needed.
7 Unfortunately this does not necessarily mean that these activities will be taken seriously. A few women discussed the idea of asking for funds from UNAG to buy an automatic corn-grinder. This is an activity which took up an enormous amount of energy and time, an alleviation of which would then allow the women to concentrate on other activities. However most of the brigadistas and members of UNAG itself felt this would be an uneccessary investment as it would not contribute to 'production' on the farm. The women, very aware of how the grinder would benefit everyone, were nonetheless seen as frivolous.
8 The dilemma of what to do when being asked for gifts (e.g. newspapers, food, batteries, candles, water containers) plagued the group consistently throughout our stay. It was interesting that despite being told many times by the director of UNAG (who had been living in Nicaragua and doing this type of work for many years) not, under any circumstances, to give gifts, that most of the volunteers did so anyway, causing certain tensions among families. There was also a food incentive for hosting a brigadista, which created the discomfort of realising that one is not simply a guest but also a meal-ticket. For the volunteer, this challenges white liberalist notions of cross-cultural experiences; it illuminates the underlying economic exploitation of the exchange process (economic benefit in exchange for 'authentic' overseas experience).

   Other tensions revealed themselves in terms of notions of 'productivity' which were connected to activity. The group in general was very impatient and the work project was viewed as unorganised and inefficient. Many consequently equated a *mañana* mentality (do it tomorrow) with laziness and also typical of the 'lack of motivation among the poor.' The issue of vegetarianism was also problematic in a location where certain foods are scarce, meat is considered a luxury, and the offering of meat is to celebrate special occasions and functions as a gift for guests. Volunteers struggled with the dilemma of how, not whether, to tell their families not to kill their last chicken for them. Interestingly enough, many volunteers reported that their 'host mothers' prepared meat anyway, regardless of being informed of a vegetarian diet; also during festive occasions cows were slaughtered and eaten.

REFERENCES

Abu-Lughod, L. (1993) *Writing Women's Worlds: Bedouin Stories*, Berkeley, CA: University of California Press.

Aleman, P. P. (1991) 'Women's Movement, Crisis, and Food: The Case of Nicaragua', *Alternatives: Women's Visions and Movements* 2: 79–112.

Anon. (1991) 'Women in Nicaragua: The Revolution on Hold', *Envio: The Monthly Magazine of Analysis on Nicaragua* 10(119): 30–41.

Brock-Utne, B. (1989) 'Women and Third World Countries: What do We Have in Common?', *Women's Studies International Forum* 12(5): 495–503.

Collins, P. H. (1991) 'Learning from the Outsider within:The Sociological Significance of Black Feminist Thought', in M. M. Fonow and J. A. Cook (eds) *Beyond Methodology: Feminist Methodology as Lived Research*, Bloomington IN: Indiana University Press.

de Groot, J. (1991) 'Conceptions and Misconceptions: The Historical and Cultural Context of Discussion on Women and Development', in H. Afshar (ed.) *Women, Development and Survival in the Third World*, London: Longman.

Ferguson, A. (1991) 'Lesbianism, Feminism, and Empowerment in Nicaragua', *Socialist Review* 21(3–4): 75–97.

Jaquette, J. (1976) 'Female Political Participation in Latin America', in J. Nash and H. Icken Safia (eds) *Sex and Class in Latin America*, New York: Praeger.

Kandiyoti, D. (1988) 'Bargaining with Patriarchy', *Gender and Society* 2(3): 274–290.

Mohanty, C., Russo, A. and Torres, L. (1991) *Third World Women and the Politics of Feminism*, Bloomington, IN: Indiana University Press.

Mohanty, C. (1988) 'Under Western Eyes: Feminist Scholarship and Colonial Discourses', *Feminist Review* 30: 16–34.

Molyneux, M. (1985) 'Mobilization without Emancipation? Women's Interests, the State, and Revolution in Nicaragua', *Feminist Studies* 11(2): 227–54.

Moser, C. and Peake, L. (1987) *Women, Human Settlements and Housing*, London: Tavistock.

Moser, C. O. N. (1993) *Gender Planning and Development: Theory, Practice and Training*, New York: Routledge.

Nash, J. and Safia, H. I. (1979) *Sex and Class in Latin America*, New York: Praeger.

Randall, M. (1981) *Sandino's Daughters*, Canada: New Star Books.

Sen, G. and Grown, C. (1987) *Development, Crises, and Alternative Visions: Third World Women's Perspectives*, New York: Monthly Review Press.

Skiar, H. (1989) 'The New Dawn', *Spare Rib* 203: 11–22.

Stead, M. (1991) 'Women, War and Underdevelopment in Nicaragua', in H. Afshar (ed.) *Women, Development and Survival in the Third World*, London: Longman.

Vance, I. (1987) 'More than Bricks and Mortar: Women's Participation in Self-Help Housing in Managua, Nicaragua', in C. O. N. Moser and L. Peake (eds) *Women, Human Settlements and Housing*, London: Tavistock.

FURTHER READING

I have included here specifically those works which attempt to address the various issues of positioning and power within disciplinary methodologies. For example, Lila

Abu-Lughod's (1993) *Writing Women's Worlds: Bedouin Stories* illuminates the problems of being an anthropologist situated in the First World and researching women from 'her culture' living in the Third World. Patricia Hill Collins (1991) elaborates, within a different context, on the fluidity of insider and outsider constructs in 'Learning From the Outsider Within: The Sociological Significance of Black Feminist Thought', in M.M. Fonow and J.A. Cook (eds) *Beyond Methodology: Feminist Methodology as Lived Research.* Joanna de Groot's (1991) 'Conceptions and Misconceptions: The Historical and Cultural Context of Discussion on Women and Development', in H. Afshar (ed.) *Women, Development and Survival in the Third World,* points to the connections between colonialism and post-colonialism and discourses of development. See also Chandra Talpade Mohanty, Ann Russo and Lourdes Torres (eds) (1991) *Third World Women and the Politics of Feminism.* In particular, Mohanty's 'Under Western Eyes: Feminist Scholarship and Colonial Discourses' (reprinted from *Feminist Review*) focuses on constructions of Third World women and the Third World Woman, problematising monolithic understandings of feminism and the subsequent universalising of Western frameworks. Naila Kabeer's (1994) *Reversed Realities: Gender Hierarchies in Development Thought* (London: Verso) elaborates on gender and development studies approaches, including analyses of the debates around the 'household', WID methods, and strategic/practical divides.

Chapter 6

Chinese women
Media concerns and the politics of reform

Delia Davin

Women's issues have attracted an enormous amount of attention in post-reform China in all types of publications from the most popular magazines to serious academic journals. What is striking about this writing is its great diversity. Some is complacent about the present situation of women in China; much is quite critical. It is written from many perspectives, some feminist, many which are not and some which are clearly anti-feminist. The variety of this writing in terms of standpoint, subject-matter and objectives marks it out sharply from most writing on women which appeared in the first three decades of the People's Republic.

Although reform of the organs of party and state in China in the 1980s was superficial and hesitant, there was a significant growth in alternative sources of power, influence and information in the form of a freer press and publishing industry, the establishment of private companies, voluntary associations, private schools and other institutions as a result of what are usually referred to in China simply as 'the reforms'. Despite the obvious existence of limits and constraints there is also a much greater tolerance for private or grassroots debate or dissent. Some analysts argue that this has produced the beginnings of a civil society in China (White 1993). This process has allowed the development of a more complex and interesting discourse on many topics including those of women and women's issues.

After 1949, most writing on women closely reflected current party policy (Davin 1978; Stacey 1983). Policy on women did undergo changes and development over the years but in most periods writing on women's issues was stereotyped and predictable in its focus, shifting in accordance with changes in broader party concerns rather than women's specific needs. It informed its audience about policy and contrasted the misery and oppression suffered by women in the old society with the enormous improvements offered under the new. These improvements were to be brought about by a range of measures among which the most important were the reform of the old arranged marriage system through the marriage law, and the drawing of women into paid employment outside the home to give them economic independence and social respect. Accordingly the marriage law and women's employment were given detailed media coverage. If inequalities or injustices to women were reported at all they were explained in terms of remnants from the old society and a lack of thoroughness in implementing communist policy; the possibility that the policy itself was inadequate was not considered.

By contrast, writing on women in contemporary China is not informed by a consistent policy or line. It deals with a great range of topics and is produced by a wide variety of people from feminist academics to journalists and officials. It is useful for what it can tell us both about actual problems for women today and the differing ways in which these problems are viewed. In this chapter I propose some explanations for the widespread concern with women's issues now current in China and discuss some examples of recent writing on women's issues.

IDEOLOGY AND WOMEN'S ISSUES IN POST-REFORM CHINA

Since the introduction of the economic reforms at the end of the 1970s, China has experienced extraordinarily rapid social, economic and even political change. Gross national product has soared, and standards of living have risen with it. The average Chinese is very much better off in the mid-1990s than the early 1980s. But change has inevitably brought its own stresses and strains. The benefits of growth are unevenly distributed, giving rise to glaring inequalities. Inflation and price reform create great anxieties for those on salaries and pensions. Generation gaps have opened up. The young tend to take for granted and participate fully in the newly developing acquisitive, consumerist society while older people criticise their greed and extravagance. Corruption is widespread, crime rates are rising and prostitution is obvious in all the big cities. Migrants have left the countryside in their millions in the hope of a better life in the towns. In the general atmosphere of uncertainty, and even anxiety, moral panics are easily generated, and, as elsewhere, are often focused on such issues as family life, child-rearing, sexual mores, women's roles and female comportment. To some extent, therefore, the concern with gender divisions and women's issues can be read as reflecting a deeper and more pervasive concern about what is happening in Chinese society.

In 1983, official concern about the impact of the reforms on women, especially women in rural society was demonstrated when the Central Secretariat of the Chinese Communist Party convened a special meeting to discuss women's issues and decided to give high priority to protecting the interests and rights of women and children (Siao and Chao Yuanling 1994). Between 1983 and 1989, of China's thirty provincial-level legislatures, twenty-eight passed regulations on the protection of women's and children's rights and interests. In 1992, a national law was promulgated (Law Yearbook 1993). These regulations vary considerably in length and detail, but have the common purpose of reaffirming the equality of women in the family and in society at large, and forbidding the abuse and ill-treatment of women. They insist on a woman's right to choose her marrige partner, prohibit the sale and purchase of women, and lay down that infanticide should be treated as homicide. The regulations reflect official puritanism, for example many of them lay down that anyone who has an affair with someone they know to be married to another person is liable to punishment, either by the courts or the Public Security Bureau. Prostitutes and their clients are liable to fines or to re-education through labour. Most of the regulations also deal with employment rights and with equality of treatment when land is contracted out in the countryside. As no machinery was set up to monitor or enforce the implementation of these laws, their efficacy is open to doubt. However they do give useful pointers to the main areas of official concern about women in China. They also confirm that broadly speaking the official line continues to be that there should be no discrimination against women.

Nonetheless if one looks at other official and semi-official literature, the messages are mixed. Some articles continue to urge that there should be no discrimination, and that women should be treated equally at work, at home and in education (Party Official 1988). But since the beginning of the reforms, official sources have often emphasised the special role of women and their physiological limitations, implying or even arguing that at least a degree of division of labour based on gender is necessary and desirable (*Tianjin Daily* 1980). An officially backed campaign for women to be 'virtuous wives and good mothers' (a Confucian concept once condemned in Maoist China), and to create good harmonious families has flourished since the early 1980s (Feng Bian 1984). Even more extreme, early in the reform era two economists suggested that women should withdraw from the labour force leaving their jobs to men (Secretariat of the All-China Women's Federation 1981; and Wang Shulin 1983). The party-led Women's Federation expressed strenuous opposition to this idea but it has been brought up again quite frequently again since the mid-1980s. A later article in the same vein urged that the 'natural division of labour' should be respected with women doing lighter work or part-time work to allow them time for household chores (Ji Zheng 1986). On the other hand, there have been some vigorous attacks on discrimination against women in employment which has become very pronounced in the wake of the reforms. Women are urged to overcome it by working and studying harder and building up their self-confidence (Anhui Provincial Women's Association 1985). Whatever the line taken, articles of this type from official or semi-official sources tend to be didactic and written in a tone of great certainty. The fact that they offer such contradictory views reflects the comparative lack of consensus on social development in China today.

POLITICAL PARTICIPATION

Women's political participation has been another area of concern both in the official press and in women's studies publications. It is noted that the reforms appear to have reduced women's political activity at all levels from village committees right up to provincial and central level government.[1] Women were badly under-represented in politics even in the pre-reform era, what is disturbing about contemporary China is that they are losing ground not gaining it. Female membership of the Central Committee peaked in 1973 at 10.3 per cent, by 1992 it was down to 7.5 per cent (Research Institute of the All-China Women's Federation 1991; Rosen 1993a). While women were 25 per cent of the members of the Standing Committee of the National People's Congress of 1975, they made up only 9 per cent of the Standing Committee in 1993. Data from many sources indicate that this trend is typical at all levels of government. There is a debate about whether this problem is best addressed by quotas which were used formally and informally in the past, especially in the Cultural Revolution era of the early 1970s, but are not applied at present. In the past also it was normal for only one candidate to stand in an election. The introduction of multi-candidate elections in 1987 appears to have disadvantaged women. Where there is a choice, voters prefer men. Analyses of the appointment of rural cadres indicate that women are appointed as to posts customarily reserved for females only because they are seen as women's business such as women's representative or birth control worker.

The explanation for women's lower participation in all kinds of political activities is again the change in the political climate. There is no longer any real pressure to appoint even token numbers of women to political office and indeed male political officials may be reluctant to see them in plum jobs. On the other hand women are less willing than in the past to take on the voluntary political responsibilities of a party member or a low-level street committee member because it is no longer regarded as praiseworthy for them to take this time away from family responsibilities.

GENDER AND EMPLOYMENT ISSUES SINCE THE REFORMS

There can be no doubt that although women as part of the general population have benefited from China's growing prosperity, the reforms have adversely affected women in certain specific ways. Growing discrimination against women has been noted in many spheres of employment (Honig and Hershatter 1988: ch. 7). There have been many reports of companies and government offices demanding to be allocated male rather than female graduates (Yang Xingnan 1985). Investigations of discrimination against women in employment usually come up with the explanation that women's reproductive functions make them expensive to employ since they will require paid maternity leave and time off to care for sick children. In the era of economic reform when enterprises still usually bear the costs of welfare provision, but are also responsible for their own profit and loss, this is obviously an important consideration. Nevertheless it is not wholly satisfactory as an explanation. First, urban women in present-day China rarely bear more than one child and therefore their time off for maternity leave and child care is comparatively short. Second, in urban China it is normally the man's employers who are expected to provide a newly married couple with rented accommodation. This heavy welfare cost does not apparently discourage employers from recruiting men. It is difficult not to conclude that once the political pressure not to discriminate was reduced, employers simply felt freer to follow their prejudices.

There are other areas of employment, new since the economic reforms, for which women are actively recruited. These include factory and sweatshop work in the Special Economic Zones and other newly industrialising areas where cheap Chinese labour has attracted foreign and Chinese investors. Working conditions in these enterprises are known to be poor and their safety record is bad as demonstrated in the appalling loss of life in two factory fires at the end of 1992 (Gittings 1993). Complaints in the official press and investigations follow such accidents but they continue to occur. The women employed are often migrants from poor inland provinces tempted by earnings higher than they could hope to obtain at home and unlikely to demand safer conditions. Migration was very strictly controlled in the pre-reform era and is still officially restricted. Many rural migrants in cities do not have the necessary urban residence permit and live in fear of being departed to their places of origin. This insecurity makes them vulnerable to bullying and exploitation.

The maidservants who undertake domestic work in the homes of urban families in the big cities are another group of vulnerable migrant workers (Wan Shanping 1992). These women are much discussed in the media, usually from the employers' point of view. They are therefore characterised as greedy, lazy, ignorant, unskilled and so on. It is rarely pointed out that these girls, who are usually young and far from home, may be very vulnerable and have little defence against unreasonable demands or ill-treatment. The only space they can call their own is often a bed partitioned off from the family living area by a curtain. If employed for child care they may spend their days alone with a baby, frequently isolated in a high-rise building. On the other hand, women who have been in the city long enough to find their way around can take advantage of the fact that there is now a shortage of maids to bargain for shorter hours and their better pay. Maids who return to the countryside may take with them enough savings and knowhow to set up small enterprises and become very much more prosperous than their peers who stayed in the countryside.

GENDER ISSUES IN EDUCATION

At primary and secondary level girls' school enrolment rates are significantly lower than those of boys. Pragmatic peasants see no advantage in paying fees to educate girls who will be lost to the family when they marry, and prefer to set them to work on the family plot or to earn money in rural industry. For both sexes enrolment falls with age, but it is always lower for girls and the gap is increased in the higher grades. For example in 1983, throughout China, 59.15 per cent of 7-year-old girls were in school against 64.9 per cent of boys. For 13 year olds it was 38.0 per cent of the female cohort in school against 51.2 per cent of the male cohort (Population Census 1990: 184–7; Research Institute of the All-China Women's Federation 1991: 209). Moreover the need for the girls' labour was overwhelmingly the reason given by parents for keeping girls out of school. In China 80 per cent of illiterates are female (Population Census 1990: 180). Women are also only in a minority in higher education although their numbers have moved from under one-quarter to around one-third (Population Census 1990: 675). This under-representation partly reflects their smaller numbers among those who finish secondary school, but there are other factors. Many colleges admit that they require higher admission grades of female than of male applicants. This is most often justified by the argument that females are disciplined about learning by rote and thus perform better in exams than men, whereas the latter, with a stronger and more lively intelligence, ultimately have the greater potential (Pepper 1984: 112–14). Sometimes employers' preferences are used to justify discrimination. For example, a school of foreign trade claimed that if it admitted too many women, graduates would end up unemployed however good their grades because employers in this field wished to recruit men (Ju Ning 1990). At post-graduate level women's numbers are even smaller. It is widely reported that men are reluctant to marry women more highly qualified than themselves and this is thought to deter women from taking post-graduate courses.

WOMEN AND POPULATION POLICY

Unlike many other gender issues, population policy is discussed in the press only in rather limited ways.[2] As this is not an area in which the state would tolerate dissent, opposition to the policy is not openly expressed, although its strictness has occasionally been obliquely questioned in academic journals. In newspapers and magazines read by the general public, campaigns are supported, demographic data are reported and news of successes and infringements is printed.

Most Chinese couples are required to limit their families to one child although two or even three are allowed in certain defined circumstances. For example, since the late 1980s, most peasant couples whose first child is a girl have been permitted a second birth (Davin 1990). Faced with the situation that the birth of a daughter will mean that they are not allowed to try again for a son, some couples resort to desperate measures. There were many reports of female infanticide in the early years of the policy. More recently, sex determination tests and selective abortion have been used to assure the birth of a son. Such procedures are forbidden and those carrying them out are subject to considerable penalties, but some experts argue that they are common enough to be statistically significant (Zeng Yi *et al.* 1993). The 1990 census certainly recorded a distorted sex ratio among the youngest age groups although it is impossible to tell which of the possible factors contributed in what proportion to this (Hull 1990). It may be that some of the missing girls were simply not registered by parents who hoped to have a second child unnoticed and thus unpenalised by officialdom. Another widely reported evil produced by population policy is the ill-treatment or beating of women who give birth to girls and are then punished by disappointed husbands or in-laws. Writers of popular science columns insist that women are not responsible for the sex of their babies but apparently this problem persists (Davin 1987a).

Because it has given rise to such tragic phenomena, the restrictive birth policy has focused attention on the strength of son preference in China. This has made it impossible to argue as was sometimes claimed in the past that gender equality has already been achieved. It has also forced a careful consideration of factors underlying son preference such as patrilocal marriage, an old-age support system in which parents depend heavily on their sons, the generally higher earning capacity of males over females and so on. Media coverage of these issues has produced a greater awareness of the structures underlying son preference, though no real solutions have been found.

WOMEN IN THE MARKET-PLACE

In contemporary China as elsewhere in the world everything from clothes to washing machines is now sold by the use of images of pretty young women in advertising. The Women's Federation protested against this practice on the grounds that it was demeaning to women when it became commonplace in the early 1980s but commercial interests proved too strong. The issue is still debated in the press, notably in the splendidly titled article, 'Love one's wife = Buy her a washing machine? On male chauvinism in television commercials' (He Dong 1992). Unfortunately there is no evidence that protests have any effect on practice.

The commercialisation of both marriage and sexual relations has also become more apparent since the reforms. Since 1949 the communist government has consistently argued that the custom of giving a bride-price and the exchange of large amounts of money or property at the time of marriage amounted to the sale of women or 'mercenary marriage'. Despite repeated campaigns these customs were never wholly eliminated. However, it is widely acknowledged that both bride-price and the amounts spent on equipping the new couple's home and on the wedding feast rose enormously in the 1980s. The rise in bride-price perhaps in part reflects the higher value of the girl's labour to her family who have to be compensated for its loss. The huge amounts spent on furnishing and equipping a home for the new couple are to be explained by rising expectations and new consumerist values. The uneven sex ratio in the younger cohorts affected by the population policy seems likely to ensure that in future families will have to spend more and more to secure a bride for their son. Political calls for frugality are still made, but in the new climate they are quite ineffective (Yang Zhangqiao 1987).

A clearer example of the commoditisation of women is the trafficking in women which has been reported from many places in China (Zhuang Ping 1993). Poor rural women are taken sometimes by coercion, sometimes as volunteers, across hundreds or even thousands of miles to be sold as wives to strangers. The women are recruited in the poorest parts of China and sold in wealthier regions where bride-price for local women is high and imported women offer a cheap alternative for men who would otherwise be unable to afford a wife. The explanation for the traffic is both demographic and economic. Unmarried men of marriageable age outnumber women everywhere in the Chinese countryside and the working of the market ensures that men in the wealthier areas are able to draw in women from poor regions. One may infer from the migration figures gathered in the 1990 census that female marriage migration across provincial boundaries occurs on an enormous scale (Messkoub and Davin 1993). No doubt this is often consensual, but in such matches women are vulnerable and may be duped, abused or exploited. Many prosecutions of traffickers have been reported, but the trade basically reflects the magnitude of regional economic inequality in China and it will be difficult to eliminate in the near future. Similar factors have no doubt contributed to the increase in prostitution which has been very widely observed and debated in China.

EXTERNAL INFLUENCES

The discussion and treatment of women's issues in China has been influenced from the outside in various ways. China is part of a global culture to a far greater extent than ever before. Though 'Western feminism' is frequently decried as bourgeois in China, or more politely rejected as irrelevant, there can be no doubt that some of its ideas and methods have had an influence both direct and indirect. Many Chinese now travel or study abroad. Some, especially among the women, have been influenced by women's movements in other countries. They are of course a tiny minority in China's vast population, but they are significant among the serious writers on women's issues today. Female academics have set up women's study and discussion groups on many campuses and women's studies centres have been established in various universities, notably at Beijing University, Zhengzhou University and Tianjin Normal University. The women involved in these groups are familiar with trends in feminist scholarship elsewhere and are influenced by its ideas, although some are quick to insist that their task is to develop a new women's studies adapted to Chinese conditions. Their work tends to be more open, scholarly and analytic than earlier writing on women in the People's Republic.

Large women's studies conferences were held at Zhengzhou University in 1989 and at Beijing University in 1992 with some international participation (Beijing Municipal Women's Federation 1992).

Development and aid agencies are another source of outside influence. Many of these now make the condition that a certain part of their aid should be targeted on women. Thus the growing sensitivity to gender issues among those working in development internationally has its parallel in China.

In 1995, China played host to the UN Conference on Women. Official planning for the conference began very early, as with other such international events, because high priority was given to making them run smoothly. It was hoped that foreign delegates would depart with good impressions of China and of the treatment of women in China. Some independent women's activists complained that only official voices would be heard at the conference and that there was no room for a diversity of views. They were probably right. What the authorities wish to be said about Chinese women at the conference would be informed first by their pride in what has been achieved for Chinese women for which they believe they should be given credit internationally, and second, by their desire for international prestige. Although there are limits to what they are prepared to do to get it, such prestige does matter to the Chinese government.

Even before China was open to the outside world, the Chinese authorities were extremely sensitive to foreign commentaries on and criticisms of China. This remains the case today. Chinese reaction to a Canadian study of the position of women which placed China 132nd in the world illustrates this sensitivity. It was reported in the Chinese press and the Women's Federation was funded to do a large-scale survey with the implicit aim of refuting the Canadian study (Rosen 1993b; 1993c). The six indicators chosen for this 1988 study made it inevitable that China's position in the ratings would be low. They were: attitude towards male and female infants, rates of school enrolment of boys and girls, rate of employment of young men and women, proportion of women among the top leaders in state organs, position of women in their homes, and percentage of women's personal property in social wealth. If we look at them one by one, it is obvious that China would do badly on the first as the strength of son preference has been highlighted by the introduction of the extremely restrictive birth policy. Girls' school enrolment rates compare badly with those of boys. Discrimination against the recruitment of women in employment and the fact that the majority of rural migrants who go to the cities to seek jobs are young males produces a higher employment rate for young men. It is not clear how position in the family was assessed, *de facto* power in the Chinese family varies with individual circumstances, but for formal purposes it is still usual to name the oldest male or the oldest working male as the household head. The only women likely to be identified as household heads are widows, divorcees or women whose husbands have been absent for a long time. Women are poorly represented in political office at the highest levels. Finally, there is little personal wealth in China: the major form of property by tradition is family property. The government has recently tried to introduce the idea of marital and personal property and to reinforce women's property rights and rights of inheritance but without much success (Davin 1987b).

It seems only fair to point out that China might have done much better on some other selection of criteria, for example, the proportion of women amongst students studying engineering, the proportion of doctors who are female, women's life expectancy and legal rights, or access to maternal and child health services. Nonetheless the study was taken seriously in China.

The Women's Federation survey commissioned as a response to the Canadian study was based on 42,000 interviews involving almost equal numbers of male and female and urban and rural respondents. It covered employment, education, family status, attitudes and the respondents' own assessment of gender inequality in China.

The findings compared women both to their mothers and to men. For example 87.21 per cent of the female respondents were either working or had retired from a job, 8.9 percentage points lower than for men but 20.7 points higher than for their mothers' generation. Of women under 40, only 5.18 per cent were engaged solely in housework whereas for their mothers' generation the figure had been 27.54 per cent. Employed women in urban areas earned 81.68 per cent of what the males earned. The level to which women had been educated varied with age being much higher among younger people. Of the women surveyed 53.32 per cent were able to name the party general secretary, the premier and the president as against 74.78 per cent of the men.

Differences in attitudes between the sexes towards women's proper place were quite small. For example 48.16 of the males and 51.21 per cent of the females disagreed with or doubted the validity of the saying that a man's place is in society and a woman's place is in the family. Asked whether women should avoid surpassing their husbands in social status, 65.50 per cent of the males and 67.79 per cent of the females expressed disagreement or doubt. Asked where equality had been established, 81.07 per cent thought it greatest in the area of legal rights. Only 40.39 per cent thought it had been established in ideas and concepts. Asked about the sorts of inequalities they had observed, the survey respondents came up with a list which corresponds closely with the issues already mentioned in this chapter. Women who gave birth to a girl were felt to be looked down on (35.91 per cent), women suffered discrimination in employment (33.09 per cent), it was hard for daughters to inherit property (20.56 per cent), and there was inequality in the score required of males and females to enter schools and colleges (19.74 per cent).

The treatment of time spans in the survey masks the fact that many of the improvements which it found in women's employment and education status and in attitudes towards women probably dated from before the reforms. It has little to tell us about the specific impact of the reforms on women with which the media coverage discussed in this chapter is so concerned.

CONCLUSION

The considerable volume of writing about women and gender issues published in China since the mid-1980s is to be explained by several factors. First, in a society undergoing rapid change, the questioning in the writing stands for a more general unease. Although the party line on population is not open to challenge, comparative freedom of discussion is permitted on other gender issues which the state does not seem to regard as threatening. Second, the reforms have had a specific and sometimes negative effect on women. The examples looked at in this chapter are employment, education, population control, and the commoditisation of women. Among many omissions the most notable one is the position of women in the peasant household which I have discussed elsewhere but have not included here for reasons of space (Davin 1991). Third, as the reforms have resulted in a much freer gathering and dissemination of information, the educated elite who do the writing are probably more aware of social problems affecting women than in the past. Finally, Chinese are now far more aware of trends in the world outside China and of foreign commentary on China. This has also contributed to the growing awareness of gender issues. The development of this awareness, and the debates and discussion to which it has given rise, are just one example of the political spin-off from China's primarily economic reforms.

NOTES

1 The whole issue of *Chinese Law and Government* 1993 26(5) is devoted to translations of articles on this subject.
2 For a more detailed study of population policy see Aiping Mu, Chapter 7 in this volume.

REFERENCES

Anhui Provincial Women's Association (1985) 'How Women Can Become Achievers', translated in *Chinese Sociology and Anthropology*, 1987, 20(1): 32–8.
Beijing Municipal Women's Federation (1992) *Women's Theoretic Studies in China 1981–1990*, Beijing: Chinese Women's Press (in Chinese).
Davin, D. (1978) *Woman-work: Women and the Party in Revolutionary China*, Oxford: Oxford University Press.
Davin, D. (1987a) 'Gender and Population in the People's Republic of China', in H. Afshar (ed.) *Women, State and Ideology*, London: Macmillan.
Davin, D. (1987b) 'China: The New Inheritance Law and the Chinese Peasant Household', *Journal of Communist Studies* 3(4): 52–63.
Davin, D. (1990) 'Never Mind If it's a Girl You Can Have Another Try', in J. Delman *et al.* (eds) *Remaking Peasant China*, Aarhus University Press.
Davin, D. (1991) 'Chinese Models of Development and their Implications for Women', in Haleh Afshar (ed.) *Women, Development and Survival in the Third World*, London: Longman.
Feng Bian (1984) 'On the Concept of Good Wife and Mother in the 1980s', *Women of China*, 7 July: 3–4, translated in E. Honig and E. Hershatter (1988) *Personal Voices: Chinese Women in the 1980s*, Stanford, CA: Stanford University Press.

Gittings, J. (1993) 'Sixty Die as Blaze Engulfs Chinese Factory', *Guardian*, 20 December.

He Dong (1992) 'Love One's Wife = Buy Her a Washing Machine? On Male Chauvinism in Television Commercials', translated in *Chinese Education and Society* 1993, 26(3): 86–8.

Honig, E. and Hershatter, E. (1988) *Personal Voices: Chinese Women in the 1980s*, Stanford, CA: Stanford University Press.

Hull, T. (1990) 'Recent Trends in the Sex Ratio at Birth in China', *Population and Development Review* 16(1): 63–81.

Ji Zheng (1986) 'Deviation of Women's Liberation in China and a Tentative Plan for Instituting a New System of Female Employment', *Society* 6 December, translated in *Chinese Sociology and Anthropology* 1988, 20(3): 105–6.

Ju Ning (1990) 'My Perspective on the Discrepancy between the Respective Scores for Admission of Men and Women for Colleges and Universities in the Shanghai Region', *Shanghai Women* 10 July, translated in *Chinese Education and Society* 1993, 26(2): 48–55.

Law Yearbook (1993) *Zhongguo Falu Nianjian*, Beijing Legal Publishing House (in Chinese).

Messkoub, M. and Davin, D. (1993) 'Migration in China, Results from the 1990 Census', unpublished conference paper.

Party Official (1988) 'Party Official says Policy on Women Remains Unchanged', Xinhua News Agency 12 January, reprinted in *Chinese Sociology and Anthropology* 1989, 21(3): 9–10.

Pepper, S. (1984) 'China's Universities: Post-Mao Enrolment Policies and their Impact on the Structure of Secondary Education', Center for Chinese Studies, University of Michigan.

Population Census of China for 1990 (1991) *10 % Sampling of the 1990 Population Census of China*, Beijing: China Statistical Publishing House (in Chinese).

Research Institute of the All-China Women's Federation (1991) *Statistics on Chinese Women 1949–89*, Beijing: Chinese Statistical Publishing House (in Chinese).

Rosen, S. (1993a) Editor's Introduction, Women and Politics in China, special issue of *Chinese Law and Government*, 1993, 26(5): 3–5.

Rosen, S. (1993b) 'Women and Reform', *China News Analysis*, 15 January: 1–9.

Rosen, S. (1993c) 'Preliminary Analysis Report on the Survey of the Social Status of China's Women', translated with an introduction by Rosen in *Chinese Education and Society*, 1993, 26(3): 3–15.

Secretariat of the All-China Women's Federation (1981) Letter of August 15 from the Secretariat of the All-China Women's Federation to comrades Wan Li and Peng Chong, in All-China Women's Federation (ed.) (nd) *Selected Women's Movement Documents from the Period of the Four Great Modernisations 1981–3*, Beijing: Chinese Women's Press (in Chinese).

Siao, R. and Chao Yuanling (1994) Editors' Introduction, Compilation of English Translations of Sixteen Provincial Regulations on the Protection of Women and Children in *Chinese Law and Government*, 1994 27(1).

Stacey, J. (1983) *Patriarchy and Socialist Revolution in China*, Berkeley, CA: University of California Press.

Tianjin Daily (1980) 'Men and Women are Different: Cultivate Strengths and Avoid Weaknesses', *Tianjin Daily* 15 October, translated in E. Honig and G. Hershatter (1988) Personal Voices: Chinese Women in the 1980s, Stanford, CA: Stanford University Press.

Wang Shulin, (1983) 'The Question of Urban Employment for Women', *Management Modernisation* 1, translated in *Chinese Sociology and Anthropology*, 1987, 20(1): 68–78.

White, G. (1993) *Riding the Tiger: The Politics of Economic Reform in Post-Mao China*, London: Macmillan.

Yang Xingnan (1985) 'Rejection of Female College Graduates must be Stopped', *Chinese Women* 27 February, translated in *Chinese Sociology and Anthropology* 1987, 20(1): 62–4.

Yang Zhangqiao (1987) 'Mercenary Marriages in Rural Zhejiang Province', *Youth Studies*, February, translated in *Chinese Sociology and Anthropology* 1989 21(3): 65–6.

Wan Shanping (1992) 'From Country to Capital: A Study of a Female Migrant Group in China', unpublished PhD thesis, Oxford Brookes University.

Zeng Yi *et al.* (1993) 'Causes and Implications of the Recent Increase in the Reported Sex Ratio at Birth in China', *Population and Development Review* 19(2): 283–302.

Zhuang Ping (1993) 'On the Social Phenomenon of Trafficking in Women in China', *Sociology Research*, May 1991, translated in *Chinese Education and Society* 1993, 26(3): 33–50.

FURTHER READING

Emily Honig and Gail Hershatter's (1988) *Personal Voices: Chinese Women in the 1980s* is the best study of Chinese women in post-Mao China. Based largely on a wide reading of the Chinese press and on the observations of two years' residence in China, it focuses mainly on urban women. It includes chapters on courtship, marriage, education and work, and on women and violence.

Ellen Judd's (1994) *Gender and Power in Rural North China* (Stanford, CA: Stanford University Press) is a study based on fieldwork in Shandong Province in the 1990s. It concentrates on gender relations in the rural household which after the end of collectivism in the early 1980s became once more the basic economic unit in the villages. It pays particular attention to the ways that women organise and construct strategies to encourage change with positive implications for women.

Chapter 7

Social policies and rural women's fertility behaviour in the People's Republic of China, 1979–90

Aiping Mu

Childbearing in China was traditionally regarded as an essential obligation for women from which the family expected to increase labour or income and gain old-age support. Since 1949, although the Chinese government has taken great efforts to eliminate these ideas and traditions, there have been different changes in terms of women's fertility patterns between urban and rural areas. This is mainly attributed to the separated social and economic policies which apply to the two areas over the period. For example, in the context of social and economic development, the status of urban women has been greatly improved, particularly as a result of the opportunities provided for employment as well as pension schemes for employees. But at the same time, such improvements did not occur in most parts of rural China. As the majority of rural women were still engaged in traditional agricultural production, the perceived unequal economic values associated with males and females continued to be upheld regarding their physical capability. In addition, as long as sons are regarded as the major supporters for parents in old age, which is the case in rural China, their role in the family could not be matched by that of daughters. Daughters would eventually join their husbands' families after marriage, and would therefore not support their own parents. Consequently, both family size preferences and fertility rate are substantially different between urban and rural areas.

Since the implementation of the one-child family planning policy after 1978, childbearing has become a highly political issue not only for women, but also for their families. Women's fertility behaviour has to be unified and restricted, as the government's one-child policy demands delaying marriage and practising contraception. On the other hand, following the introduction of the rural economic reform policies during the same period, the perceived economic values associated with children have changed through individual household production, which result in more demand for family labour. In addition, the introduction of a market economy created more employment opportunities and mobility regarding economic activities. Women have gained greater autonomy and thereby changing attitudes towards reproductive issues, which would eventually influence the patterns of fertility behaviour.

This chapter attempts to examine rural women's fertility behaviour under the implementation of the two policies prevailing in China during 1979–90. Some aspects are particularly discussed, such as the performance of women's fertility behaviour; their desire regarding childbearing and the impact of the social policies on women's fertility. The data were collected during late December 1991 to early January 1992 from twenty-five villages in two counties, Wujiang county in the south of Jiangsu province, an eastern coastal developed area, and Chongqing county in Sichuan province, an inland and less developed area (see Figure 7.1). The survey collected information from 1979 to 1990. There was a random sample of 240 married rural women aged between 30 and 39 (about 10 women in each village) and the gathering of social and economic data involved 240 families. Each woman completed a constructed questionnaire, 80 being further selected for in-depth interviews.

Before discussing the results, the one-child family planning policy and the rural economic reform policies are briefly described.

ONE-CHILD FAMILY PLANNING POLICY

As the largest country in the world in terms of population size, China contained more than 20 per cent of the world total population, about 1.185 billion at the end of 1993 (SSB 1994: 2). Rapid population growth especially in rural areas has been regarded as one of the major problems in social and economic development, as China is still a primarily developing country with about three-quarters of the population residing in rural areas (SSB 1990: 41–6). In the late 1970s, the government set a demographic target to control its population size within 1.2 billion by the year 2000. In view of both the size as well as the age structure of the population (64.44 per cent being under the age of 30 in 1982 – SFPC 1985: 3), the government began to reward couples who chose to have only one child, and subsequently enlarged the practice and made the concept of a 'one-child one couple' as the central theme of the family planning programme (Hua 1979: 25; 1980: 26).

The major aspects of the one-child policy are: the majority Chinese (Han Chinese) are encouraged to delay marriage by three years after the legal marriage age (20 years for females and 22 for males), and by so doing, to delay childbearing. Married couples are encouraged to have only one child, but under certain conditions, some are allowed to have a second child (Davin 1985: 37–82; 1987: 111–29). Under any circumstances, a third or subsequent birth is forbidden. For most 'minority Chinese', the number of children is restricted to two. However, this provision was hardly implemented during the 1980s.

Detailed regulations were formulated by each provincial government. Generally speaking, the major variation in provincial regulations is authorisation for the birth of a second child in rural areas. In most of the modified documents by the end of the 1980s, more conditions or exceptions have been

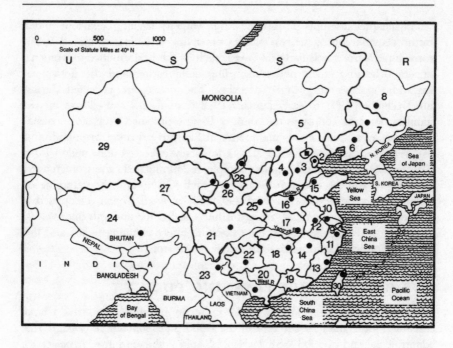

Provinces

1 **BEIJING MUNICIPALITY** ■ Beijing	9 **SHANGHAI MUNICIPALITY** ● Shanghai	17 **HUBEI** ● Wuhan	25 **SHAANXI** ● Xian
2 **TIANJIN MUNICIPALITY** ● Tianjin	10 **JIANGSU** ● Nanjing	18 **HUNAN** ● Changsha	26 **GANSU** ● Lanzhou
3 **HEBEI** ● Shijiazhuang	11 **ZHEJIANG** ● Hangzhou	19 **GUANGDONG** ● Guangzhou	27 **QINGHAI** ● Xining
4 **SHANXI** ● Taiyuan	12 **ANHUI** ● Hefei	20 **GUANGXI** ● Nanning	28 **NINGXIA** ● Yinchuan
5 **NEI MONGGOL** ● Hohhot	13 **FUJIAN** ● Fuzhou	21 **SICHUAN** ● Chengdu	29 **XINJIANG** ● Urumqi
6 **LIAONING** ● Shenyang	14 **JIANGXI** ● Nanchang	22 **GUIZHOU** ● Guiyang	30 **TAIWAN** ● Taibei
7 **JILIN** ● Changchun	15 **SHANDONG** ● Jinan	23 **YUNNAN** ● Kunming	
8 **HEILONGJIANG** ● Harbin	16 **HENAN** ● Zhengzhou	24 **XIZANG** ● Lhasa	

Note:
Capital ■   Provincial Capital ●

Figure 7.1 Map of China

set to allow rural couples to have a second child within a given time after the birth of a first child (normally between four and eight years). This development has emerged as a result of the tremendous difficulties in promoting the one-child family concept in rural areas. Looking at the provincial regulations regarding a second birth, there are three different categories in terms of conditions. The first applies to couples who have special difficulties, such as the handicap of the only child due to a non-hereditary disease. The second is for rural couples whose only child is a girl. In the third, all rural couples are free to have a second child regardless of the sex of the first one (Yu 1991: 6–10). The formulation of these regulations were mainly based on local situations such as population, natural resources, geographical location, economic development, the proportion of minority residents as well as the link with Overseas Chinese.

One of the major methods of implementing the programme is to adjust the costs and benefits associated with childbearing through incentives and disincentives. For example, one-child families are granted a subsidy of 4–6 Yuan (about £0.5–£0.7 in 1990) monthly until the child is 14 years old. They also enjoy preferential treatment in getting medical care, enrolment of children to nurseries and schools. In urban areas, the mothers enjoy longer maternity leave with full pay. In rural areas, the families have priority in getting loans for economic production, employment opportunities, and the allocation of land for residential construction. The major disincentive is a fine for the couple with 'out-of-plan' born children (the birth which is not approved within the official plan).

To implement the one-child policy, the government has provided free and sufficient contraceptive services to all married couples, including free abortion services. Contraceptives are mainly distributed through a network of government Family Planning Commission outlets, together with health care agencies and pharmaceutical stores all over the country. In theory, people are free to choose whatever method they like. In practice, however, the government has proposed that rural women have IUDs inserted after the birth of the first child, while those with two or more children have ligations.

After nearly twenty years of implementing the one-child policy, China's population reached 1.2 billion in February 1995, five years earlier than targeted (Fan 1995: 8). As the average total fertility rate (TFR) – the average number of children that would be born alive to a woman – from 1980 to 1987 was 1.33 in urban areas but 2.84 in rural areas (Li 1989: 10–12), it is clear that the policy has been difficult to accept by the majority, namely, the rural population.

RURAL ECONOMIC REFORM POLICIES

China's rural economic reform policies have been introduced by the government since 1979. As the Chinese leadership insisted, the reforms essentially attempted to eradicate poverty and backwardness in rural areas and to increase agricultural production as soon as possible (Du 1984: 14–17). Four major changes have occurred in rural China since 1979.

Transformation of the agricultural management system and the rural administrative system

The previous system was based on the three-tiers of rural administration: the people's commune, the production brigade and the production team. This system more or less dominated all aspects of socio-economic and political life in rural society. Since 1979, a new administrative system replaced the original three-tier one. This again was made up of three levels: town government, village administration and villager group. The major obligations of the present system are more limited than before. Town government is the government administration at the grassroots level. It is responsible for co-ordination of local economic production only at the previous level of the people's commune. Village administration replaced the production brigade as a self-organised committee at village level. It is responsible for co-ordination of economic production and communal interests among villagers, such as the distribution of water supply and the welfare of the village. The villager group is at the previous level of the production team. It is operated under the jurisdiction of the village administration.

Transformation of the economic production unit from collective to individual households

Prior to 1979, with everyone getting roughly the same remuneration, known as 'eating out of the same big public pot', rural economic production took place collectively, and peasants' income was distributed through the collective economic unit (the production team). Since 1979, land, orchards, forests and agricultural machinery have been allocated to individual households within the collective ownership. Peasants may exploit the land during the period of the contract with the local government, but they are not allowed to sell it themselves or use it for non-agricultural production. Therefore, rural households have taken over full responsibility for economic production, income is not collectively calculated and distributed as before.

Transformation of agricultural production patterns

As a consequence of previous agricultural policies such as 'take grain production as the key link and effect the all-round development of agriculture', the development in other areas of agricultural production was severely restricted, such as economic crop or sideline production (including animal husbandry, fishery and forestry). Since the reforms, rural economic production patterns have been diversified as encouraged by the government, hence, peasants have undertaken various economic sidelines apart from grain plantation.

Development of township or village industries and free markets

The responsibility system not only raised productivity, but also created a labour surplus. Peasants have been encouraged to develop the productive processes and trade which would absorb some of the labour and contribute to the rural economy. Between 1984 and 1987, an additional 3 million township or village enterprises were set up each year, hence about 85 million jobs were created. Rural enterprise output values grew by 40 per cent annually during 1984 to 1987, and exceeded the agricultural output value for the first time ever in 1987 (Ji 1988: 11–13). During the same period, a number of peasants also moved outside of agriculture to specialise in forms of private commodity development, such as street selling.

OCCUPATIONAL TRANSFORMATION

The survey data show that the implementation of the rural economic reform policies have brought about significant changes in women's economic activities. Interestingly, although women's participation in economic production has been regarded as a major indicator in terms of social and economic development, there was not much change in the incidence of employment in both counties. This was mainly due to a very high level of female employment rates throughout the twelve-year period. In Chongqing, the proportion of women in the survey who did not participate in economic production was only 6.7 per cent in 1979, fell to zero in 1980, and has remained at that level ever since. While in Wujiang, the figure moved from less than 2 per cent prior to 1986 to zero afterwards. This situation may be attributed to three reasons. First, women aged 30–39 at the time of the survey were at their prime of economic production during 1979 to 1990. Second, women's participation in economic production has been promoted since 1949 in China. Third, as the average income was extremely low under the previous economic system, women's economic activities had made an essential contribution to the family economy in 1979.

Consequently, it may be argued that the major changes in economic activities were not in terms of employment rates, but rather, related to women's occupational patterns and forms of employment. These occurred differently in the two communities under investigation. In Wujiang in terms of the occupational patterns, there was an increasing movement from being almost dependent on agriculture to a situation where non-agricultural production assumes a growing significance. During the period of rapid industrialisation from 1979 to 1990, the percentage of women who worked in the agricultural sector fell from 86.6 per cent to 37.5 per cent, while industrial workers increased from 6.7 per cent to 50.0 per cent. But in Chongqing, the majority (70.7 per cent), even in 1990, were still engaged in grain production. Major forms of employment also differed between the two counties. In 1990, collective units still prevailed in Wujiang, while village or township industries were also common; but in Chongqing, individual household working on contract land emerged as the predominant form of employment.

From 1979 to 1990, women's average annual income increased 9.5 times in Chongqing and 14 times in Wujiang. Since 1984, women contributed to more than 40 per cent of their families' total annual income in both occupational groups. When compared with agricultural workers, non-agricultural women received better income and made greater economic contributions to their families.

FERTILITY BEHAVIOUR

Given the innovations in economic activities, it is necessary to compare the impact of the one-child family planning policy on rural women's fertility behaviour between the agricultural and the non-agricultural sector. The following discussion highlights women's age at first marriage, contraceptive practice, the incidence of induced abortion and the 'out-of-plan' born children.

For social and cultural reasons, sex relationships outside marriage were not common among the majority of rural Chinese, thus, age at first marriage can be regarded as the commencement age of regular sexual activities, which is an important variable for fertility level. In this survey, the marriage age was very similar among women who married since 1979 (the year in which the one-child family planning policy was introduced). In Chongqing, it was 23 years old for women working in agriculture and 22.8 in non-agriculture; in Wujiang, it was 23.1 and 23.3 respectively. These figures were very close to the officially proposed marriage age for females (23 years old) rather than the legal marriage age (20 years old). Looking at the major reason for their choice regarding marriage age, the majority of women stated that they delayed to marry mainly due to the influence of the one-child policy. However, the incidence concerning such a reason was higher in the non-agricultural (80.0 per cent in Chongqing and 90.9 per cent in Wujiang) than in the agricultural sector (66.3 per cent and 77.2 per cent respectively).

In 1990, women's contraceptive prevalence rate was as high as 100 per cent in the two communities. Among the users, 62.6 per cent had IUDs, 27.3 per cent were sterilised and a further 6.3 per cent were married to husbands who had undergone vasectomy. The total percentage of the three methods was higher than the national statistics in 1991 (39.0 per cent, 38.9 per cent and 12.1 per cent respectively – Peng 1992: 2–8). While only 3.8 per cent in the survey used other methods, such as the pill and condoms. Surprisingly, a certain number of ligations (sterilisation or vasectomy) were reported by women with one child only (30 out of the 160 one-child mothers). This was especially so amongst non-agricultural workers where it accounts for 100 per cent of the ligations in Chongqing and three-quarters in Wujiang, which was in contradiction with the government guideline regarding the condition for ligation. It suggests that the policy was radically implemented in the two communities, reflecting the frequent birth control campaigns in the 1980s.

Despite the restrictive influences of the one-child policy on fertility behaviour, it is interesting to note that a number of women who had IUDs inserted were found to be the mothers of two children. They should have been ligated in line with the government guideline. All cases occurred among agricultural women in both counties, which account for 19 per cent of the total with two children in this occupational group.

Induced abortion is practised in China's family planning programme as a back-up against contraceptive failure and also undertaken by women in the absence of contraceptive practice. Previous research shows that the majority of Chinese women experienced at least one abortion in their reproductive years (Hull and Yang 1991: 163–87). In this survey, the average abortion rate was 0.46 per woman during 1980–90. However, the figures for non-agricultural women were relatively higher than the average (0.55 in Chongqing and 0.60 in Wujiang); but this was reversed for agricultural women, especially in Wujiang (0.44 and 0.31 respectively). Data showed a higher proportion of non-agricultural workers (81.8 per cent in Chongqing and 77.4 per cent in Wujiang) than those involved in agriculture (78.8 per cent and 63.6 per cent respectively), stating that 'No permission for childbearing' was the major reason for their abortion. Information from the interviews suggests that it was very rare for rural women to have their first pregnancy aborted, because most of them would start childbearing within three years of marriage. In addition, since most women delayed their marriage age, it was easy for them to obtain official permission for the first birth. Thus, most of the abortions were regarded as the termination of second or subsequent pregnancies, which would certainly not have been authorised in many cases.

In terms of the number of the 'out-of-plan' births between 1980 and 1990, only three out of the twenty-two cases were from non-agricultural workers, while nineteen cases were from agricultural women. The occurrence rate was 3 per cent and 13 per cent respectively for the two groups. Referring to their abortion rate, it showed that there was a difference in terms of carrying on non-authorised pregnancies (pregnancies occurred without the permission of childbearing) between the two occupational groups, which indicates the role of 'employers' in rural industries in terms of implementing the national population policy.

In general, data from this survey revealed different influences of the one-child policy on women's fertility behaviour between the two occupational groups. It suggests that there was relatively less control on women in agriculture than in non-agriculture with respect to the implementation of the one-child policy.

DESIRED FAMILY SIZE AND FERTILITY LEVEL

In the context of desired family size, the reaction of women in the survey may be interpreted not only as an expression of women's individual choice, but also in terms of their families' expectations which could be decisions made with their husbands and even parents-in-law (Greenhalgh 1992: 16; Mu 1995: 213–16). This is because Chinese culture regards reproduction as a matter not only for the individual woman, but also for the family into which she marries.

With respect to the preferred number of children, 40.7 per cent favoured one child only and 59.3 per cent expressed a preference for two children in Chongqing. In Wujiang, the percentages were 28.3 per cent and 71.7 per cent respectively. None indicated a desire for more than two children. In the context of the preferred sex, all expressing a preference for two children favoured a son and a daughter rather than two boys or two girls. This reflects the strong influence of traditional attitudes towards childbearing, summarised in the traditional saying: 'the great joy is having both sons and daughters'. Among those expressing a one-child preference, seventy-one out of the seventy-eight cases said that they would like to have a son, while only seven favoured a daughter. This suggests that although the preferred number of children has decreased to a level which is close to the national policy requirement, women would not stop childbearing spontaneously unless their children were already of the desired sex, particularly in the case of male children.

Of the 214 available responses, 160 women had one child only in 1990, 50 women had two children while 4 were with three children. Considering about 40 per cent of women in this study were married before 1979, it has to be appreciated that fertility levels among them might not have been entirely restricted by the policy. Looking at fertility levels in terms of economic activities, Tables 1 and 2 divide all respondents into two groups, namely those married before 1979 and those who were married between 1979 to 1986 (the latest year in which their marriage took place).

Table 1 Fertility by occupation and preferred family size in Chongqing, 1990

Women grouped by year of marriage and occupation		Number of children per woman	
		Preferred	TFR
Before 1979	Agricultural (N = 41)	1.65	1.73
	Non-agricultural (N=5)	1.20	1.00
1979–86	Agricultural (N=42)	1.59	1.07
	Non-agricultural (N=15)	1.59	1.00
Subtotal	Agricultural (N=83)	1.62	1.40
	Non-agricultural (N=20)	1.50	1.00
TFR of total sample			1.32

TFR: Total Fertility Rate

Table 2 Fertility by occupation and preferred family size in Wujiang, 1990

Women grouped by year of marriage and occupation		Number of children per woman	
		Preferred	TFR
Before 1979	Agricultural (N = 29)	1.86	1.72
	Non-agricultural (N=9)	1.80	1.44
1979–86	Agricultural (N=21)	1.48	1.00
	Non-agricultural (N=52)	1.72	1.00
Subtotal	Agricultural (N=50)	1.69	1.42
	Non-agricultural (N=61)	1.73	1.07
TFR of total sample			1.23

TFR: Total Fertility Rate

Among women married before 1979, fertility was lower in the non-agricultural than in the agricultural sector. The explanation would appear to be that the occupational transformation from agriculture to non-agriculture which commenced since 1979 primarily concerned women with one child, and emphasised the movement towards lower fertility. This happened during the implementation of both the rural economic reform policies and the one-child policy. Since the reforms, there has been increasing employment opportunities within the non-agricultural sector, but as an incentive, women with one child only have been given priority for such emerging job opportunities. Thus, they are either involved in employment in industry or given permission to practise in private business outside agriculture. A similar situation prevailed even before 1979. Under the then family planning policy of the 'later (marriage age) – longer (space between two births) – fewer (number of children)' during the 1970s, especially in the late 1970s, priority for employment in the non-agricultural sector was already seen as a major family planning incentive. In areas such as Wujiang where rural industrialisation started before the reforms, women who had two or fewer children (the required number of children at that time) obtained easier access to employment. Consequently, a fertility rate of 1.44 may be observed among Wujiang women in non-agriculture who were married before 1979 (see Table 2). Thus, the occupational movement from agriculture to non-agriculture has been mainly influenced by women's fertility behaviour, rather than other factors concerning their potential capability in economic production, such as skills or educational levels. Therefore, fertility behaviour becomes an important criterion for employment in these areas during the course of economic development. This argument is further strengthened by the fact that women with little education were able to find jobs in rural industries (Mu 1995: 124–5).

However, Tables 1 and 2 show that amongst those who were married between 1979 and 1986, there was not much difference in terms of fertility rate between the two occupational groups. This may mainly be attributed to

the strong state intervention in terms of fertility behaviour in both occupations. In addition, since fertility was a major criterion for employment, women
had to accept the one-child policy in order to gain access to non-agricultural
jobs. A problem is that even though women had only one child, ironically,
the opportunities for non-agricultural jobs are relatively limited. Hence, despite
the incentive, many women's objectives cannot be achieved.

It is very interesting to find that in spite of the enormous differences in
income, education and socio-economic development, fertility levels were
similar among women as a whole in each occupational group between
Chongqing and Wujiang (1.40 to 1.42 in agriculture and 1.00 to 1.07 in non-
agriculture). Therefore, the relatively lower fertility rate in Wujiang (1.23) may
be mainly attributed to rural industrialisation which has provided sufficient
job opportunities for women in the non-agricultural sector.

Tables 1 and 2 also show that for most women, there was a clear gap
between their preferred family size and fertility level. This is especially so for
women who were married between 1979 and 1986. In other words, the gap
was wider among those whose fertility was already limited to one child. It
shows again that among those women, there was not much difference between
occupational groups in terms of the state intervention on childbearing. In
general, most women were not satisfied with their current fertility levels. This
was true even in the relatively more developed economy of Wujiang.
Considering the preferred sex of children among women as a whole, one
daughter and a son were regarded as ideal by the majority. Of those who
wanted one child only, a son was desired; while only a few women expressed
satisfaction with only a girl. With such goals, some families would need to
have three children in order to get one of each sex or a boy; the truly unfortunate would need to have more. The actual gap between preference and
reality would be even wider.

The fact that the gap was greater among women as a whole in non-agriculture
than in agriculture, indicates that the ability of women to achieve their ideal
family size was relatively more restricted in the non-agricultural sector.

ENFORCEMENT OF THE ONE-CHILD POLICY

The major reason accounting for the relative control which women had over
their own fertility was that the one-child policy was more vigorously enforced
in the context of rural industries. It is assumed that there is a balance between
the high cost and the anticipated economic benefit in the process of decision
making among women as well as their husbands. In order to influence women's
fertility behaviour, state intervention must be able to adjust the perceived
economic values associated with childbearing. Previous research has generally
emphasised the negative consequences of rural reforms in implementing the
one-child policy (such as Whyte 1987: 284–317). But this study suggests
that the family planning policy has effectively adjusted the costs and benefits

associated with childbearing among rural women who have transferred to the non-agricultural sector as industrial workers.

Existing literature highlights the major mechanisms by which the post-1978 reforms are likely to have undermined family planning policy enforcement (such as Greenhalgh 1990: 11–12). It argues that the rise in peasant incomes impaired family planning implementation, as it enabled couples to pay the fines imposed for violating the family planning policy rules without suffering great hardship. This, however, is not evident in this survey as the enormously high level of fines occurred. For example, for an out-of-plan birth, where the stipulated fine is between three and six times a couple's total *annual income* in Jiangsu Province (JFPC 1990: 8–11). In such cases, it was virtually difficult for violators to meet the fines from either the non-agricultural or the agricultural sector.

Since the reform of accounting system from collective economy to individual household economy, peasants' income is not distributed through the production team as it had been the case before. Thus, the system of economic incentives and disincentives by which the one-child policy was to be enforced has been adversely affected. For example, there was a lack of public funds to provide incentives to rural couples who claimed the one-child certificate, such as the financial subsidy or possible social security provision for old age. But this study shows that most of the village or township industries, where the majority of non-agricultural women worked, were still based on a collective economy. Adjustments regarding the costs and benefits of childbearing have therefore improved in these rural firms, as compared with the pre-reform era. In fact, economic penalties can be easily deducted from the workers' salary or other benefits provided by the firms, thus cadres did not loss control over women's income as a guarantee for collecting fines. In addition, firms have themselves instituted what can be described as 'supplementary' incentives which augmented those prescribed in the national programme. Hence, women with only one child in the non-agricultural sector have been able to obtain more benefits than others.

It has been argued that commune reform exacerbated implementation difficulties by reducing the power and prestige of local cadres. For example, as local cadres were included in the distribution of land, cultivating their plots was more rewarding than promoting birth control (a task for which they received only nominal compensation), hence depressing their commitment to their official work. Evidence from the rural industrial sector suggests that this was not as serious as was reported, due to the fact that family planning agencies in local government still had access to administering the birth control programme in these collective economy based firms. With government's intervention, negligence of such a responsibility could affect a firm's benefits through the allocation of raw material resources, as well as by the imposition of fines on the firm. Consequently, family planning came to be regarded as part of the normal administrative responsibility of such rural industries.

Regarding the various regulations introduced by different firms, it is difficult to describe the details which have influenced the adjustment of the
perceived values of children for these non-agricultural workers. The following
points provide only a general picture. Regarding the major incentives, in addition to the official monthly subsidy of 4–6 Yuan for the one-child parents
(which was difficult to implement in some rural areas due to a lack of
resources), the possible benefits that non-agricultural workers could receive
from village or township industries include

1   reducing the costs of childbearing through
    • free medication and hospitalisation during pregnancy and parturition
    • maternity leave for at least eight weeks with full pay
    • the opportunity of going back to work early after maternity leave by
      being given priority for crèche or nursery services provided by the firm
    • free or discount rates for crèche, nursery, children's schooling and
      medication
2   providing additional services for old-age support.

Disincentives in the context of rural industries, in addition to a fine which
women would experience at the time of an 'out-of-plan' birth, could include

• self-finance for medication and hospitalisation during the pregnancy and
  parturition
• non-paid maternity leave
• self-financing crèche, nursery, children's schooling and medication
• losing the opportunity for promotion or even being down-graded
• being discharged from the firm.

Obviously, as compared with women in agriculture, non-agricultural workers
were able to gain from having one child. Although the promise of old-age
support from the firm may not be sufficient to convince them thoroughly,
there were clearly many more 'indirect' incentives to persuade them to comply
with the one-child policy, especially as the additional costs for going against
the policy were considerably high, given the possible threat of losing their job
and hence losing a good income.

CONCLUSION

This chapter looked at women's fertility behaviour in the context of two important social policies in rural China. The general conclusion is that during rural
industrialisation following the economic reforms, the occupational transformation
from agriculture to non-agriculture has resulted in different fertility behaviour
patterns among rural women. In the collective economy based rural industries,
the one-child family planning policy was more vigorously enforced, thus fertility
behaviour was more effectively controlled among these industrial workers than
was the case for those in individual household-based agricultural production.

The analysis also suggests that although the desired family size has been reduced, there was a clear gap between individual preferences and the goals of the national population policy. Therefore, it is still difficult for the majority of rural couples to accept the concept of a one-child policy, even in Wujiang where social and economic development has gone much further than in most of China. Conflict over fertility control between rural couples and the state authorities is likely to continue for a long time. This is as true for rural industrial workers who have become economically better off and have gained greater access to social security services since the reforms, as it is for agricultural workers.

REFERENCES

Davin, D. (1985) 'The Single-child Family Policy in the Countryside', in E. Croll, D. Davin and P. Kane (eds) *China's One-child Family Policy*, London: Macmillan.

Davin, D. (1987) 'Gender and Population in the People's Republic of China', in H. Afshar (ed.) *Women, State and Ideology*, London: Macmillan.

Du, Runsheng (1984) 'Rural Economic Reforms: Questions and Answers', *China Reconstructs* 33(6): 14–17.

Fan, You (1995) '15th February: 1.2 billion population in China', *Chinese Science News – Overseas Edition* 25 February.

Greenhalgh, S. (1990) *The Peasantization of Population Policy in Shaanxi: Cadre Mediation of the State–Society Conflict*, Working Papers 1990–no. 21, New York: Research Division, Population Council.

Greenhalgh, S. (1992) *Negotiating Birth Control in Village China*, Working Papers 1992a–no. 38, New York: Research Division, Population Council.

Hua, Guofeng (1979) 'Government Work Report of the 2nd Session of 5th National People's Congress (Excerpts)', *Almanac of China's Population (1985)*, Beijing: Chinese Social Science Publishing House.

Hua, Guofeng (1980) 'Government Work Report of the 3rd Session of 5th National People's Congress (Excerpts)', *Almanac of China's Population (1985)*, Beijing: Chinese Social Sciences Publishing House.

Hull, T. H. and Yang, Quanhe (1991) 'Fertility and Family Planning', *Population and Development Planning in China*, Sydney (Australia): Allen & Unwin.

Ji, Yecheng (1988) 'Renewed Emphasis on Agricultural Reform', *China Reconstructs* 37(6): 11–13.

JFPC (Jiangsu Family Planning Commission) (1990) *Family Planning Regulations of Jiangsu Province* Najing (unpublished).

Li, Tieying (1989) 'Speech at the meeting of the provincial (autonomous regions and municipalities) governors (Excerpts)', *Family Planning Yearbook of China (1990)*, Beijing: Academic Press.

Mu, Aiping (1995) 'Rural Women's Economic Activities and Fertility Behaviour in Selected Areas of China during 1979–1990', unpublished PhD thesis, University of Glamorgan.

Peng, Peiyun (1992) 'Population Problems in China and the Countermeasures', *Population Review* 4: 2–8.

SFPC (State Family Planning Commission) (1985) *Population Situation and Policy*, Beijing: SFPC.

SSB (State Statistical Bureau) (1990) 'Communiqué of the State Statistics Bureau of the People's Republic of China on major figures of 1990 Population Census (no.1)',

Major Figures of the Fourth National Census of China, Beijing: China Statistical Publishing House.

SSB (State Statistical Bureau) (1994) 'Communiqué on economic and social development statistics 1993', reported in *People's Daily Overseas Edition* 2 March.

Whyte, T. (1987) 'Implementing the One-Child-Per-Couple Population Programme in Rural China: National Goals and Local Policies', in D. M. Lampton (ed.) *Policy Implementation in Post-Mao China*, Berkeley, CA: University of California Press.

Yu, Yan (1991) 'General Analysis on Provincial Family Planning Regulations in China', *Population Information* 12, Beijing: China Population Information and Research Centre.

FURTHER READING

Delia Davin's (1985) 'The Single-child Family Policy in the Countryside', in E. Croll *et al.* (eds) *China's One-child Family Policy*, is a comprehensive account of the implementation of the one-child policy in rural China.

Susan Greenhalgh's (1990) *The Peasantization of Population Policy in Shaanxi: Cadre Mediation of the State–Society Conflict* examines the evolution of state–society relations in rural China in the area of population control by using retrospective field data from three villages in the north-western province of Shaanxi.

Susan Greenhalgh's (1992) *Negotiating Birth Control in Village China* takes a close look at the implementation of the one-child policy through a field research in a village in Shaanxi province.

Chapter 8

Women and the politics of fundamentalism in Iran

Haleh Afshar

This chapter is concerned with understanding what Islamic fundamentalism means to women who choose to adopt it and how, if at all, it could be used as a means for political struggles. The intention is to move away from the usual condemnatory approach to Islamic fundamentalism and consider it in the light of the views and activities of its adherents. Specific examples will be given with reference to Iran and the women's organisations and their activities in that country.

WHAT IS FUNDAMENTALISM?

Fundamentalism has for long been associated with greater or lesser degrees of oppression of women. Given the rise of fundamentalism and the decision of many women to consciously reject feminisms of various kinds and adopt the creed, it is important for some of us to consider what it is and why so many have chosen it. We should stand back and separate state and theocratic policies from choices made by some women. It is worth while to consider the reasons that the Muslim women have offered for adopting Islamic fundamentalism and 'returning to the source' both in the UK and elsewhere.

Part of the problem of understanding fundamentalism has been in terms of definitions and terminology. Muslims themselves do not use the term 'fundamentalist' at all; the twentieth-century Islamists argue that they are revivalists, and are returning to the sources of Islam to regain a purified vision, long since lost in the mire of worldly governments. Shiias, who are a minority school of Islam, but form 98 per cent of the Iranian population, have for long seen themselves as the guardians of the poor, the dispossessed and those trampled on by unjust governments (Momen 1985). For them revivalism is merely a matter of succeeding in their centuries-long struggle against injustice.

Thus fundamentalism for the Muslims is a return to the roots and a recapturing of both the purity and the vitality of Islam as it was at its inception. In this pursuit of the past, the Muslims, like all those glorifying their histories, are returning to an imaginary golden episode to lighten the difficulties of their present-day existence (Chhachhi 1991). The golden age for the

Shiias is the short-term rule of the Prophet, about a decade long, and the even shorter one of his nephew and son-in-law Ali, who ruled for less than five years. The Sunnis, who accept the first four caliphs of Islam as being pure and worthy of emulating, can lay claim to about forty years of just rule; from the *hijrat*, the Prophet's move to Madina in 622 to Ali's death in AD 661. In addition all Muslims claim to adhere absolutely to the Koranic laws and accept the Koran as representing the very words of God as revealed to his Prophet Muhammad.

> The Koran which is divided into 114 Suras, contains expressly or impliedly, all the divine commands. These commands are contained in about 500 verses and of these about 80 may be regarded by WESTERN lawyers as articles of a code.
>
> (Afchar 1987: 86).

Thus in their pursuit of the golden age the Muslims are equipped with fifty years of history and 500 verses of a holy book, and a clutch of legal clauses, perhaps as good a resource as those offered by any other ideologies or utopists' vision.

But like all utopias the past and the holy book have difficulties adjusting to the present. It is in the domain of interpretation and adjustments to history that Islam is deemed to have become degraded. Yet without such adjustments, it would find it hard to survive as a creed. Thus the notions of return and revivalism are very much anchored in the processes of interpretations and adjustments. They seek to present new interpretations, puritanical inter-pretations, interpretations that wipe out the centuries of misdeed and hardship and open the way for the future.

WOMEN AND REVIVALISM

In the twentieth-century domain of interpretations, women have been active in their own right. Although the bulk of Islamic theology has been adapted and interpreted by male theologians, who have claimed exclusive rights to instituting the Islamic laws, *Shari'a*, women have always maintained a pres-ence, albeit a small one, in the domains of politics and theology (Abbott 1942; Ahmed 1992; Keddie and Baron 1991; Mernissi 1991). They have consis-tently and convincingly argued that Islam as a religion has always had to accommodate women's specific needs. Since the first convert to Islam was the Prophet's redoubtable and wealthy wife Khadija, no religion which she accepted could discriminate against women. Khadija, who was nearly twenty years older than the Prophet, had first employed him as her trade represen-tative and subsequently commanded him to marry her, overcoming his reserve and reluctance by informing his uncle that she was the very best wife that he could ever have. Their marriage was a happy one and the Prophet did not take another wife till after her death.

Thus some fourteen centuries ago Islam recognised women's legal and economic independence as existing and remaining separate from that of their fathers or husbands and sons. Islamic marriage was conceived as a matter of contract between consenting partners (Koran 4:4, 4:24), and one that stipulated a specific price, *mahre*, payable to the bride before the consummation of marriage. Women must be maintained in the style to which they have been accustomed (2:238, 4:34) and paid for suckling their babies (2:233).

Beside having personal and economic independence, women were also close confidantes and advisers to the Prophet. Khadija supported him in the early years and undoubtedly her influence protected the Prophet against the various Meccan nobles who wished to quench Islam at its inception. After her death Muhammad's favourite wife Aishah, who married him as a child and grew up in his household, became not only his spouse, but also his closest ally and confidante. She is known as one of the most reliable interpreters of Islamic laws.

Besides being a renowned source for the interpretation and extension of Islamic laws, Aishah was also an effective politician and a remarkable worrier; like many of the Prophet's wives, she accompanied him on his campaigns. After his death she ensured that her father Abu Bakre, and not Muhammad's nephew Ali, succeeded to the caliphate, and led the Muslim community. Subsequently, when Ali became the Caliph, Aishah raised an army and went to battle against him, taking to the field herself. Although she was defeated, Ali treated her with respect, but begged her not to interfere in politics.

Thus, if fundamentalism is about returning to the golden age of Islam, Muslim women argue that they have much reason for optimism and much room for manoeuvre. Furthermore many highly educated and articulate Muslim women regard Western feminism as a poor example and have no wish to follow it. Not only do they dismiss Western feminism for being one of the many instruments of colonialism, but also they despise the kind of freedom that is offered to women under the Western patriarchy (Ahmed 1992; al-Ghazali nd; Rahnavard nd). Using much of the criticism provided by Western women themselves, the Islamist women argue that by concentrating on labour market analysis and offering the experiences of a minority of white affluent middle-class women as a norm, Western feminists have developed an analysis which is all but irrelevant to the lives of the majority of women the world over (Afshar 1994a; 1994b). They are of the view that Western-style feminist struggles have liberated women only to the extent that they are prepared to become sex objects and market their sexuality as an advertising tool to benefit patriarchal capitalism (al-Ghazali nd; Rahnavard nd). They are particularly critical of the failure of Western feminism to carve an appropriate, recognised and remunerated space for marriage and motherhood. They argue that by locating the discussion in the domain of production and attempting to gain equality for women, Western feminists have sought and failed to make women into quasi men. They have failed to alter the labour market to accommodate women's needs and at the same time have lost the benefits that women had once obtained in matrimony. Thus Western feminists have made women into permanent second-class citizens. Not a model that most women, in the West as elsewhere, would choose to follow.

By contrast the Islamist women argue that they can benefit by returning to the sources of Islam. They are of the view that Islamic dictum bestows complementarity on women, as human beings, as partners to men and as mothers and daughters. They argue that Islam demands respect for women and offers them opportunities, to be learned, educated and trained, while at the same time providing an honoured space for them to become mothers, wives and homemakers. They argue that unlike capitalism, and much of feminist discourse, Islam recognises the importance of women's life cycles: they have been given different roles and responsibilities at different times of their lives and at each and every stage they are honoured and respected for that which they do. They argue that Islam at its inception has provided them with exemplary female role models and has delineated a path that can be honourably followed at each stage. For all Muslims Khadija is a powerful representative of independence as well as being a supportive wife. Muhammad's daughter Fatima, for the Shiias in particular, provides an idealised and idolised role model as daughter to the Prophet and wife to the imam, Ali. The Sunnis admire Aishah for her powerful intellect as well as her political leadership. Thus, the revivalists contend, Muslim women have no need of Western examples, which are in any case alien and exploitative. They have their own path to liberation which they wish to pursue.

Islamist women are particularly defensive of the veil. The actual imposition of the veil and the form that it has taken is a contested domain (Mernissi 1991). Nevertheless many Muslim women have chosen the veil as the symbol of Islamification and have accepted it as the public face of their revivalist position. For them the veil is a liberating, and not an oppressive, force. They maintain that the veil enables them to become the observers and not the observed; that it liberates them from the dictates of the fashion industry and the demands of the beauty myth. In the context of the patriarchal structures that shape women's lives the veil is a means of bypassing sexual harassment and 'gaining respect'.[1]

As post-modernism takes hold and feminists deconstruct their views and allow more room for specific and differing needs, demands and priorities of women of different creeds and colours (Afshar 1995; Mirza 1989) it is no longer easy to offer pat denials of the Islamic women's positions.

IRAN AND THE PRACTICAL POLITICS OF ISLAMIST WOMEN

Like all political theories, the Islamist women's has had difficulties in standing the test of time. Although Islam does provide a space for women, it has been as difficult for Muslim women, as for their Western counterparts, to obtain and maintain their rights. The throng of women who supported the Islamic revolution in Iran were no exception to this rule. On its inception the Islamic Republic embarked on a series of misogynist laws, decrees and directives which rapidly curtailed the access of women to much of the public domain. Female judges were sacked the faculty of law closed its door to female applicants and Article 163 of the Islamic constitution stated that women cannot become judges.

Subsequently the Islamic laws of retribution, *Qassas*, severely eroded women's legal rights. Not only are two women's evidence equated with that of one man, as required by the Koran (2:82), but women's evidence, if uncorroborated by men, is no longer accepted by the courts. Women who insist on giving uncorroborated evidence are judged to be lying and subject to punishment for slander (Article 92 of the *Qassas* laws). Murder is now punished by retribution; but the murderer can opt for the payment of *dayeh*, blood money, to the descendants of the murdered, in lieu of punishment (Article 1 of the *Qassas* laws). Furthermore the murderer can be punished only if the family of the victim pays the murderer's blood money to his descendants:

Should a Muslim man wilfully murder a Muslim woman, he must be killed, the murderer can be punished only after the woman's guardian has paid half of his *dayeh* (blood money, or the sum that the man would be worth if he were to live a normal life; this is negotiated with and paid to the man's family;)

(Article 5 of the *Qassas* laws)

Whereas killing a man is a capital offence, murdering a women is a lesser crime. The same logic dictates that women murderers should have little or no blood money and must be executed (Article 6). Similarly if a man attacks a women, and maims or severely injures her, he can be punished only if the injured or her family pay retribution money so that the assailant can be similarly mutilated; this is to ensure that his dependants have secured the income lost through the implementation of the retribution laws. No such money is paid to the dependants of women assailants (Article 60).

What is worse, fathers, who are recognised as the automatic guardians of the household, have the right of life and death over their children. Fathers who murder their children are 'excused' from punishment, provided they pay blood money to the inheritors (Article 16); however, there is no specific blood money stipulated for children. Fathers who murder one or more of their children, are to pay themselves the blood money! Khomeini decided to return to all fathers their Islamic automatic right of custody of children on divorce, which they had lost under the 1976 Family Laws in Iran. By doing so and legislating the *Qassas* laws, the post-revolutionary state endowed fathers with the undisputed right of life and death over their children. Men gained the right to kill anyone who 'violated their harem'. Men who murder their wives, or their sisters or mothers, on the charge of adultery, are not subject to any punishment. But women are not given any such rights. Nor do they have the right of life and death over their children.

In addition the access of women to almost 50 per cent of university departments was barred and they were encouraged to abandoned paid employment (Afshar 1982: 79–90; 1992; Tabari and Yeganeh 1982). They could not be employed without the formal consent of their husband, a rule that after much struggle was extended to apply to both marriage partners before the revolution, but was revised in favour of men afterwards. Politically too women were marginalised; Article 115 of the Islamic constitution follows Ayatollah Khomeini's instructions in insisting that the leader of the nation, *Valayateh Faqih*, would be a man, and so would the president. Since its inception the Islamic Republic has never had a female member of the cabinet and the numbers of female *Majlis*, (parliamentary) representatives had been fewer than five in all but the last *Majlis*, when they reached twelve.

Thus with the arrival of the Islamic Republic, with the notable exception of the vote, Iranian women lost all they had struggled for over a century. The situation seemed grim indeed.

THE POLITICS OF FEMINIST FUNDAMENTALISM

But to despair of the plight of women is to fail to recognise the formidable resilience of Iranian women. They refused to be daunted by this onslaught of patriarchy, as they had been for the past hundred years or more. Although some bowed to the pressures of the Islamic Republic, many remained firm, both as women and as believers in the faith. There has been a long and determined struggle by secularist women. But it was as devout Muslims that elite women in Iran (Moghissi 1994) have most successfully countered the demands made of them by the Islamic Republic. Given the Islamic nature of the national political discourse,[2] the defenders of the faiths of women took the republic to task for failing to deliver its Islamic duties. For post-revolutionary Iranian elite women, revivalism has almost literally been a God-send. They have used it to fight against their political, legal and economic marginalisation. Although victory is yet to come, they have won considerable grounds and are continuing to do so. Throughout, their arguments have been anchored in the teachings of Islam, the Koranic laws and the traditions and practices of the Prophet of Islam.

Using the Koranic instruction that all Muslims must become learned, women have finally succeeded in removing many of the bars placed on their education. Women who gained their training and expertise in the pre-revolutionary days of equality now command high salaries and many run their own successful businesses in the private sector (Afshar 1992). Private sector schools have simply defied the laws of gender segregation and employed male science and mathematics teachers to teach girls. As a result Iranian girls regularly come top in the university entrance examinations in most subjects.

THE STRUGGLE FOR EQUAL EMPLOYMENT OPPORTUNITY

Before the revolution Iranian women had, at least on paper, obtained the right to equal employment. But although the post-revolutionary state accepted this right, in practice Islamification has led to a severe cut-back in female employment rates (Afshar 1992). Nevertheless neither the public nor the private sector could operate without female employees, nor for that matter could most households survive without the women's income. Thus despite the government's policies, women continue to have a presence in the workforce, though in terms of percentage, it is much lower than before the revolution; whereas according to the 1966 and 1976 censuses some 13 to 14 per cent of women of working age were in paid employment, the post-revolutionary census of 1986 indicated that only 9 per cent were in paid employment. This was a clear reflection of the government's policies which disapproved of the entry of women into all but a few 'suitable' professions such as teaching and nursing and the refusal of the civil service to employ women in other fields. In addition the segregation of work places and public transport, the cutting back on child care provisions and unfavourable tax systems all made it harder for women to participate fully in paid employment.

These discriminatory practices were legitimised by some women appointees who had no difficulty in using Khomeini's teachings to support such activities. A clear example is Shahla Habibi who, in 1991, was appointed to the newly created post of presidential adviser on women's affairs.

Typically her previous post had been with the national Islamic Propaganda Organisation. She reminded the public that Khomeini had placed women in the home and had declared that:

> Women, whatever qualifications they may have or however learned they may be, must remain the pivotal core of the family and play their parts as exemplary housewives.
>
> (*Zaneh Rouz* 7 January 1992)

In this she was fully supported by the government sponsored Women's Organisation. In December 1990 it had already declared:

> As the imam [Khomeini] has repeatedly said good men are raised in the laps of good women. If we follow this example then we'd find our true station in life and recognise that motherhood is a sacred and holy duty of women.
>
> (*Zaneh Rouz* 25 December 1990)

A view shared by the High Council of Women's Cultural and Social Affairs which was appointed by the High Council of Cultural Revolution to co-ordinate government policies on women. It was staffed with women like Soraya Maknoun, university professor who headed the Council's Employment

Research Group. Maknoun chose to disregard her own highly paid position and blithely denounced all demands for equal opportunities as corruptive and pro-Western:

> I am totally against the view that women's success depends on gaining access to equal opportunities in all sectors of the economy. . . . The truth is that our society does not have a women's problem and it's just pro-Western critics who have invented such a problem and imposed it on our lives.
>
> (*Zaneh Rouz* 27 January 1990).

Marzieh Mohamadianfar, who was appointed to head the Council's Employment Committee, held a similar view. In a country where the staple food is rice, a grain which is almost entirely cultivated by women, Marzieh Mohamadianfar declared:

> You see there are some activities which are based on physical strength and so are beyond women . . . we cannot deny that men are physically stronger. So there are jobs like cultivation and agricultural work which women simply cannot do.
>
> (*Zaneh Rouz* 27 January 1990)

Not surprisingly the Employment Committee of the High Council of Women's Social and Cultural Affairs declared itself satisfied with the segregation of the labour market. It came to the conclusion that women were physically ill suited to certain tasks. Mrs Mohamadianfar declared that the existing restrictions on female employment were not disadvantageous, but merely reflected the 'nature' of the female condition:

> The existing laws and regulations are not detrimental to the rights of working women and we do not need to revise them. It is not the law that is deficient, it is its implementation.
>
> . . . It is the male employers who won't employ women. Of course women do cause their own problems. When they are giving birth or suckling their babies, they cannot work. That is why men prefer to employ men. So women graduates cannot hope to get the kinds of jobs that are offered to men and earn similar salaries even in the fields that are open to them to work in.
>
> . . . We must also be aware that if we insist on welfare and special facilities for female employees, then the managers would simply refuse to employ women.
>
> (*Zaneh Rouz* 27 January 1990)

So the government's supporters condemned special welfare provisions for women and condemned women themselves for being potential mothers and therefore inefficient workers. With such friends in high places, Iranian women do not need any enemies. As a teacher told the weekly women's magazine *Zaneh Rouz*:

Some of the women in positions of influence forget how they got there and in doing so not only they fail all other women, but also they weaken the very fabric of our society.

(27 January 1990)

But the women supporters of the government have been firmly and continuously opposed by women such as Azam Taleqani, the campaigning daughter of the late Ayatollah Taleqani and member of the first post-revolutionary *Majlis*. Azam Taleqani founded the Women's Society of Islamic Revolution, which has been ceaselessly defending women's rights. She is an extremely well-informed, outspoken and tireless critic of the government's discriminatory policies:

Two-thirds of women in this country live and work in the rural areas and carry a major burden of agricultural activity. Nevertheless we do not allow our women to study agricultural sciences at the University.

(*Zaneh Rouz* 25 December 1990)

Similarly Zahra Rahnavard, a leading Islamic feminist and the wife of the previous Iranian Prime Minister, Mir Hussein Mussavi, denounced discrimination against women on religious and political grounds:

Our planners say 'we don't have the means to invest equally in men and women and must spend our limited resources on those who provide the highest return for our society. Therefore as women's natural obligations, in giving birth and raising their children, means that they work less, we cannot allocate too great a portion of our resources to them.'

We respond that this is wrong since all Muslim are required to pursue knowledge regardless of their gender. It is of the essence, in terms of religious requirement and social well-being, that no barriers be put between women and their quest for knowledge.

(*Zaneh Rouz* 10 February 1990)

By placing the argument squarely in the Islamic domain, Rahnama, Taleqani and others succeeded in gaining the support of some of the leading politicians, like the long-serving, enlightened Minister of Interior, Hojatoleslam Nateq Nouri. He declared:

Islam places no limitation whatever on the participation of women in the public, political and cultural domains.

(*Zaneh Rouz* 14 March 1985)

In fact women have retained their entitlement to equal rights of access to the labour market in Iran after the revolution. They had even been promised a less discriminatory future at the inception of the Islamic Republic. Article 43 of the Constitution undertakes to provide employment opportunities for all and states that full employment is a fundamental aim of the revolution. Thus, even after the revolution, the Constitution, Labour Laws and the State Employment Laws make no distinction between men and women. As Azam Taleqani explained:

> Article 28 of our constitution declares that anyone can choose any profession that they wish, provided they do not contravene Islam and public and social interests. The government must provide equal opportunities for every one in every job according to social needs. The failure to implement this law properly has destroyed the trust of women in Islam and the government. When you ask a woman civil servant what do you think about Islam? The only answer is 'they have destroyed me! You only have to read the notices that are plastered all over the walls, you only have to see the way that they are treating me. They think of me as an easily exploitable being. They have reduced me to the level of beasts of burden; they have no respect for me, or for what I do!' This is the heart felt cry of working women and there is no one to hear them, they have destroyed the women workers, squeezed the working day, squeezed the very life out of them and destroyed their self respect.
>
> (*Zaneh Rouz* 25 December 1990)

Of course in practice women do not benefit from equal pay for equal work provisions. Married women pay higher taxes on their incomes than do married men; and women pay higher child insurance premiums than do men. It is the men who benefit from the married man's entitlement whereas it is usually women who end up paying for nursery care of their children. Men get larger bonuses, because it is assumed that they are the head of household, and they are entitled to cheap goods from the civil service co-operatives; their share increases with the numbers of their children. Not so for women who do not even get a share for themselves.[3]

Zahra Rahnavard warned the government that such discriminations eroded much of women's support for the regime. By 1990 she had to admit that at least the government, if not the revolution, had failed women:

> We have no strategy for including women in this country's destiny and in this respect we have fallen far short of our political aspiration. . . . In the five years plan women are only mentioned once . . . despite all our protests we have remained invisible. It is essential that women's role in the development process is clearly delineated.
>
> (*Zaneh Rouz* 10 February 1990)

THE POLITICS OF ACTIVISM, RESISTANCE AND COMPROMISE

Activists such as Rahnavard and Taleqani persevered and eventually found a foothold in the High Council of Cultural Revolution, which determines policies at a national level. There they managed to formulate an Islamic female employment policy. On 11 August 1992, seventeen months after Zahra Rahnavard had joined the Council, it issued an official document on female employment. Despite President Rafsanjani's directives to the Council 'to educate women about the correct ways of dealing with their husband and children' (*Zaneh Rouz* 26 December 1991) the Council chose to educate the rulers about women's liberation, by making concessions and focusing on areas where it was possible to make gains. Its statement applauded the revolution for returning women to the pedestal of honour and respectability:

> Women in society who under the past regime had, in the name of freedom, suffered great oppression and lost many of their human and Islamic rights have had the opportunity to free themselves of the cheap Westoxificated voyeuristic societal gaze and find their real and pure Islamic status. . . . Thus the Muslim Iranian woman is on the one hand faithfully fulfilling her pivotal social task in the familial context. . . . On the other hand where there has been a need and a correct context Iranian women have remained active in the educational, social and economic domains.

The High Council accepted that women's first priority was to remain within the home and care for the family. But it argued that Islam offered women the opportunity of fulfilling all their potentials and was capable of enabling them to live their life cycles to the full. Therefore the Committee requested that 'suitable jobs' be provided for women in fields such as:

> midwifery and similar medical posts as well as teaching (Article 5A).
>
> Jobs which best suit the nature and temperament of women such as laboratory work, electronic engineering, pharmacology, welfare work and translation work (Article 5B).
>
> Employment where men and women are equally suitable such as simple workers in service and technical industries. In such cases experience and qualifications, rather than gender must be the determining factor for selection of the work force (Article 5C).

Where the Council's resolution is of interest is that it argues that the government should enable women to fulfil both their domestic and their paid duties. In addition to equal pay for equal work, in the segment of the labour market allocated to women, the government should also allow women paid time off to enable them to fulfil their 'mothering obligations'. They should be entitled to shorter working hours and an earlier retirement age; measures which would recognise women's double burden of unpaid domestic work and paid employment.

It is worth noting that in 1985 the government had passed a Bill to facilitate half-time working for mothers of young children. Since the law required full-rate contributions towards their pension funds, and the state made no tax allowance for part-time workers, only 1 per cent of the female civil servants chose this option. Most women simply could not afford to give up half of their salary.

If, as the Council has suggested, the recognition of 'mothering duties' results in some flexibility in working hours, without cut-backs in pay, then women workers would indeed fare much better. At the moment, despite all the lip-service paid to complementarity in marriage and women's special qualities, Iranian women workers have to work as a 'manpower' in an inflexibly male labour market. For example work and schools start at the same time, as do nurseries. There are few workplace nurseries and so most women have to travel considerable distances during rush hours depositing and collecting their children. As a result they are usually late for work. Most factories have two fortnight-long holidays, one for the Persian new year in late March and one during the summer. The factories close for that period. Women are not allowed to use their paid holiday leave in small portions to deal with a sick child or do their 'mothering' duties; all such obligations have to be shouldered as unpaid leave. Furthermore anyone who accumulates more than four months' unpaid leave in any working year can be sacked, even from tenured posts.

If the High Council's recommendations go through, at least some of these problems may be alleviated. In addition the proposal demanded that working women be entitled to job security, unemployment benefits and welfare provisions (Article 10). Women who are heads of household are to be entitled to special retraining programmes to enable them to return to the labour market (Article 11) and the government is urged to provide co-operative type organisations to facilitate home working for women who wish to combine their paid and unpaid jobs (Article 12). Thus, in return for accepting women's domestic obligations, the Council's proposal sought to extract concessions which would enable women to fulfil both their paid and unpaid duties. Its declaration forms part of the slow, but continuous progress of women in Iran in clawing back the rights that were summarily curtailed by the post-revolutionary state.

WOMEN IN PUBLIC AND POLITICS

Although they fought shoulder to shoulder with men, women were not given high office by the revolutionary government. It has never appointed a woman to a ministerial post, a point made by Zahra Rahnavard in 1990 when she complained:

> Women have been and continue to be present at times in larger numbers than men, in our public demonstrations, for the revolution and in its support. But when it comes to public appointments, they are pushed aside. ... Women like myself have continuously campaigned for better conditions. We have made our demands in the *Majlis*, in the press and in the public domain. But no one has taken any notice and our voices are not heard.
>
> (*Zaneh Rouz* 10 February 1990)

But getting elected is only the first step, women members of *Majlis* are severely constrained by the ideological views that designate them as inferior, demands of them to be modest, silent and invisible (Milani 1992), and defines them as interlopers in the public domain. Maryam Behrouzi, a veteran representative who had served a prison sentence before the revolution and whose 16-year-old son was 'martyred' in the Iran–Iraq war, still found herself firmly discriminated against. She pointed out that women are never elected to high-powered committees. Nor did they become chair or officers of other parliamentary committees (*Zaneh Rouz* 30 January 1988). Azam Taleqani, who gained a seat in the first post-revolutionary *Majlis*, explained that women were expected to be 'naturally modest' and this prevented them from 'saying too much in the *Majlis*' (*Zaneh Rouz* 20 January 1991).

In April 1991, as the country was preparing for the parliamentary elections, Maryam Behrouzi demanded that Bills allowing an earlier retirement age for women, reforming some of the more draconian divorce laws (Mir-Hosseini 1993a: 59–84; 1993b) and provision of national insurance for women and children be put before the next session of the *Majlis*. Behrouzi also asked for the laws to be reformed to allow single women to travel abroad to continue their studies. This request was not endorsed by Habibi; she stated that such an act would devalue Iranian women and knock them off their perch of purity:

Since women are the public face of our society and the guardians of our honour, we must not intentionally dispatch them to a corrupt environment [i.e. the West].

(*Zaneh Rouz* 29 October 1990)

In the subsequent *Majlis* twelve women were elected. They have been fighting hard on women's issues. Although they lost their demands for the establishment of a Parliamentary Women's Committee, they have made some gains.

In a remarkable move, *Majlis* representatives Behrouzi, Monireh Nobakht and Marzieh Vahid Datgerdi managed to alter the divorce laws to make it more expensive for men to leave their wives at will. The Islamic government had restored the male prerogative to easy divorce. But, except for a brief period, the post-revolutionary government had not succeeded in closing down the Family Courts set up before the revolution to curb divorce, or defend the aggrieved party, who was usually the wife, in familial disputes. By using the marriage contract, and insisting on the Koranic right to fair treatment, many Iranian women had continued using the Family Courts as bargaining counters in their divorce proceedings (Mir-Hosseini 1993a; 1993b). On the whole the courts favoured the men and on divorce women were not entitled to any of their husband's property. Activists such as Azam Taleqani had gone on arguing fiercely against the gender-blind attitudes of the courts:

Unfortunately after the revolution ... the government and the religious institution have not paid enough attention to women as full human beings.

All their efforts has been concentrated on making women stay at home, at all cost; to make them accept self sacrifice, oppression and submission. Even when they go to court to get their due, I am not saying that the courts are totally patriarchal; but unfortunately there are these tendencies. So the problem is presented in a way that does not illuminate the truth.

(*Zaneh Rouz* 25 December 1990)

In the event Behrouzi and her colleagues insisted that the *Majlis* should give women their Islamic dues. The 1993 Bill sought to curtail men's automatic right of divorce, by demanding that men who 'unjustly' divorce their 'obedient' wives should do their Koranic duty and pay 'wages' for the wife's domestic services during their married years.

Behrouzi also succeeded in pushing through a Bill which allowed women to retire after twenty years of active service, while the men still had to serve twenty-five years. Her success was in part achieved because it permitted women to return to their proper sphere, that of domesticity, all the sooner.

For those who were actively campaigning for women, this Bill was a remarkable success, since the path of women's liberation has been less than smooth. In 1991 the Women's Cultural-Social Council, despite its conservative membership, still submitted thirteen women's projects to the High Council of Cultural Revolution; but only one of these was considered and ratified by the Council. It was a proposal to eliminate the prejudicial treatment of women in higher education and in the selection for degree courses. This was no mean feat since there were discriminatory measures against women in 119 academic subject areas (*Zaneh Rouz* 31 August 1991).

WOMEN'S ORGANISATIONS

It was in quangos and organisations outside the direct control of the government that women activists were most successful in struggling for better economic and political opportunities. Although in the public domain success depended on espousing an Islamic stance, Islam itself is sufficiently flexible to allow a diversity of interpretation and much leeway for women. Azam Taleqani, for example, set up the Women's Society of Islamic Revolution, a non-governmental activist group, whose members have included Zahra Rahnavard, the path-breaking Islamist writer and the wife of the long-serving post-revolutionary Prime Minister Musavi, as well as more conservative women such as *Majlis* representative Gohar Dastqeib, and Monireh Gorgi, a woman representative in the Assembly of Experts, which is responsible for nominating the national leader.

Within the civil service it was younger women in the lower echelons of the governmental organisations who fought effectively for the cause. By 1992 the Minister of Interior had been prevailed upon to set up women's affairs committees to serve the social councils in all the provinces. Women working on these committees were much clearer about their aims than Mrs Habibi ever could be. A good example is Jaleh Shahrian Afshar, a member of Western Azarbaijan's women's committee, who told the press that first and foremost the women wished to be independent, furthermore they sought better employment opportunities and needed more facilities to embark on a wide-ranging family planning programme (*Zaneh Rouz* 29 August 1992). They had taken their demands directly to the *Majlis*. But the only one of their suggestions to meet with approval was the family planning one.

THE POPULATION DEBATE

By 1987 the Statistical Centre of Tehran was indicating that 96 per cent of the urban women of child-bearing age were married and only 1 per cent had never married. The non-literate women married at around 16 and literate women at 17.5. But only 7 per cent of married women used any form of family planning. The average age for the first birth was 19, but it increased to 21 for women with secondary education. On average mothers had four live births, rather more than their stated desired average of two in urban areas and three in rural areas. Interestingly over half of the women questioned did not mind whether they had a son or a daughter; 14 per cent actually preferred to have a daughter and only 31 per cent had a marked son preference.[4]

Thus by 1990 the Iranian population reached 59.5 million and was growing at an average annual rate of 3.9 per cent. Although there was some disquiet, the devout were not panicking. Nevertheless both the high birth rates and temporary marriages came under new scrutiny. The daily newspapers warned that the country had only 12 million hectares of cultivable land which would feed 30 million people at most (*Zaneh Rouz* 18 September 1991). But some people like the *Majlis* deputy Mrs Gohar Dastqeib were unperturbed:

> The previous regime used to say 'fewer children a better life'. We do not say this. ... As the late Ayatollah Mottahari had repeatedly stated this 1,647,000 square kilometres of land in our country could feed 150 million people ... you only have to look around there are lots of empty spaces in Sistan and Baluchestan [Eastern provinces bordering on the central desert].
>
> (*Zaneh Rouz* 12 May 1990)

But already in 1988 the Islamic government had introduced a Bill for population control and a year later a five-year programme was announced to curb the explosion. By 1990 Ayatollah Yousef Saneyi was advocating birth control. He told the population control seminar in Isfahan that he had come to the conclusion that

> None of the wise and learned people has ever said that it is good and desirable to have lots of children.
>
> (*Zaneh Rouz* 3 February 1990)

His preferred solution was 'to tie up women's tubes and untie them whenever it's necessary'!

The population crisis posed a severe dilemma for the Islamic government. It had long since outlawed the pre-revolutionary abortion law and dismantled the family planning clinics. Suddenly it found itself with families averaging five or more children and no clear policy for halting the momentum. In July 1991 the government decreed that for a fourth birth, working women were not entitled to their three months' paid maternity leave, nor could a fourth child be allowed any rations or a ration card. Any family that chose to have a fourth child would have to share out its resources and spread it more thinly, with no help from the state. At the same time the Minister of Health Dr Reza Malekzadeh suggested to husbands that they should choose to have a vasectomy. A year later the courts decided to reconsider the abortion laws:

> It remains absolutely illegal to have an abortion or to carry out an abortion. Article 91 of the Criminal code imposes the death penalty, according to the Islamic laws, for anyone murdering an unborn child 'if that child possesses a soul'. But 'before the soul enters the body of a being' if a doctor is of the opinion that it is dangerous to continue with the pregnancy and issues a certificate to that effect; then the pregnancy can be terminated.
>
> (*Zaneh Rouz* 1 August 1992)

At the same time the newspapers published a list of fifty hospitals in the country offering free vasectomy and female sterilisation.

By 1993 the Ministry of Health had its own population control bureau, with a 20 billion rials budget that was 300 per cent higher than that of the previous year. Assisted by an additional $300 million loan from the World Bank the bureau launched a massive population control campaign offering free services at national, provincial and rural levels. The aim was to reduce population growth to 2.7 per cent per annum (*Zaneh Rouz* 18 April 1993).

A year later academia was mobilised to provide evidence in support of population control. Dr Mohab Ali Professor and head of research on productivity and efficiency *bahrevari* of Alameh Tabatabyi University announced that

> Women who have too many children would not find the time to think and work properly and have to devote themselves to cleaning and feeding the household. For a woman to have time to think properly about the education of her children and to create a suitable home environment she must have few children – ideally a maximum of two adults and two children per family – since the fewer the children the more time a mother has for each and the higher the rate of efficiency and productivity of that mother.
>
> (*Zaneh Rouz* 4 May 1994)

Azam Taleqani seized the opportunity to point out the close links between polygamy and increasing birth rates. Before the revolution Iranian women had managed to curb men's right to polygamy, by making remarriage subject to the consent of the first wife and ratification by Family Courts. Khomeini had restated men's right to permanent and temporary marriages and his successor Rafsanjani had endorsed this position during the war.

But women's opposition to polygamy continued. In this they were assisted by the Koranic dictum that no man, other than the Prophet of Islam, could treat all his wives equally and therefore it was advisable for them to take only one (4:3, 4:4, 4:129). As Azam Taleqani stated:

> There are 500,000 fewer women than men in our country. . . . Yet we are told that we must accept that our husbands have the right to remarry. I even went to some of our religious leaders and asked them whether they were backing the family or planning to destroy it? Since it is obvious that the moment a second wife steps in, effectively the first wife is discarded and her life is ruined. . . . But they are forcing women in this country to accept polygamy, if they don't then they are told that they have to quit and divorce the husband. . . . How can you have such a policy and still claim that women are respected and valued? What is there left of such a women? How can she become a good mother and raise a healthy family?
>
> (*Zaneh Rouz* 25 December 1990)

Although during the war the religious institution had been largely supportive of polygamy, afterwards, with the population explosion, some of its more enlightened members conceded Taleqani's point. In February 1990 Ayatollah Yousef Saneyi asked:

> Who says there are no barriers to polygamy in Islam? You should study Islamic law and then see whether you can make such a claim. The only thing that some men know about the Koran is the right to polygamy.
>
> (*Zaneh Rouz* 3 February 1990)

As yet polygamy has not been outlawed. But the prospects of curbing it have improved. What has been a marked success is the decision in the summer of 1993 to revise the *Qassas* laws and make honour killings punishable. The newly elected women members of *Majlis*, Azam Taleqani's Women's Movement and Zahra Rahnavard, all made a concerted effort to outlaw honour killings. They documented the growing numbers of murders and atrocities committed by husbands, fathers and brothers on their unsuspecting womenfolk and demanded that the judiciary defend women. Finally the head of the judiciary Ayatollah Mohamad Yazdi issued a decree revising the laws and making male murders, be they kin or not, subject to state prosecution. He agreed to remove the requirement that made the male 'guardians' responsible for seeking justice in such cases. The decision was a landmark; it demonstrated that the *Qassas* laws, supposedly Islamic and eternal, were, like other aspects of the Islamic rule, responsive to pressure and subject to change.

SELF-IMMOLATION

Although it is the Islamist women who have succeeded in changing some of the more repressive anti-feminist laws they have been assisted in their battle by secular women's resistance groups as well as the rising numbers of tragic self-immolations. Increasingly Iranian women are choosing to burn themselves rather than tolerate the misogynist rules concerning their private and public lives. Daughters forced into unacceptable marriages, young brides caught in difficult marriages, wives faced with their husbands' polygamous marriages, and more recently women barred from employment for failing to observe the Islamic dress code.

A tragic example was Professor Homa Darabi Tehrani, who set herself on fire to protest against the draconian misogynist rule of the Islamic government; she died as she had lived, campaigning for liberty. On 21 February 1994, Darabi tore off her headscarf and her Islamic long coat in a public thoroughfare near Tajrish Square in the Shemiran suburb of Tehran. She gave an impassioned speech against the government's oppressive measures which disempower and undermine women; calling for liberty and equality she poured petrol on herself and set herself alight. Homa Darabi, a popular teacher and respected researcher, had been dismissed from her post as Professor of Psychology in Tehran University for 'non-adherence to Islamic conduct and dress code' in December 1991. Although in May 1993 the decision was overturned by the 'Employment and Grievance Tribunal' the university refused to reinstate her.

Her death led to widespread protests in Iran and abroad. An estimated thirty thousand people attended her memorial service on 24 February 1994, at the Aljavad Mosque in Tehran. The meeting was held despite the government's intention to ban it. A letter of condemnation signed by about seventy leading Iranian academics working in the West was sent to the government in Tehran and activists abroad organised well-attended protest meetings in her memory in London, Paris, Los Angeles and other cities in the USA and Canada. They have also been writing letters condemning the denial of human rights to Iranian women.

CONCLUSION

The rule of Islam in Iran has not been easy on women. They lost much of the ground that they had won over the previous century and the way to recapturing some of those rights has been slow and barred by prejudice and patriarchal power. Undaunted Iranian women have struggled on. Some have actively opposed the Islamic dress codes and put their own lives on the line in support of their principles. Others have for the moment conceded the veil and its imposition in the name of Islam, though they have done so reluctantly and have continued the discussions about its validity, relevance and the extent to which it should be imposed. But the bargain that they have struck (Kandiyoti

1988) has enabled them to negotiate better terms. They have managed to revert the discriminatory policies on education, they are vociferously attacking the inequalities in the labour market and demanding better care and welfare provisions for working mothers. Of course in this, as in all other issues concerning women, the demise of Khomeini was in itself of the essence. Although the road to liberty is one that is strewn with difficulties, Iranian women, as ever, have come out fighting and have proved indomitable.

NOTES

1 As one of many examples this statement was made by a woman interviewee in Algeria, for the *Today* programme (21 September 1993).
2 It is worth noting that some commentators such as Ghassan Salame are of the view that the 'the Islam of the Islamists may be nothing but a discourse' (1994: 7–8).
3 Jaleh Shahriar Afshar, feminist researcher interviewed by *Zaneh Rouz* 29 August 1992.
4 The 1978 sample survey of childbearing women, carried out by the Statistical Centre and reported in February 1987.

REFERENCES

Abbott, N. (1942) *Aishah The Beloved of Mohamad*, Chicago: University of Chicago Press.
Afchar, H. (1987) 'The Muslim Concept of Law', *International Encyclopedia of Comparative Law*, Tubingen, The Hague and Paris: J. C. B. Mohr.
Afshar, H. (1982) 'Khomeini's Teachings and their Implications for Women', in A. Tabari and N. Yeganeh (eds) *In the Shadow of Islam*, London: Zed.
Afshar H. (1992) 'Women and Work: Ideology not Adjustment at Work in Iran', in H. Afshar and C. Dennis (eds) *Women and Adjustment Policies in the Third World*, London: Macmillan Women's Studies at York Series.
Afshar, H. (1994a) 'Muslim Women in West Yorkshire, Growing Up with Real and Imaginary Values amidst Conflicting Views of Self and Society', in H. Afshar and M Maynard (eds) *The Dynamics of Sex and Gender*, London: Taylor & Francis.
Afshar H. (1994b) *Why Fundamentalism? Iranian Women and their Support for Islam*, Working paper no 2, York: University of York Department of Politics.
Afshar, H. (1995) 'The Needs of Muslim Women and the Dominant Legal Order in the UK'
Ahmed, L. (1992) *Women and Gender in Islam*, New Haven, CT, and London: Yale University Press.
Al-Azmeh, A. (1993) *Islam and Modernities*, London: Verso.
al-Ghazali, Z. (nd) *Ayam min hayati*, Cairo: Dar al-shurua, quoted by V. J. Hoffman, 'An Islamic Activist: Zeinab al-Ghazali' in E. Warnok Fernea (ed.) (1985) *Women and the Family in the Middle East*, Austin, TX: University of Texas Press, and L. Ahmed (1992) *Women and Gender in Islam*, New Haven, CT, and London: Yale University Press.
Al-Khayyat, S. (1990) *Honour and Shame Women in Modern Iraq*, London: Saqi.
Chhachhi, A. (1991) 'Forced Identities: The State, Communalism, Fundamentalism and Women in India', in D. Kandiyoti (ed.) *Women, Islam and the State*, Philadelphia, PA: Temple University Press.
Kandiyoti, D. (1988) 'Bargaining with Patriarchy', *Gender and Society* 2(3): 271–90.

Keddie, R. and Baron, B. (eds) (1991) *Women in Middle Eastern History: Shifting Boundaries in Sex and Gender*, New Haven, CT, and London: Yale University Press.

Lemu, B. A. and Hareen, F. (1978) *Women in Islam*, Leicester: Islamic Council of Europe Publication.

Mernissi, F. (1991) *Women and Islam: An Historical and Theological Enquiry*, Oxford: Blackwell.

Milani, F. (1992) *Veils and Words: The Emerging Voices of Iranian Women Writers*, London: Tauris.

Minces, J. (1982) *The House of Obedience: Women in Arab Society*, London: Zed.

Mir-Hosseini, Z. (1993a) 'Women, Marriage and the Law in Post-revolutionary Iran', in H. Afshar (ed.) *Women in the Middle East*, London: Macmillan.

Mir-Hosseini, Z. (1993b) *Marriage on Trial, A Study of Islamic Family Law*, London: Tauris.

Mirza, K. (1989) 'The Silent Cry: Second Generation Bradford Women Speak', *Muslims in Europe* 43, Centre for the Study of Islam and Christian–Muslim Relations.

Moghissi, H. *'hoquqeh zan v bonbasthayeh farhangi, ejtemayi jomhurieyeh eslami'* (Women's Rights and the Sociocultural Problems in the Islamic Republic), *Cesmandaz* 13 spring 1773 [1994]: 42–53

Mojahedin Khalq (1980) *Zan dar Massyreh Rahayi* ('Women on the Path of Liberation'), Tehran: Mojahedin's Publication.

Molyneux, M. (1985) 'Mobilization without Emancipation? Women's Interests, the State, and Revolution in Nicaragua', *Feminist Studies* 11(2): 227–54.

Momen, M. (1985) *An Introduction to Shii Islam*, New Haven, CT: Yale University Press.

Mottahari, A. M. (1980) *Nezameh Hoquqeh Zan dar Eslam*, Qum: Islamic Publication.

Omid, H. (1994) *Islam and the Post Revolutionary State in Iran*, Basingstoke: Macmillan.

Rahnavard, Z. (nd) *Toloueh Zaneh Mosalman*, Tehran: Mahboubeh Publication.

Radcliffe, S. A. and Westwood, S. (1993) *'Viva': Women and Popular Protest in Latin America*, London: Routledge.

Salame, G. (1994) *Democracy Without Democrats: The Renewal of Politics in the Muslim World*, London: Tauris.

Shariati, A. (nd) *Zaneh Mosalman*, Tehran: Shirazi Foundation.

Tabari, A. and Yeganeh, N. (compilers) (1982) *In the Shadow of Islam*, London: Zed.

FURTHER READING

For a thorough historic overview of women in Islam it is well worth reading Leila Ahmed's (1992) scholarly book *Women and Gender in Islam*, which provides an excellent overarching historical perspective of both the secular and the Islamist movements of Middle Eastern women, as well as providing a millennial historical view of their political engagements. Nadia Abbott's (1942) *Aishah The Beloved of Mohamad* presents an excellent analysis of the life of one of the leading women of Islam and should be read along with Fatima Mernissi's (1991) *Women and Islam: An Historical and Theological Enquiry*, which provides an in-depth analysis of the meaning and imposition of the veil in terms of both the Prophet's life and the subsequent interpretations placed on the injunction on the relatives of the Prophet of being dressed modestly.

Haleh Afshar's (1994) *Why Fundamentalism? Iranian Women and their Support for Islam* looks at the arguments presented by the female advocates of Islamism for rejecting the Western options of feminism and choosing the Islamic way for women. Amrita Chhachhi's (1991) 'Forced Identities: The State, Communalism, Fundamentalism and Women in India', in D. Kandiyoti (ed.) *Women, Islam and the State*, complements this by offering a critical analysis of why women would hark back to a golden past in order to come to terms with a bleak present.

For the Iranian case it is useful to look at Homa Omid's (1994) *Islam and the Post Revolutionary State in Iran*, which provides a historical and political framework for understanding the post-revolutionary state in Iran, and Azar Tabari and Nahid Yeganeh's (eds) (1982) *In the Shadow of Islam*, which looks at the plight of women in the post-revolutionary state.

Haleh Afshar's (1982) 'Khomeini's Teachings and their Implications for Women', in Tabari and Yeganeh's *In the Shadow of Islam*, looks critically at the Ayatollah's specific interpretations of Islamic laws; and her (1992) 'Women and Work: Ideology not Adjustment at Work in Iran', in H. Afshar and C. Dennis (eds) *Women and Adjustment Policies in the Third World*, analyses the implications of these interpretations in terms of women's labour market participation in Iran.

Ziba Mir-Hosseini's (1993) 'Women, Marriage and the Law in Post-revolutionary Iran', in H. Afshar (ed.) *Women in the Middle East*, looks at the way in which women have used their Islamic rights to negotiate better terms for themselves in the marriage courts, while Mir-Hosseini's (1993) *Marriage on Trial: A Study of Islamic Family Law* compares the Iranian cases with their Moroccan counterparts.

Chapter 9

Women and politics in post-Khomeini Iran

Divorce, veiling and emerging feminist voices

Ziba Mir-Hosseini

In September 1993, a lawyer friend in Tehran arranged for me to meet the new president of the Special Civil Courts. These are the post-revolutionary family courts which I studied between 1985 and 1988, when they were located in an old building near the Bazaar. They had recently moved to a modern building in affluent north Tehran. My friend could not remember the name of the street, but told me, 'Come to Vanak Square, you'll find it: the entrance will be packed with women waiting for the door to open at 8.30.' Near Vanak Square, I saw a women in a *chador*, carrying freshly baked bread, one of those so-called 'traditional Iranian women'. I asked her for directions to the courts. She looked at me in horror, and said 'Oh no! why you?' Feeling defensive and somehow ashamed, I explained in an apologetic tone that I was just meeting a lawyer friend who would introduce me to the new court president. Disbelief showing on her face, she told me to come with her, as she lived in a nearby street. Taken aback by my own reaction, as we walked together, I tried to make a case for divorce, for women such as those whose court cases I had studied, women who shared my view that divorce is a lesser evil than staying in an unhappy and unfair marriage. My guide disagreed: 'What makes you think you'll find fairness in another marriage; divorce doesn't change anything, the next husband will be just as bad as the first one; it is up to a woman to make the best of her life.' I protested that there were surely standards and limits: 'What if he takes another wife?' I knew from my court attendance that this is where most women, and even judges, draw the line. She paused and said, 'Too bad; but if she leaves, the children will turn against her; if she stays, she will keep them for ever; they matter to a woman more than a husband.'

This encounter seems to me to reveal the basic similarities and differences between two major discourses on women in Iran today. My reactions were typical of the 'modernist' position – which has been discussed extensively in the growing literature on Iranian women; my guide's position, on the other hand, although that of perhaps the majority of Iranian women, has received little attention, and is little understood outside Iran. I begin with this encounter not only because it indicates what marriage, as defined and regulated by the

Shari'a, can entail for women in Iran, but also because it tells something of the ways in which women relate to and deal with its patriarchal rules. It is against the background of the opposed discourses implicit in the encounter that I examine in this chapter the working of the *Shari'a* as it concerns women in Iran today – where one version of the Islamist vision has been realised.

One unpredicted outcome of the Islamic revolution in Iran has been to raise the nation's gender consciousness. Since the revolution, whatever concerns women – from their most private to their most public activities, from what they should wear and what they should study to whether and where they should work – are issues that have been openly debated and fought over by different factions, always in highly charged and emotional language. The result has been a breakdown of all kinds of easy dichotomies, including that of public versus private. Consciously or not, everyone has been drawn into these debates and somehow forced to take a position. It is almost impossible not to, if you happen to be an Iranian woman, whether living inside or outside the boundaries of the Islamic Republic.

There is now a substantial literature on women in post-revolutionary Iran, largely produced by Iranian women educated in the West and living in exile.[1] Most of them, especially those writing in the 1980s, see the impact of the revolution as having been detrimental to women. Basing their case on the changes brought about in the law to ensure the rule of the *Shari'a* and on the restrictions imposed by compulsory veiling, they argue that women lost many rights they had before the revolution. More recent writers, especially since 1990, are less polemical and more willing to explore the complexity of the situation. Yet there has been little examination of the processes through which the changes in law have been implemented in practice, and the paradoxical ways in which the whole process has come to empower women.

To explore the actual field of operation of the *Shari'a*, I shall examine two of its features in today's Iran, namely divorce law and dress codes: not only are they among the most visible and debated Islamic mandates, but also they are the yardsticks by which women's emancipation or repression in Islam are measured. Both have been the subject of intense debates in Iran since the turn of the century; and in both areas the legislations of both the former and present regimes have aroused deep emotions and diverse reactions. However, as we shall see, whereas on divorce laws the Islamic Republic has gradually retreated from its early position and suppressed debates have now fully re-emerged, the same has not happened with the issue of dress.

I argue that, contrary to what the early literature contends, and what remains implicit in the later wave, the impact of the revolution on women has been emancipatory, in the sense that it has paved the way for the emergence of a popular feminist consciousness.[2] By feminism, here I mean a broad concern with women's issues and an awareness of their oppression at work, in the home and in society, as well as action aimed at improving their lives and changing the situation (Moore 1988: 10).[3] Such a consciousness, most active in the private domain of the family, is now extending to the public domain. What facilitates such extension is the widening gap between the ideals and realities of the *Shari'a* as defined and enforced by a modern state.

DIVORCE LAWS: A CHANGE OF HEART

In December 1992, the *Majlis* (Iranian parliament) ratified a law which represents a radical interpretation of *Shari'a* divorce provisions. Entitled 'Amendments to Divorce Regulations', this law outlaws the registration of a divorce without a court certificate, and allows the appointment of women as advisory judges to work in co-operation with the main judge. Above all it enables the court to place a monetary value on women's housework, and to force the husband to pay her *ujrat al-mithl* (literally, wages in kind) for the work she has done during marriage, provided that divorce is not initiated by her or is not caused by any fault of hers. The amendments further require every divorcing couple to go through a process of arbitration. If the arbiters, one chosen by each side, fail to reconcile the couple, the court allows a man to effect a divorce – which has to be of *ruj'i* type[4] – only after he has paid his wife all her dues: dower (*mahr*), waiting period (*'idda*) maintenance and *ujrat al-mithl* (domestic wages). The registration of a *ruj'i* divorce is also made contingent upon the production of another certificate confirming that the wife spent her *'idda* period (three menstrual cycles, or until delivery if she is pregnant) in the marital home and was provided for by the husband.

By introducing the concept of domestic wages and substantially restricting men's right to repudiation (*talaq*), the 1992 amendments not only break new ground in *Shari'a* divorce provisions but also amount to a complete reversal of an early ruling of the Revolutionary Council dismantling the Family Protection Law of 1967, which had introduced substantial reforms in *Shari'a* divorce provisions.

Before discussing how and why such a reversal came about, a brief note is needed on the history of the Family Protection Law (FPL) and how it was dismantled. There is a tendency to take the *Shari'a*-based rulings in Iran at face value and to overlook both the processes involved and the extent to which they are translated into practice.[5] As we shall see, although the FPL itself was denounced in rhetoric, after the revolution a large portion of its reforms was retained in practice.

The FPL, enacted in 1967 and amended in 1975, received international acclaim and was even described as the most radical reform in *Shari'a* laws of divorce (Bagley 1971; Hinchcliffe 1968). It was part of a series of legal reforms begun earlier in the twentieth century aimed at creation of a totally secular judicial system. The most radical step was in 1936 during the reign of Reza Shah, when all serving judges in the newly created Ministry of Justice were required to hold a degree from either Tehran Faculty of Law or a foreign university. The result was that, almost overnight, the remaining *Shari'a* judges lost their positions. In the same year, the *Majlis* approved the final draft of the new Civil Code, based on Western judiciary models, namely, those of France and Belgium. Meanwhile, the Marriage Law of 1931 had made marriage subject to state provisions by requiring the registration of all marriages and divorces and denying legal recognition unless they were registered in civil bureaux. Otherwise in matters relating to marriage, family and inheritance, the Civil Code still deferred to the *Shariʿa*; the only departure was those articles prohibiting marriage of girls under 13 (Banani 1961: 73–4).

In 1967 substantial reforms in the *Shariʿa* provisions were attempted. This was done through a legislation entitled Family Protection Law, which restricted men's rights to divorce and polygamy, and more importantly gave women easier access to divorce. The reforms were achieved through procedural devices, that is by simply changing the regulations for registration of marriage and divorce, and leaving intact the provisions of the *Shariʿa* as reflected in the Civil Code. New courts, headed by civil judges (some of them women), were established to deal with the whole range of marital disputes. The registration of divorce and polygamous marriage without a certificate issued by these courts became an offence, subject to a penalty of six months' to one year's imprisonment for all parties involved, including the registrar.[6] In 1975 a new version of FPL, which formally repealed all laws contrary to its mandate, in effect provided these courts with discretionary power to disregard all the provisions of the Civil Code on divorce and child custody with impunity.

In February 1979, soon after the victory of the revolution, a communiqué from the office of Ayatollah Khomeini declared the FPL to be non-Islamic, and demanded its suspension and the reinstitution of the *Shariʿa*.[7] There followed a period of uncertainty during which FPL courts continued to function, until September 1979, when they were replaced by Special Civil Courts (*dadgahha-ye madani-ye khass*). Established by a legislation with the same name, the new courts are in effect *Shariʿa* courts and they are presided over by a *hakem-e sharʿ* (a judge trained in *fiqh*, Islamic jurisprudence). 'Special' here denotes the freedom of these courts from the law of evidence and procedure contained in the Civil Procedure Code, investing them with the same degree of discretionary powers as the pre-revolutionary FPL courts.

The point that needs to be made is that in 1979 the return to the *Shariʿa* was achieved exactly in the same way as it had been abandoned in 1967, that is by manipulating the procedural rules. In this way, neither the Pahlavi regime nor the Islamic Republic had to address the theory of the *Shariʿa*, while both were able to achieve their objectives through changing its practice. Legally speaking, like the Civil Code articles on marriage and divorce under the Pahlavis, FPL was never formally repealed by the Islamic Republic. Some of its procedural rules continued to govern the registration of marriages and divorces, although to different degrees. For instance, in theory registering a polygamous marriage without a court order is still an offence, but in practice the penalty for doing so has been removed: in August 1984 a ruling of the

Council of Experts declared this penalty anti-*Shari'a*. Now it is left to the conscience and outlook of the marriage registrars whether or not they require a court order to register a polygamous marriage.

The same has not happened with respect to the registration of divorces, where only two changes were effected. First, whereas between 1967 and 1979 no divorce could be registered without first producing a Certificate of Impossibility of Reconciliation, issued by the FPL courts, between September 1979 and December 1992 a divorce could be registered if both parties reached a mutual agreement. The only cases that needed to appear in court were those where one party, either the husband or the wife, objected to the divorce or its terms. Second, in conformity with the *Shari'a* mandate of divorce, whereas men are not required to provide a ground, women can obtain a divorce only upon establishing one of the recognised grounds, which are basically the same as those available to them under the FPL. These grounds are much broader than those recognised by classical Shi'a law, which are only two: the husband's impotency and his insanity. Using the legal device of *talfiq*, that is adopting provisions from other schools of the *Shari'a*, the 1936 Civil Code had made three other divorce grounds available to women: husband's failure to maintain his wife, his failure to perform marital duties (sexual), his affliction by a disease endangering her life, and his maltreatment of her to the extent that continuation of marriage is deemed to cause her harm. To further broaden these grounds and yet not to break with the *Shari'a* provisions for divorce, the 1967 FPL resorted to another legal device, which could in theory put women on the same footing as men in terms of access to divorce. This was the insertion of stipulations into the marriage contract which give the wife the delegated right to divorce herself on behalf of her husband after recourse to the court, where she must establish one of the inserted conditions. In this way a divorce stipulation became an integral part of every marriage contract, whereas in the past it was up to the woman, and in effect her family, to negotiate such a right for her, which seldom happened and was confined to the property-holding middle classes.

This aspect of the reform not only was retained after the revolution, but also was further expanded to provide women with financial protection in the event of an unwanted divorce. In 1982 new marriage contracts were issued which carry, in addition to the divorce stipulation, another one which entitles the wife, upon divorce, to claim half the wealth that her husband acquired during marriage, provided that the divorce was not initiated or caused by any fault of hers. The only difference is that now the husband can refrain from signing any of these stipulations. This is in conformity with the *Shari'a* mandate of divorce: a man is free to divorce, to delegate or refrain from delegating this right. But in practice, as I saw in the courts, the presence or absence of his signature under each clause has no effect on the woman's right to obtain a court divorce, as the decision lies with the judge. The amended version of Article 1130 of the Civil Code provides him with discretionary power to issue or withhold a divorce requested by a woman (Mir-Hosseini 1993: 65–71). However, I have not yet come across any case in which the wife has received any portion of the husband's wealth, so the new stipulation is in practice ineffective.

As evident even before the 1992 amendments, as far as divorce laws were concerned, there has been more continuity than break with the pre-revolutionary situation. In fact the 1992 amendments are but the completion of a U-turn from the direction indicated in the early rhetoric of the revolutionary regime on women, with parallels in other spheres of law. What is significant about the 1992 amendments is that they also mark a shift in rhetoric. To appreciate the importance of this U-turn, the amendments should be juxtaposed with a decree issued by Ayatollah Khomeini when the FPL came into effect in 1967, which reads:

> the 'Family law' (FPL), which has as its purpose the destruction of the Muslim family unit, is contrary to the ordinances of Islam. Those who have imposed [this law] and those who have voted [for it] are criminals from the stand-point of both the *Shari'a* and the law. The divorce of women divorced by court order is invalid; they are still married women, and if they marry again, they become adultresses. Likewise anyone who knowingly marries a woman so divorced becomes an adulterer, deserving the penalty laid down by the *Shari'a*. The issue of such unions will be illegitimate, unable to inherit, and subject to all other regulations concerning illegitimate offspring.
>
> (Algar 1985: 411)

These are not simply strong words, they constitute a *fatwa*, bearing the same sanction as the one Khomeini issued when Salman Rushdie's *The Satanic Verses* came to his attention. Yet it has vanished into thin air. None of the thousands of divorces issued by the Family Protection courts was annulled when the Islamic Republic was created, and no one was charged with adultery or was declared illegitimate. This in itself is clear evidence of the error of taking *Shari'a* rhetoric at face value, and the futility of engaging in debates on theological grounds.[8]

To understand *Shari'a* as a lived experience, I believe we need to shift the focus from the ways in which *Shari'a*-based ideology is oppressive to women to the ways in which its embedded contradictions are empowering to women. In so doing we need to distinguish between what those armed with its discourse say when they are in opposition and what they end up doing when in power. Once in power in Iran, the custodians of the *Shari'a* found themselves caught by their own rhetoric. They had blamed the Pahlavi regime for denying women their full rights, disparaged Western models of gender relations as degrading to women and harmful to the family, and argued that only Islam can give women back their dignity and secure their rights by restoring morality and upholding the family unit within which they have a secure and valued place.

It was not until they assumed power that they were hit by the paradoxical nature of their agenda. There was no way to uphold the family and value women's position within it, and at the same time to uphold men's *Shari'a* rights to extra-judicial divorce and polygamy. Since men could not be deprived of their prerogatives, the only solution was to protect women in the face of them; hence the 'amendments' to the divorce laws.

There were also other factors at work, some of more political and others of more socio-economic import. As the coalition of forces that brought the revolution about rapidly broke down, the custodians of the *Shari'a* came to rely more and more on popular support, including large numbers of women.[9] This need was intensified with the onset of war with Iraq, and the coming of other internal and external challenges. Thus, not only could women not be excluded from the political arena, as happened for instance in Algeria after independence, but also the 'women's question' became even more central to the Islamic polity in Iran. This, I believe, has little to do with any specific Islamic position on women's role in politics, for instance Shi'ism versus Wahabism. Rather it has to do with the fact that Islamic discourses on women in Iran became an element in the opposition to the Pahlavis who had made women's rights and their unequal status in the *Shari'a* a major issue in order both to appease secular forces and to discredit any religiously based opposition. Once in power, the Islamic regime, like the Pahlavis, found that the 'women's question' would not go away but rather was appropriated by opposition factions and thus re-emerged in a different guise.[10] This time, whereas the Pahlavis had to deal with *Shari'a*-based opposition to its gender policies, the Islamic regime had to deal with secular and liberal types of argument invoked by the opposition – both inside and outside Iran – to criticise the regime for its gender policies. In this way, the Islamic regime unwillingly had to engage in a dialogue with secular discourses on gender, whose premises were radically different from their own. Such engagement naturally has meant both negation and adoption of some features of the pre-revolutionary discourses.

As far as women were concerned, this became a double-edged sword; while it prevented them from being marginalised in political discourse, they had to bear the burden of policies whose only rationale and justification were that they were opposite to those of the Pahlavis, and by extension anti-Western. In the process, many Islamic women who at the beginning genuinely, although naively, believed that under an Islamic state women's position would automatically improve, became increasingly disillusioned. These included intellectuals like Zahra Rahnavard, activists like Azam Taleqani, and later on establishment women like Monireh Gorji. These women strongly opposed the previous regime's gender policy because of its Western and non-Islamic orientation. They played an instrumental role in discrediting and destroying the existing women's press and organisations, and did this with the conviction that they were being replaced with better ones, free from the corruption that marked

them under the Shah. In reviewing a decade of activities of the Islamic
Organisation of Iranian Women, Azam Taleqani gives a revealing account
of the ways in which she and her associates took over the pre-revolutionary,
state-sponsored Women's Organisation of Iran, how they carried out purges
in the process of which she lost the support of some of her associates, and
how at the end she and her own Islamically orientated organisation were
let down by the provisional government which axed their budget (Taleqani
1991).[11]

On the socio-economic front, women did not lose their public persona after
the revolution. It is true that women in government offices bore the brunt of
early purges, but it is equally true that a larger number of women have found
types of employment that were not available to them before.[12] Whereas a large
majority of women working in ministries or the private sector before the
revolution came from the 'Westernised' and highly educated middle and upper
classes, now they come from the so-called 'traditional' middle and lower
classes. These women were previously excluded from such jobs, because of
their family values, which defined working outside the home as corrupting,
and because of their not being part of the patronage system which has always
been the main way of finding a job in Iran. The revolution removed both
obstacles: its moralistic rhetoric and the new compulsory veiling made work
outside the home respectable, and it created a new patronage system with a
lower-middle-class bias.

Further, the long-drawn-out war with Iraq, and the subsequent economic
crisis, have meant a wider participation for women in the outside economy.
Women played an active role during the war; some joined the fronts as fighters,
nurses and cooks. Those who lost their husbands as martyrs in the war received
rewards and pensions, and became effective heads of household. Also, inflation has forced 'traditional' housewives into the labour market, as petty traders,
cooks, dress-makers, hair-dressers and so forth. One income in the family is
no longer enough to make ends meet. Contrary to prevailing assumptions,
women today have a much wider presence and are economically more active
outside the home than before the revolution.[13] They might be engaged in
marginalised activities in comparison to their pre-revolutionary sisters, but this
does not mean that they are politically marginalised. These women form a
force that the Islamic Republic cannot afford to alienate: it is indebted to
them. It is they who have come out to demonstrate, whenever needed. Some
are wives and mothers of martyrs, some gave their dowries and jewellery to
help pay the cost of the war. It is they who would pay the heaviest price if
their husbands were given a free hand in divorce and polygamy; and it is
their voice that has found a sympathetic ear among the authorities, as affirmed
by Nateq Nuri, the *Majlis* Speaker. In a recent interview, he referred to the
plight of women whose husbands had divorced them as the driving force for
introducing deterrents such as entitling women to claim 'domestic wages'
(*Zan-e Ruz*, 13/9/1372: 15).

A melange of three factors has made 'the plight of divorced women' a central issue in the *Majlis*, bringing about legislation which confronts the iniquity of men's *Shari'a* rights. The first is an unwritten gender code governing *Majlis* proceedings which assumes the constituencies of its female members to comprise solely women. Such an assumption not only has ensured that women's grievances are aired in the *Majlis* but also in time has become a strong lobbying force in defence of women's rights. The pattern appears to have been set from the start. In her analysis of the proceedings of the first *Majlis*, Esfandiari notes that, apart from Azam Taleqani (who was not elected in later rounds), other women deputies tended to confine their remarks to Bills relating to women's issues (Esfandiari 1994: 77). Given the quest to enhance the 'Islamic' aura and composition of the *Majlis* as the legislating body of the Islamic Republic, this early tendency became stronger in the subsequent *Majlis* where women parliamentarians came to devote all their energies to women's issues. This is also in line with the ethics of women deputies, who mostly came from established religious families where the segregation code is accepted.[14] In the present *Majlis* (convened summer 1992) not only are there more female deputies (nine as opposed to four in the first three), but also, as can be inferred from the interview with the *Majlis* Speaker, they are both more vocal and more active on all fronts.[15]

Second, what enables female deputies to argue for legislation to protect women is the contradictory terms of the early revolutionary discourse on women and the ways in which they continue to define the regime's gender policies. The discourse makes gender a central issue of an Islamic polity; makes the private public, the personal political and in this way politicises every aspect of women's life; it gives opportunity for political activity to some women, in particular the so-called traditional women who saw politics as outside their realm. Yet it remains adamant in adhering to the *Shari'a* and in treating women differently, and it denies them some rights that they used to take for granted. These contradictions not only marked the early post-revolutionary rulings, but also found their way into the Constitution of the Islamic Republic. For instance, on the one hand, the Constitution places men and women on the same footing in matters such as protection in law, rights to vote and be elected, access to education and employment (Articles 3, 20), on the other, it subordinates these rights to the supreme rule of the *Shari'a* which restricts women and treats them as second-class citizens (Articles 4, 91, 93).[16] The family, as the basic unit of Islamic society, soon became the arena where all these contradictions came to the surface. The discourse promotes domesticity and motherhood for women as ideal roles; the constitution promises to guard the sanctity of the family (Article 10);[17] yet the return to the *Shari'a*, as embodied in the Civil Code, which gives men a free hand in divorce and polygamy (Article 1133),[18] in effect subverts the very sanctity of the family as understood by women, thus going against the Constitution's promise.[19]

Such a patent contradiction prompts female deputies to argue that the family must be protected by containing men's *Shari'a* prerogatives. In so doing, they were in effect articulating the anxieties of their constituents – assumed to consist largely of 'traditional' housewives, who are most affected by the gap between the ideals and practices of the *Shari'a* under the Islamic Republic. They did not have to look far, since the same rhetoric which advocated domesticity and motherhood as primary roles of a woman could be invoked to give them protection in marriage.

The third factor making divorce a central issue in the *Majlis* is a legacy of the FPL, which established a legal frame of reference in which women could be treated on equal grounds with men in matters of divorce and child custody. This frame of reference was well known and welcomed by women – at least in urban areas – from all walks of life, even religiously-orientated women, some of whom later became part of the establishment.[20] As Esfandiari found in the *Majlis* transcripts, women parliamentarians 'complained bitterly about the operations of the Special Civil courts'; they objected to the ease with which men could obtain divorce; and challenged the assertion that 'God's command is such that any time a man wants to divorce his wife, she has to accept his wish and leave' (1994: 77).

In the early 1980s, when I first started attending Tehran branches of the Special Civil Courts, women who came to court because of their husbands' request to register a divorce were astonished to learn that their husbands now could divorce them without first securing their consent. Some remained incredulous and would ask more than one authority: 'Can he really divorce me, just like this?' In 1985, when I resumed my court attendance, although no longer incredulous, women were insistent on voicing their discontent; some used every occasion to remind the Islamic judge of the injustice of a system which could afford them no protection. On this they often had the judge on their side, especially when a man would insist on exercising his right to divorce and the wife was entirely dependent on him, with no source of income or nowhere to go. It was common to hear women asking the judge: 'Is this how women are honoured in the Islamic Republic? Is this how Islam rewards motherhood? Is this the justice of 'Ali that he can throw me out just because he has found a younger wife? Where do I go now? Who is going to take care of me? What will become of my children?' To these questions, the judges had nothing to reply, apart from assuring the women that the court would make sure that they received all their dues. Some judges would employ every available legal device to protect these women against what they deemed an unfair and unjustified divorce. But no judge could prevent a man from exercising his prerogative: they had to uphold the *Shari'a* mandate of divorce, as reflected in Article 1133 of the Iranian Civil Code, enabling a man to divorce whenever he wishes.[21] Many judges – certainly not all – felt that they were in a moral dilemma. Not only did they have to witness the plight of women on a daily basis but also they could not help but feel implicated, as women constantly reminded them of their own role as custodians of the *Shari'a*. In this way, the dismantling of the FPL became not only one of the most tangible evidences of the violation of women's rights in Iran, but also a measure of the Islamic Republic's failure to deliver its promise to honour and protect women.

Although it is too early to draw conclusions about the actual working of the 1992 divorce amendments, one can point to ways in which they differ from the FPL, in terms of the rationale of the law, its intentions and its probable impact. Whereas the spirit of the FPL was that of according women the same right as men in matters of divorce and child custody, the spirit of the 1992 amendments is to protect the family by making divorce less accessible to men. A central objection to the FPL – voiced only by the clergy but felt by many men – was that by making divorce easy for women, it harmed the institution of the family. In a 1993 seminar on Family Laws and Women, held to coincide with the Birthday of the Prophet's daughter Fatima, which is also Women's Day in Iran, this objection was phrased by an eminent lawyer, Dr Safa'i: 'many felt that the FPL, instead of protecting the family, simply served to protect women' (*Zan-e Ruz* 27/9/1372: 27).

Despite its different intention and rhetoric, the 1992 law, in practice, is bound to have a very similar impact to the FPL. By making divorce contingent upon the husband's payment of marital dues, the new amendments place the wife in a better bargaining position to negotiate the terms of her divorce than under FPL. If she is the party who seeks the dissolution of the marriage, by forgoing her *mahr* – which as practised in Iran is not only substantial but also legally payable upon her request – she is in a better position to obtain a *khul'* divorce. If he is the one who wants to terminate the marriage, by demanding her *ujrat al-mithl*, she can make her husband change his mind or even force him to provide her with a kind of alimony. However, by requiring every divorcing couple to go through the process of arbitration, these amendments are further complicating the whole process of negotiation that precedes any divorce, as well as creating a great deal of work for already overworked judges.

No study has been published (and probably none was ever done) of the actual working of the dismantled FPL in pre-revolutionary Iran, and we do not know how its courts operated, and to what extent men were prevented from exercising their right to divorce. What we do know is that its main beneficiaries were working middle-class women, who were seeking divorce and wanted to keep their children. In the Special Civil Courts (prior to the new amendments), by contrast, as my own work suggests, the beneficiaries are non-working women, entirely dependent on their husbands for support, and women who present no overt challenge to the patriarchal structure of the family. It remains to be seen to what extent these women can use the amendments, and the courts as an arena, to renegotiate the terms of their *Shari'a* marriage contracts. What is clear at this stage is that, at least in theory, the 1992 amendments do offer a better deal than the FPL did to women who enjoy little economic independence. It does make it impossible for men to exercise their *Shari'a* prerogatives with impunity. This sanction, I believe, can serve women such as my guide in Vanak better than equal rights in matters of divorce and child custody.

HEJAB: THE LAST DITCH

Let me now turn to a second field of operation of the *Shari'a* mandates in Iran, that of veiling or *hejab*. Unlike in the issue of divorce, here the early discourse rules supreme and there is no dissent, at least overtly. To understand why no debate is tolerated on *hejab*, we need to place it in context of the former regime's policies.

In 1936 Reza Shah banned the veil as part of his modernising crusade. Veiled women were arrested and had their veils forcibly removed. This not only outraged clerics but some ordinary women to whom appearing in public without their cover was tantamount to nakedness. Yet it was welcomed by others, both men and women, who saw it as a first step in granting women their rights. Since then, the *hejab* issue has become a deep wound in Iranian politics, arousing strong emotions on all sides. It also became a major arena of conflict between the forces of modernity and Islamic authenticity, where each side has projected its own vision of morality.[22]

Later the rules were relaxed, and after Reza Shah's abdication in 1941 the compulsory element in the policy of unveiling was abandoned, though the policy remained intact throughout the Pahlavi era. Between 1941 and 1979 wearing *hejab* was no longer an offence, but it was a real hindrance to climbing the social ladder, a badge of backwardness and a marker of class. A headscarf, let alone the *chador* (see p. 155), prejudiced the chances of advancement in work and society not only of working women but also of men, who were increasingly expected to appear with their wives at social functions. Fashionable hotels and restaurants refused to admit women with *chador*; schools and universities actively discouraged the *chador*, although the headscarf was tolerated. It was common to see girls from traditional families, who had to leave home with the *chador*, arriving at school without it and then putting it on again on the way home.

Just as the rules and meanings of *hejab* became more subtle and nuanced, so did the ways of promoting and defying it. In the 1970s, *hejab* represented what the Pahlavis had rejected, a symbol of both vice and virtue.[23] Apart from Islamist students, many middle-class urban working women took up the scarf to show their own rejection of the Shah's regime, which had good reasons to count on them as allies. Few of these women imagined that veiling would become obligatory if the Shah went (Betteridge 1983; Tabari 1986). In March 1979, when the intentions of the new regime became clear, these women once again took to the streets, this time to protest against the veil; but it was too late, and gradually but surely *hejab* became compulsory. In 1983, appearing in public unveiled became an offence, punishable by the 'Islamic' penalty of up to seventy-four lashes.[24] In 1994, there was not a single bare-headed woman to be seen in public anywhere in Iran. No woman could imagine venturing out without a head cover.

No one can doubt that the Islamic Republic has succeeded in veiling women (just as Reza Shah succeeded in unveiling them earlier), yet it is clear that it has failed to sell the ideal of *hejab* to many women, especially to the younger generation (just as the Pahlavis failed to obliterate it).[25] The *hejab* issue continues to dominate the political scene: the problem is now that of *bad-hejabi*, that is 'incorrect veiling'. The phenomenon is not confined to the middle-class streets of northern Tehran, where the latest hair-styles and fashions constantly push back – literally – the edges of the veil. It is most prevalent among school-girls, who started their schooling in a fully 'Islamised' system, the post-revolutionary generation who have not been exposed to the corrupting influences of the past.

Alarmed by the spread of *bad-hejabi*, in December 1987, the Women's Association of the Islamic Republic, whose general director is Zahra Mostafavi (Ayatollah Khomeini's daughter), took upon itself to establish a *Hejab* commission. After some deliberations, the commission – a number of women with close ties to the ruling elite – decided to tackle the problem in two 'moves', or operations. The first, designed to have an immediate and cutting impact, was accomplished by holding the rally of 'Vanguards of Chastity' (*tali'eh-daran-e 'efaf*). The second operation, intended to have a deep and long-term impact, entailed the creation of six subcommittees charged with conducting research in historical and contemporary aspects of the problem (*Neda* 1369, no. 3: 36–9).

The activities of one subcommittee, that responsible for Research on Ways to Combat the Banal Western Culture in Society, were outlined by its head in winter 1991. The research, which involved reviewing and indexing over 135 books, 32 radio programmes and 6 periodicals, focused on three major issues: factors leading to Western cultural penetration; people's disposition to them; and ways to counter Western cultural banality. The results on the first issue, as published in the form of three articles in consecutive numbers of the Association's journal *Neda* (1370/1, nos 8, 9 and 10), can be best described as a partial but orthodox version of the history and dynamics of Iran's relation with the West. The first article discusses the exploitative nature of these relations from the time of Shah 'Abbas, the Safavid King, to the present day; the second deals with the evolution of the clergy's opposition to Western culture; and the third explores the entry points through which Western culture penetrated into Iranian society, which include intellectuals, modern arts, media, and finally dress forms.[26]

In 1989, a more rigorous sociological investigation of the reasons for *bad-hejabi* was commissioned by the Social Affairs division of the Tehran Governor's Office. This initiative is noteworthy, not only as a response to the increasing defiance of *hejab* by young women in Tehran, but also in that it recognises the problem for the first time as socio-cultural rather than religious and contains some interesting insights. Until then the only strategies for confronting 'bad-veiling' were indoctrination (through schools, wall slogans and the media) and intimidation (by organised attacks on women in the street). The study is a revealing document in its own right, using the latest state-of-the-art socio-logical methodology to produce a totally non-sociological analysis.

Conducted by a team of university researchers, the study aims to uncover the underlying reasons behind the 'deviant behaviour of Tehrani women with respect to Islamic dress'. A random sample of 3,030 women are graded according to the degree of correctness of their *hejab*. The highest grade, that is the most correct form, goes to a black *chador* and *maqna'eh* worn together (*chador* is the traditional Persian veil, a loose sheet of cloth which covers the entire body except the face, and needs to be held by one hand under the chin; and the *maqna'eh* is a new kind of headgear which is secured under the chin and over the forehead). The second highest grade goes to *maqna'eh* on its own plus tunic and matching trousers; a non-black *chador*, that is a *chador* either slightly patterned or coloured, gets the same mark. The third grade goes to a plain scarf and tunic. The lowest grade goes to a coloured or patterned scarf or *chador*. Each of these four grades of dressing are further qualified by three other factors: the tightness of the outfit worn, together with the extent of hair shown; the heaviness of the make-up worn: and the thickness of stocking worn. On the basis of the above, the women in the sample are divided into categories in terms of the correctness of their *hejab*: extremely good *hejab*, good *hejab*, moderate *hejab*, bad *hejab*, and extremely bad *hejab*.

The findings were written up in a report of 361 pages, which includes 180 statistical tables, relating *hejab* to all conceivable socio-economic factors. Over 48 per cent of women are found to be 'bad-*hejab*', 23 per cent are 'good-*hejab*', and the rest moderate. (In the tables the categories of very good and good, or very bad and bad are respectively collapsed into good and bad *hejab*.) One of the major findings of the study is that 'in the category of moderate and good *hejab*, women follow an established model, thus they enjoy social cohesion, but *bad-hejab* women lack this cohesion and betray a great deal of diversity and individualism'. From this finding, the study concludes that *hejab* is now institutionalised, and that since *bad-hejabi* is not, it is possible to contain and eventually to eradicate it. Altogether seventeen recommendations are made, such as:

- women's status in society should be raised in harmony with cultural tradi-tions in order to prevent the sudden descent into *bad-hejabi* which appears to coincide with the start of a woman's marital life
- there should be no further investment in trying to change the attitudes of older women who lived under the previous regime

- the consumerist habits of the middle and upper middle classes should be controlled by means of the redistribution of wealth
- there should be a return to traditional forms of urban planning, to narrow streets and culs-de-sac, as wide streets and apartment blocks are found to be correlated with *bad-hejabi*.

The remaining thirteen recommendations are of the same genre, some of which, if taken seriously, would require another revolution on a much wider scale to ensure the full enforcement of *hejab*.

I have described these two initiatives in some detail so as to give an idea of the state of the debate over *hejab*, which, unlike that over divorce laws, not only lacks sophistication but also is detached from social reality.[27] This was not the case early in the revolution. A prominent woman physicist, who herself wore *hejab*, resigned in protest when it became compulsory in government offices. In her resignation statement she declared that the rule had no religious sanction and would ultimately negate the very purpose of *hejab*, whose observance must remain a personal decision, incumbent only on those who believe in it.[28] But today there is nothing of this scope and level in any of the women's papers, which choose not to bring the subject up.[29] Why?

Hejab is a powerful metaphor, capable of taking many shades of meaning and performing many functions. At an abstract level, some of the issues raised have been explored by others, notably Milani's (1992) study of the relationship between the veil and the literary silence of women in Iran. But at the tangible level of this chapter, I suggest that *hejab* has its own payoffs; and in the context of social life in Iran today it is an empowering tool for women.[30] What tends to be neglected here is that the enforcement of *hejab* can be as empowering as its ban, and that *hejab* is one of those issues where one group of women claims the right to speak for all women. As in other Muslim countries, in Iran the current orthodox form of *hejab* is largely an urban phenomenon, and an issue for educated and working women, marking the ascendancy of anti-Western and popular strands over those which prevailed a generation ago.

Also neglected is that, unlike on the issue of divorce, women in Iran have always been widely divided on the question of *hejab*. While it undoubtedly restricts some women, it emancipates others by giving them the permission, the very legitimacy for their presence in the public domain which has always been male-dominated in Iran. Many women today owe their jobs, their economic autonomy, their public persona, to compulsory *hejab*. There are women who have found in *hejab* a sense of worth, a moral high ground, especially those who could never fare well in certain elitist and Westernised sections of pre-revolutionary Iran, which was self-consciously obsessed with the display of wealth and beauty. This obsession goes a long way to explain the current regime's obsession with *hejab*, one of the aims of which is to keep beauty and wealth hidden. (It is a commonplace in current anti-*hejab* discourses in Iran that those women who support *hejab* are themselves either plain-looking or of modest circumstances or both.) In fact, one of the pleas for wearing *hejab*, as made in a guide for the young bride, tells her, 'sister, have mercy on those unfortunate women who might not be endowed with your youth and beauty; by not displaying your beauty and attracting the admiring eyes of their husbands, you are also keeping their marriage intact' (Division for Struggle Against Social Corruptions nd: 3). In a convoluted way, this is a plea for solidarity, which, although made by men on behalf of women, appeals to many women.

In a bizarre way, *hejab* has even empowered those whom it was meant to restrain: Westernised middle-class women. The regime's obsession with its enforcement has given these women, now marginalised, the means for making a mockery of one of its most explicit platforms. It is precisely because of the power and potential threat in such mockery that the regime cannot afford to show flexibility. There is too much at stake. This has given the traditional expression of women's power of subversion in patriarchal systems a different lease of life, a political edge that it has never had before in Iran.[31] These women have resisted the rule of compulsory *hejab* in ways similar to those described by James Scott in his *Weapons of the Weak* (1985), which lack any kind of organisation and indeed need no co-ordination or planning. Such resistance, which can be nothing more than individual acts of footdragging and evasion, may in the end make an utter shambles of the policies dreamed up by the powerful. Events in Iran in 1993–4 indicate a serious questioning of the legitimacy of the harshness with which *hejab* has at times been imposed, and that its hegemony is breaking down.

In September 1993, a 17-year-old girl was shot dead in affluent north Tehran because of her *bad-hejabi*. Although the shooting was not mentioned in the news bulletins of the day, by late afternoon everyone in north Tehran was talking about it. Two versions of the incident prevailed. In one, the girl was standing with her mother in a queue at the baker's, when a young officer from the newly created Vice Squad (*amr-e be-ma'ruf*, literally promoter of virtue) insulted her for her non-Islamic appearance: losing her temper, the girl tore her scarf off, and he shot her. In the second version, the girl was in a telephone booth when approached by the officer, who ordered her to adjust her scarf down. When she refused, he threatened her with the gun; she dared him to shoot, and he did. A crowd gathered; some took the girl to the hospital, where she died, while others attacked the officer, who barely escaped with his own life.

The rumours became so widespread that the Chief of Tehran Police (which now incorporates the revolutionary guards) had to issue a statement, aiming to set the record straight. He informed the public that the officer was not from the 'Vice Squad', whose members are not armed; he was an ordinary soldier, and it was his carelessness with his gun which led to the girl's death; it was an accident. The incident was also commented on by two women's papers, *Zan-e Ruz* (20/6/1372) and *Payam-e Hajar* (14/6/1372), the first reflecting the official version, the second using the occasion to reprimand the authorities for the non-Islamic turn which the whole issue of *hejab* has taken.

In another incident, in the city of Yazd, a Vice Squad officer, while carrying out his duty to correct a *bad-hejab* women, was beaten up by her angry husband and his friends. The incident was condemned by the Friday Prayer Leader of Yazd, and an official demonstration was held during which the safety and protection of the officers was demanded. The offender was tried and sentenced to a *diya* (compensation money) of 15,000 tomans and 45 lashes for the injuries that he caused the officer. As the officer waived the *diya*, the offender received only the lashes (*Jumhuri-ye Islami* 23/9/1372).

It is thus no exaggeration to say that what women should wear in public has become a dilemma not only for women themselves, but also for the Islamic Republic.

DEBATING WOMEN: AN EMERGING FEMINIST VOICE

Apart from the *hejab* issue, other early rulings of the Islamic Republic with regard to women have also been modified, which suggests that the early debates that were so harshly stifled a decade ago have now resurfaced (Ramazani 1993). The establishment women's press, namely *Zan-e Ruz*, has played an instrumental role in bringing about the recent *Majlis* rulings to remove the prohibitions which came into existence in 1980 barring women from studying certain subjects such as agriculture and mining. The only educational restriction that now remains is that barring female students from taking up scholarships to study abroad unless they are accompanied by either husbands or fathers/brothers.

Although limited and confined within the parameters of Islam, the current gender debates reveal a growing dissent from the earlier discourse of the Republic. In some ways one can say that recent *Majlis* rulings represent the establishment side of the debates. However, there is another side, which aligns itself with a new trend of thought in post-war and post-Khomeini Iran, grounded in a Shi'a discourse which is radically different from the official one.[32] This trend espouses a brand of 'feminism' which has the potential to change the very terms of post-revolutionary discourses on women. This is so because it is starting not only to challenge the hegemony of orthodox interpretations but also to question the very *Shari'a* legitimacy of the laws enforced by the Islamic Republic. These views are aired in *Zanan* (literally, Women), a women's magazine launched in 1992.

There are at least three significant facts about *Zanan*'s feminism and its line of argument which are novel whether in the Iranian or in the wider Muslim context. First, unlike pre-revolutionary discourses on women in Iran (both Islamic and secular), *Zanan*'s does not subordinate the women's issue to a wider political project, but advocates it in its own right. It appears to be an independent voice, not dictated by the state or a political party, advocated by women who are neither related by marriage or blood to the political elite, nor closely toeing the line of any political faction.[33]

Second, in line with feminist writings within the context of Islam,[34] and in contrast to other *Shari'a*-based writings on women,[35] *Zanan* holds that there is no inherent and logical link between patriarchy and Islamic ideals. It sees no contradiction between fighting for women's rights and remaining good Muslims, and makes no apologies for drawing on feminist sources to argue for women's rights and a new reading of *Shari'a* texts. Unlike other journals in Iran and a mass of Islamic apologetic literature elsewhere,[36] *Zanan* neither attempts to cover up nor to rationalise the gender inequalities that are embedded in many aspects of *Shari'a* law, but argues that they can all be addressed within the context of the *Shari'a* itself. However, unlike Muslim feminists elsewhere, *Zanan* discourse does not simply locate its feminist position within Islam but operates within the parameters of the political discourses and structures of an Islamic Republic. Such a position not only enables *Zanan* to break the old and tired dichotomy between Islam and feminism but also ensures that its arguments cannot be dismissed by the Islamists merely as 'corrupt and Western'.

Finally, this is made possible by the twin facts that in Iran Islam is no longer part of the discourse of opposition to the state and that those espousing *Zanan*'s brand of feminism enjoy legitimacy and argue from inside the Islamic discourse. These are women/men who not only subscribed to the *Shari'a* discourse on women as developed by Ayatollah Motahhari when it was still part of the Islamic opposition to the Pahlavis, but also helped to translate it from rhetoric to policy after the establishment of the Islamic Republic. It was during the process of this translation that some of them came to confront its inherent contradictions, a confrontation which brought about the awareness that they can find support in feminism, regardless of its Western baggage, but they can only meet resistance in patriarchy, regardless of its Islamic credentials.

Zanan's editor, Shahla Sherkat, and her colleagues were among those who helped to Islamise *Zan-e Ruz*, the glossy women's magazine of the pre-revolutionary period with the highest circulation. Sherkat was invited to join *Zan-e Ruz* in 1982 and remained its chief editor until 1991 when she was dismissed because of unresolved disagreement over the ways in which gender issues were being addressed. The first issue of *Zanan* appeared in February 1992, seven months later, to coincide with the thirteenth anniversary of the revolution. Its editorial imparts something of the nature of these disagreements which finally led to its birth. Referring to a decade of fighting against the centuries-old oppression of women in Iran, Sherkat writes:

> our experiences repeatedly tell us that awareness is a torch with which today's woman can step onto the dark paths of her destiny, without fearing the deep chasms that cross her every step. Women's awareness, without

doubt, is society's awareness, but access to this torch is impossible without the existence of freedom. The backbone of freedom is independence and the right to choose. But no independence is possible without knowledge and maturity.

(*Zanan*: 1991: 2)

Apart from consciousness-raising, *Zanan* assumes an advocacy role through addressing the disadvantages that women face in the realms of religion, culture, law and education. In culture, law and education, it argues for the urgent need for concentrated efforts to offset deep and age-old prejudices and inequalities. In religion, it argues for the urgency of progressive *ijtihad* (new rulings derived from Islamic law). Some of the articles related to *Shari'a* debates are written by a cleric in Qom, who until a year ago used a female pseudonym, Yadgar-e Azadi, which has also a symbolic meaning, 'the souvenir of freedom'. He takes issue with the very premises on which current Shi'a debates on the position of women are based, laying bare their inherent gender bias. His mastery of the Shi'a art of argumentation, coupled with his command of the sacred sources, give a different edge to his writings. Incidentally, the seminal text of this discourse, that is Ayatollah Motahhari's *Women's Rights in Islam* (1981), has its origins in a number of articles in *Zan-e Ruz* in the 1960s. Whereas then Motahhari used Western scholarship to explain the reasons and the necessity for the different treatment of women in Islam, the *Zanan* writer uses Shi'a scholarship to argue for the necessity of a new, feminist, reading of old texts.[37]

This new trend of thought appears to be having repercussions well beyond its small political base. It is even inducing its own counter-discourse, articulated by those women with close links with the political elite who have launched the first ever women's studies journal in Iran, *Farzaneh* (literally, wise or sage). As Najmabadi has observed,[38] the appearance of *Farzaneh* in autumn 1993 must be seen in connection with Sherkat's dismissal and the growing dissent within *Zan-e Ruz*, which led to the birth of *Zanan*.

In winter 1991, immediately after Sherkat's dismissal, Mahbubeh Ommi, who later became the editor of *Farzaneh*, wrote a series of articles in *Zan-e Ruz*, entitled 'Feminism from the beginning until now'. In these articles, Ommi contended that 'feminism' as a concept is alien to Islam and unnecessary to Muslim societies, although it is needed in the Western world where Judaeo-Christianity left little choice for women but to organise themselves to redress their disadvantages. In this way Ommi not only disparaged the stance taken by Sherkat and her allies, but also rejected 'feminism' as irrelevant for women in Iran. However, in an editorial to introduce the new journal, 'Why *Farzaneh*', her stance is rather different. While still rejecting organised and independent feminism, she argues for establishing the field of women's studies in Iran. Ommi writes that the 'women's question' is a universal one that stems from the 'characteristics of feminine nature' which manifests itself differently in different contexts. This makes it futile to address women's disadvantages in ways similar to those which stemmed from class, race and other differentiation. Instead she argues that the 'women's question' must be brought into the academic domain where it can be analysed and understood and where suitable strategies can be planned to redress it. Then the solutions found can be filtered into society at large, when 'experts' give their informed advice to policy-makers: in short a 'top-down' approach and prescription for feminism (*Farzaneh* 1370, 1: 4–5).

One can also detect a change of tone in *Zanan*'s rival, *Zan-e Ruz*, which has been highlighting the problems that women in Iran have to grapple with, drawing attention to gender inequalities in areas of education, health and employment, and exposing the deep-rooted misogyny evident in popular culture. Its December 1993 editorial, to mark Iranian Women's Week, was entitled 'The Presence of Women, Guarantee for the Sustainability of Development', and argued that there can be no sustainable development without women's active participation on all fronts. Similar concerns are expressed in all other journals, even in the national daily newspapers, the exception being *Payam-e Zan* (Women's Message), which is a women's monthly published in Qom. This journal, whose entire editorial board are men, is the only one which is still holding the early torch, and seems to be unaffected by these recent currents which have even caught the attention of some secular Iranian feminists who live in exile.[39]

CONCLUSION

How are these 'liberal' tendencies in Iran being viewed by the media and by women in Iran and outside, and how are they likely to develop in the years to come? Events are still unfolding and it is too early to draw firm conclusions, yet some preliminary observations can be made. First, the 1992 divorce amendments seem so far to have escaped the attention of the foreign press, which gave such acclaim in the late 1960s to the Shah's Family Protection Law. Why?

One reason must be that these developments do not fit with the image of Iran maintained in current discourses in the West. In Iran itself the recent amendments have not been met with unqualified euphoria but simply have been welcomed as a 'first step' in the right direction. In an article which appeared in *Zanan* in February 1993, Mehrangiz Kar, a woman lawyer, discusses the new amendments from a legal perspective, listing problems and legal tangles in terms of both substantive law and implementation. She contends that these amendments as they stand are not going to improve women's lot but should be viewed as a 'test'. A similar point was raised by the Women's Affairs division of the Tehran Governor's Office, two of whose members attended court sessions for a week in autumn 1993 to find out how the law was being implemented, and whether divorced women were receiving the 'domestic wages' to which the new law entitles them. In their report, they state that as long as men and women have unequal access to divorce, as long as the husband has the means to coerce his wife into giving her consent to a divorce desired by him, and as long as a woman has to compromise all her *Shari'a* rights to obtain her husband's consent to a divorce, the right to claim 'domestic wages' would offer women little protection. In another magazine article, a judge is interviewed on the implementation of the new law. Both the questions asked and the judge's response are indicative of their critical stance (*Navid-e Fazilat* no. 15, Shahrivar 1372: 10–13). The judge raises similar points to those raised by the lawyer in *Zanan*, and says that, as the law stands, the legislator's intention, which is to provide better protection for women, can easily be bypassed. He complains that the *Majlis* passed the law in haste without proper consultation with practising judges. In short, the 1992 law is seen as insufficient on its own, and more constructive changes are demanded.

When I eventually arrived at court on that day in September 1993, I learned that since the enactment of the 1992 divorce amendments there had been over a hundred cases of women demanding the *ujrat al-mithl*, 'domestic wages'. Yet the courts had not yet issued any judgement; the judges do not know what to make of the whole concept and find it legally irrelevant and inapplicable. And women coming to seek divorce are also not that happy with it; as my lawyer friend put it, 'what women need is something that puts them in the same negotiating position as their husbands'. I also learned that the new law is bound to be revised, since it is creating real legal problems for the courts. When we left the court, I told my lawyer friend what my guide had said about how children sometimes matter more than a husband to a woman. Her response was: 'Then we must suffer; we will never get anywhere unless we are prepared to leave our children behind; I promise you, it will be he who then comes begging for a compromise.'

By bringing home to women from all walks of life the harsh reality of what marriage can entail under the *Shari'a* when enforced by the modern state machinery, the Islamic Republic has acted as a catalyst for the emergence of what can be described as an indigenous – locally produced – feminist consciousness.[40] Such a consciousness has always been part of the experience of women in Iran, but, in Ardener's words (1975) in a 'muted' form, which is now slowly but surely finding its own voice, a mode of expression, and even a kind of legitimacy. More importantly, it is no longer confined to the private domain of the family, but has extended into the public arena. Today, concepts such as 'male dominance' and 'patriarchy' are increasingly used by ordinary women to make sense of their everyday experience. Interestingly, both concepts are collapsed into *mardsalari* (rule by men), which in subtle ways does not implicate all men: not a woman's father or brother, who are seen as her natural allies, but her husband whose power over her is officially encouraged, and more importantly the male political elite, who have endorsed it.[41] This term is familiar to all, debated on radio and television, and yet its meanings and connotations are different from what they used to be in pre-revolutionary Iran when the concept was taken by intellectuals from Western feminist discourses.[42]

What has facilitated this is the state's ideological understanding of Islam which, by demolishing the *de facto* divide between the personal and political, not only opens the way to challenge the hegemony of the orthodox inter-pretations of the *Shari'a* but also gives a new dimension to the tension inherent in its practice in the twentieth century. And it is this tension which has brought about the changes in divorce laws whose provisions, in theory, surpass those of pre-revolutionary laws in benefiting ordinary women. The tension is nowhere more evident than in the dispute between the *Majlis* and the Council of the Guardians over these changes. In March 1991 the Council, whose task is that of upholding the *Shari'a*, objected to the concept of 'household wages', as formulated by the law passed by the *Majlis*. The dispute between these two bodies was not resolved until November 1992, and then only through the intervention of the highest constitutional authority, the Assembly for Ascertaining the Regime's Interest (*Majma'-e Tashkhis-e Maslehat-e Nezam*). In December the new law came into effect, in an emasculated form, to the extent that it failed to achieve its objective, and became irrelevant in practice; hence there came another wave of protests, by the women's press and organisations, and even the judges, who objected that they had not been consulted. The divorce laws are once again due to be debated in the *Majlis*. It remains to be seen to what extent they will be grounded this time in court practices and the realities of marital disputes.

Meanwhile women in the courts and outside are making their voices heard and their presence felt; and the changed economic system, which has made it increasingly difficult for their husbands to be the only providers, is shaking the very foundation on which men's *Shari'a* rights rest. The changes in the divorce laws and the absence of changes in the *hejab* laws are but a moment in a process set into motion when the Islamic Republic was born. This process has inadvertently been nurturing an indigenous 'feminism' which is as much rooted in Iranian family structures as it is in the interaction of Islamic and Western ideals of womanhood. It could emerge only after challenging and rejecting the state-sponsored and Western-inspired 'feminism' of the Pahlavis, as well as the liberal-leftist feminism of 1970s women's liberation, and yet in the process assimilating some of the features of both.

ACKNOWLEDGEMENTS

An earlier draft of this chapter was presented in a lecture series on 'Feminism and Islamic Law: Contextual Approaches', convened by the Centre of Islamic and Middle Eastern Law, University of London. I am grateful to Mai Yamani, the convener of the series, and to Richard Tapper and Azam Torab for critical readings of the paper.

NOTES

1 E.g. Afshar (1982; 1987; 1989; 1994); Sanasarian (1982; 1992); Azari (1983);
  Mahdavi (1985); Nashat (1983); Tabari (1986); Tabari and Yeganeh (1982); Reeves
  (1989); Adelkhah (1991); Ramazani (1993); V. Moghadam (1988, 1993); Haeri
  (1989, 1994); Omid (1994); Najmabadi (1991; 1994); Afkhami and Friedl (1994).
   Interestingly, a large portion of the second wave of this literature is produced
  by the same authors, some of them under different names (some originally wrote
  under pseudonyms, others are now adopting them). This literature, I believe,
  should be treated as a particular discourse about Iranian women, namely that of
  the secular feminists, some with leftist inclinations, who left Iran shortly after
  the revolution. Some of these women, mainly those active in or sympathetic to
  leftist organisations, never returned to Iran but retained a keen interest in post-
  revolutionary developments as they affect women. The Persian-language feminist
  journal, *Nimeh-ye Digar*, published in North America, has been a forum for some
  of them. Elsewhere, I examine this literature and its discourse in a larger project
  of which this chapter is a part.
   Another genre of literature on women in post-revolutionary Iran is produced
  by some Western women anthropologists, such as Higgins (1985); Betteridge (1983);
  Hegland (1983); Friedl (1983; 1989; 1994); Bauer (1993).
2 For an insightful discussion of the inappropriateness of Western ideologies of
  emancipation to the Iranian situation, see Moore (1988: 173–8).
3 It is with great reservation that I use the term feminism, even in Moore's mini-
  malist definition. There is no equivalent term for it in Persian, although as a
  consciousness it has always existed. This consciousness in its indigenous forms
  remains largely unexplored in the Muslim context. Studies of feminism in the
  Muslim world predominantly deal with its expression among the Westernised and
  educated elite and align it with its Western counterpart.
4 *Talaq-e ruj'i* is a suspended form of divorce which becomes final only when the
  wife completes three menstrual cycles. All divorces are *ruj'i* unless they are initiated by the wife, who secures her husband's consent by offering him an induce-
  ment to release her (*khul'* or *mubarat*); or they meet one of the following conditions:
  if the marriage has not been consummated; if the woman is past her menopause;
  if she has not reached the age of menstruation; or if it is the third successive
  divorce. On forms and procedures of divorce in the *Shari'a* as practised in Iran,
  see Mir-Hosseini (1991: 36–41, 54–83).
5 There is also a tendency to divorce the *Shari'a* from the wider context within which
  it is meaningful, for instance as in Afshar's (1987) and Najmabadi's (1994: 374)
  evaluation of return to *Shari'a* after the revolution. As I have argued elsewhere,
  no understanding of Islamic law and what it entails for women is complete without
  examining its practice, i.e. how it is applied in courts, and how individuals use it
  to settle their marital disputes. For example, despite overt inequalities between the
  rights of men and women within Muslim marriage, there are mechanisms both
  in Islamic law and in social practice which can balance the situation. In Iran, one
  cannot examine divorce and women's access to it without considering the central
  role of *mahr* (dower, an integral part of every Muslim marriage contract), and the
  ways that women use this Islamic institution in order to determine the terms of
  continuation or dissolution of their marriages (Mir-Hosseini 1993: 72–83).
6 For an English translation of the FPL, see Naqavi (1967).
7 The letter was issued 26 February 1979; see Tabari and Yeganeh (1982: 232).
8 For instance, see Al-Hirbi (1982); Mernissi (1991).
9 For popularist bases of the revolution, see Abrahamian (1993).

10 On this, see Najmabadi (1994); Sanasarian (1992); Ramazani (1993); Haeri (1994); Moghadam (1993).

11 For an account of the Women's Organisation of Iran, see Sanasarian (1982) and for an early account of Taleqani's organisation, see Tabari and Yeganeh (1982: 223–7).

12 Those who were purged from the offices were women who were seen as following a Western model of womanhood. Some left the country, and many of those who stayed resigned or took early retirement as they found the new working conditions intolerable.

13 There are contrasting views on this; while some argue that women's higher participation in the labour force is reflected in official statistics (V. Moghadam 1988), others refute this (Omid 1994; F. E. Moghadam 1994).

14 Otherwise these women would not have qualified to stand in the first place; every candidate is screened by a pre-electoral committee which examines their 'Islamic' credentials. There is also an extended interview with two of these women in which they talk of their achievements and frustrations in the *Majlis*, confirming that they see their role as promoting women's rights on Islamic lines. For instance, Mrs Dabagh states: 'out of 270 deputies in the *Majlis* only 4 are women. No matter how hard these four try, they cannot discuss a high percentage of women's Islamic needs and rights in the *Majlis* and have them legislated' (*Neda*, 1370, no. 6: 16–30).

15 The interview is indeed a revealing account of the *Majlis*'s perception of its female members. For instance, Nateq Nuri states: 'the sisters that we have in this *Majlis* are all educated, enlightened and cultured; of course this is not to say that the sisters in the previous *Majlis* were not . . . the other day I was astonished to hear a sister saying really sensible things and expressing 'expert' opinions in a debate on . . . which was indeed a specialized topic; we have even one sister who is in our legal committee . . . sisters now take part in many debates, but they are most active with regards to matters concerning sisters and women' (*Zan-e Ruz*, 13/9/1372, nos 1437 and 1438: 15).

16 For women in the constitution, see Nashat (1983: 195–216), Sanasarian (1982: 138–9); for women's debates in the Assembly of Experts at the time of the constitution, see Esfandiari (1994: 63–9); and for how these contradictions in practice provide room for manoeuvre, see Sanasarian (1992), V. Moghadam (1993: 171–82) and Ramazani (1993).

17 Which reads: 'since the family is the fundamental unit of an Islamic society, all relevant laws, regulations and policies must facilitate its formation, guard its sanctity and ensure its relations according to Islamic rules and morals'.

18 Which reads 'a man can divorce his wife whenever he wants'.

19 Polygamy is an area of Islamic law where the conflict between law and social practice is most acute. For a discussion of the tensions involved, see Mir-Hosseini (1993: 127–8).

20 It has been suggested that the FPL 'represents a brief interlude in the otherwise continuous application of the *Shari'a*' (Higgins 1985: 479), and had no bearing on the lives of women from the popular classes. But as I have argued elsewhere, the impact of these reforms should not be sought merely in the extent to which they reach all sectors of the society, but in their power to provide a frame of reference which can be used in justifying demands and expressing grievances in the course of a marital dispute (Mir-Hosseini 1993: 191–4).

21 On the evolution and procedures of Family courts in post-revolutionary Iran, see (Mir-Hosseini 1993, especially chs 1 and 2).

22 For a discussion on this, see Najmabadi (1991; 1994); Haeri (1994).

23 For a fuller treatment of this, see the above sources.

24 Article 102 of Islamic Punishments (*ta'zirat*) passed in 1983.
25 Highly religious women, who have always worn the traditional form of *chador*, dismiss the new form of veiling, which they call *bi-hejabi* (without *hejab*). They appear to have their own definition of *hejab*, which is not the same as that promoted by the authorities. I am indebted to Azam Torab for this point.
26 The subcommittee's findings on the other two issues have not yet been made available.
27 Another study, this time by a psychologist, Shahriar Ruhani (1369/1990), purports to demonstrate why and how the observance of *hejab* can enable women to attain independence and psychological well-being, given that their psychological make-up is radically different from that of men.
28 See also speeches made by Azam Taleqani and others in 1979 (Tabari and Yeganeh 1982: 171–200).
29 There is, however, a passing reference to *hejab* in *Adineh* (a cultural and social journal) whose special 1373 *Nowruz* (Iranian New Year, 21 March 1994) issue is devoted to 'Women of Iran' (*Adineh*, no. 90–1: 73).
30 For instance, on Iran see Adelkhah (1991: 198–215); V. Moghadam (1993: 179–80); Haeri (1994: 107–14). On Egypt see El-Guindi (1981) and on Turkey, Delaney (1994).
31 Women's power to subvert the patriarchal order is well documented. For some examples, see Hatem (1986); Kandiyoti (1988).
32 This trend of thought has its clerical core in Qom, on which little has been reported; and its intellectual core in Tehran, gathered around Dr Abdul Karim Sorush. He was one of the masterminds of the so-called 'Cultural Revolution' of 1980–2. Whereas then he engaged in debates with those who were then labelled as liberals, now he is engaging a debate with those who are defined as 'hard-liners'. For a journalistic account, see R. Wright's article in the *Guardian* (1 February 1995).
33 For women in pre-revolutionary resistance movements in Iran, see S. Afshar (1983); Moghissi (1993); Shahshahani (1984); and emerging feminist voices in the wake of the revolution, see Tabari (1986).
34 For instance, secular Muslim feminists such as Mernissi (1991) and Ahmed (1992).
35 In the Shi'a context, the writings of Ayatollah Motahhari are most prominent, reproduced almost verbatim in numerous publications after the revolution. A new version of Motahhari's thesis, put forward in a book by Ayatollah Javadi-Amoli in 1992, was critically reviewed by *Zanan* (cf. Mir-Hosseini 1995). For a review of similar literature in the Sunni context, see Stowasser (1993).
36 This literature is characterised by opposition to feminism (as it is seen to advocate both secularism and Westernisation) and a defensive or apologetic tone (justifying the *Shari'a* treatment of women).
37 For an analysis of the legal articles of *Zanan*, see Mir-Hosseini (1995).
38 In a lecture delivered February 1994 at the School of Oriental and African Studies, University of London, sponsored by the Iranian Community Centre of London.
39 For instance, Najmabadi (ibid.) gave an interesting discussion of *Zanan*, in which she stated that she could enter a dialogue with the journal since she considered that it was prepared to question the 'foundationalism' of the Islamic discourse on women.
40 It is puzzling that this consciousness is either ignored in the literature, or, if it receives attention, appears to be quite misunderstood, as in Friedl's interesting but flawed discussion (1994). Friedl starts by arguing that 'women not only can be both oppressed and powerful simultaneously, but … they can derive power to effect changes in their own and others' affairs from the very relations of inequality that define their position' (1994: 151), yet she ends up concluding that in doing

so women not only fail to challenge 'the existing hierarchy of domination' but help to cement 'the gendered system of super- and subordination' (1994: 167). Her conclusions are largely shaped by the assumption that 'legitimate sources of power for women become increasingly scarce in an androcentric, male-dominated society such as the Islamic Republic of Iran' (1994: 166). Not only does she ignore the paradoxical ways in which, as we have seen, the Islamic Republic has empowered women, but also she negates the very basis of her own argument by devaluing women's strategies and seeing them as doomed.

41 For the ways in which pious women are now separating their faith from the ideology of the state, see Kamalkhani (1993); Torab (1994).

42 In summer 1994, in a village near Arak, I found myself discussing *mardsalari* with a 17-year-old girl who spends winters in Qom and summers in the village. She first heard the term in a discussion broadcast by the Voice of America on gender biases in Islam, and heard its refutation on the national radio. In her words, '*mardsalari* is when women are imposed on; and it is done in many families and in many situations, but not always, and not on every issue.' She was clearly defining the term in the light of her own experiences. Research needs to be done on how this gender concept, and others that are now gaining currency, are being constructed by ordinary women, by the press, media and the law.

REFERENCES

Abrahamian, E. (1993) *Khomeinism: Essays on Islamic Republic*, Berkeley, CA: University of California Press.

Adelkhah, F. (1991) *La Révolution sous le voile: femmes islamiques d'Iran*, Paris: Karthala.

Ahmed, L. (1992) *Women and Gender in Islam: Historical Roots of a Modern Debate*, New Haven, CT: Yale University Press.

Afkhami, M. and Friedl, E. (eds) (1994) *In the Eye of the Storm: Women in post-Revolutionary Iran*, New York: Syracuse University Press.

Afshar, H. (1982) 'Khomeini's Teachings and their Implications for Iranian Women', in A. Tabari and N. Yeganeh (eds) *In the Shadow of Islam*, London: Zed.

Afshar, H. (1987) 'Women, Marriage and the State in Iran', in H. Afshar (ed.) *Women, State and Ideology: Studies from Africa and Asia*, Albany, NY: SUNY Press.

Afshar, H. (1989) 'Women and Reproduction in Iran', in N. Yuval-Davis and F. Anthias (eds) *Women-Nation-State*, London: Macmillan.

Afshar, H. (1994) 'Why Fundamentalism? Iranian Women and their Support for Islam', Working Paper 2, York: University of York Department of Politics.

Afshar, S. (1983) 'The Attitude of the Iranian Left to the Women's Question', in F. Azari (ed.) *Women in Iran*, London: Ithaca.

Alghar, H. (1985) *Islam and Revolution: Writings and Declarations of Imam Khomeini*, Berkeley, CA: Mizan.

Anon. (nd) '*Ayam-e Mobarak-bad beh Khanevadeh-ye 'Arus va Damad*' (Congratulatory Message to the Family of the Bride and Groom), prepared and distributed by Division for Struggle Against Social Corruptions, Tehran.

Ardener, E. (1975) 'Belief and the Problem of Women', in S. Ardener (ed.) *Perceiving Women*, London: Dent.

Azari, F. (ed.) (1983) *Women of Iran*, London: Ithaca.

Bagley, F. R. C. (1971) 'The Iranian Family Protection Law of 1967: A Milestone in the Advance of Women's Rights', in C. E. Bosworth (ed.) *Iran and Islam*, Edinburgh: Edinburgh University Press.

Banani, A. (1961) *The Modernization of Iran*, Stanford, CA: Stanford University Press.

Bauer, J. (1993) 'Ma'ssoum's Tale: The Personal and Political Transformations of a Young Iranian "Feminist" and her Ethnographer', *Feminist Studies* 19(3): 519–49.

Betteridge, A. (1983) 'To Veil or not to Veil: A Matter of Protest or Policy', in G. Nashat (ed.) *Women and Revolution in Iran*, Boulder, CO: Westview.

Delaney, C. (1994) 'Untangling the Meaning of Hair in Turkish Society', *Anthropological Quarterly*, 67(4): 159–72.

El-Guindi, F. (1981) 'Veiling Infitah with Muslim Ethic: Egypt's Contemporary Islamic Movement', *Social Problems* 28(4): 464–85.

Esfandiari, H. (1994) 'The Majles and Women's Issues in the Islamic Republic of Iran', in M. Afkhami and E. Friedl (eds) *In the Eye of the Storm: Women in Post-Revolutionary Iran*, New York: Syracuse University Press.

Friedl, E. (1983) 'State Ideology and Village Women', in G. Nashat (ed.) *Women and Revolution in Iran*, Boulder, CO: Westview.

Friedl, E. (1989) *Women of Deh Koh: Lives in an Iranian Village*, Washington DC: Smithsonian Press.

Friedl, E. (1994) 'Sources of Female Power in Iran', in M. Afkhami and E. Friedl (eds) *In the Eye of the Storm: Women in Post-Revolutionary Iran*, New York: Syracuse University Press.

Haeri, S. (1989) *Law of Desire: Temporary Marriage in Iran*, London: Tauris.

Haeri, S. (1994) 'Temporary Marriage: An Islamic Discourse on Female Sexuality in Iran', in M. Afkhami and E. Friedl (eds) *In the Eye of the Storm: Women in Post-Revolutionary Iran*, New York: Syracuse University Press.

Hatem, M. (1986) 'The Politics of Sexuality and Gender in Segregated Patriarchal Systems: The Case of Eighteenth- and Nineteenth-Century Egypt', *Feminist Studies* 12(2): 250–74.

Hegland, M. (1983) 'Aliabad Women: Revolution as Religious Activity', in G. Nashat (ed.) *Women and Revolution in Iran*, Boulder, CO: Westview.

Higgins, P. (1985) 'Women in the Islamic Republic of Iran: Legal, Social and Ideological Changes', *Signs* 10(3): 477–95.

Hinchcliffe, D. (1968) 'The Iranian Family Protection Act', *International and Comparative Law Quarterly*, 17.

al-Hirbi, A. (1982) 'A Study of Islamic Herstory: Or How Did We Ever Get into This Mess?, in A. al-Hirbi (ed.) *Women and Islam*, New York: Pergamon.

Kamalkhani, Z. (1993) 'Women's Everyday Religious Discourse in Iran', in H. Afshar (ed.) *Women in the Middle East: Perceptions, Realities and Struggles for Liberation*, London: Macmillan.

Kandiyoti, D. (1988) 'Bargaining With Patriarchy', *Gender and Society* 2(3): 274–90.

Mahdavi, S. (1985) 'The Position of Women in Shi'a Iran: Views of the Ulama', in E. Fernea (ed.) *Women and the Family in the Middle East: New Voices of Change*, Austin, TX: University of Texas Press.

Mernissi, F. (1991) *Women and Islam: An Historical and Theological Enquiry*, Oxford: Blackwell.

Milani, F. (1992) *Veils and Words: The Emerging Voices of Iranian Women Writers*, New York: Syracuse University Press.

Mir-Hosseini, Z. (1993) *Marriage on Trial; A Study of Islamic Family Law: Iran and Morocco Compared*, London: Tauris.

Mir-Hosseini, Z. (1995) 'Stretching the Limits: A Feminist Reading of the Shari'a in Iran Today', in M. Yamani (ed.) *Feminism and Islamic Law*, London: Ithaca.

Moghadam, F. E. (1994) 'Commoditization of Sexuality and Female Labor Participation in Islam: Implications for Iran', in M. Afkhami and E. Friedl (eds) *In the Eye of the Storm: Women in Post-Revolutionary Iran*, New York: Syracuse University Press.

Moghadam, V. (1988) 'Women, Work, and Ideology in the Islamic Republic', *International Journal of Middle Eastern Studies* 20: 221–43.

Moghadam, V. (1993) *Modernizing Women: Gender and Social Change in the Middle East*, Boulder, CO: Lynne Rienner.

Moghissi, H. (1993) 'Women in the Resistance Movement in Iran', in H. Afshar (ed.) *Women in the Middle East: Perceptions, Realities and Struggles for Liberation*, London: Macmillan.

Moore, H. (1988) *Feminism and Anthropology*, London: Polity.

Motahhari, M. (1981) *The Rights of Women in Islam*, Tehran: World Organization for Islamic Service.

Najmabadi, A. (1991) 'Hazards of Modernity and Morality: Women, State and Ideology in Contemporary Iran', in D. Kandiyoti (ed.) *Women, Islam and the State*, London: Macmillan.

Najmabadi, A. (1994) 'Power, Morality, and the New Muslim Womanhood', in M. Weiner and A. Banuazizi (eds) *The Politics of Social Transformation in Afghanistan, Iran and Pakistan*, New York: Syracuse University Press.

Naqavi, A. R. (1967) 'The Family Protection Act', *Islamic Studies* 6: 241–66.

Nashat, G. (1983) 'Women in the Ideology of the Islamic Republic', in G. Nashat (ed.) *Women and Revolution in Iran*, Boulder, CO: Westview.

Omid, H. (1994) *Islam and the Post-Revolutionary State in Iran*, London: Macmillan.

Ramazani, N. (1993) 'Women in Iran: The Revolutionary Ebb and Flow', *Middle East Journal* 47(3): 409–28.

Reeves, M. (1989) *Female Warriors of Allah: Women and the Islamic Revolution*, New York: Dutton.

Ruhani, S. (1369/1990) *Aya hejab zarurat darad? mas'aleh-ye pushidegi az didgah-e ravan-shenashi* (Is *hejab* necessary? The question of covering from a psychological perspective), Tehran: Eshraqiyeh Press.

Sanasarian, E. (1982) *The Women's Rights Movement in Iran*, New York: Praeger.

Sanasarian, E. (1992) 'Politics of Gender and Development in the Islamic Republic of Iran', *Journal of Developing Societies* 8: 56–68.

Scott, J. C. (1985) *Weapons of the Weak: The Everyday Forms of Peasant Resistance*, New Haven, CT: Yale University Press.

Shahshahani, S. (1984) 'Religion, Politics and Society: A Historical Perspective on the Women's Movement in Iran', *Samya Shakti* 1(2): 100–20.

Stowasser, B. (1993) 'Women's Issues in Modern Islamic Thought', in J. E. Tucker (ed.) *Arab Women: Old Boundaries, New Frontiers*, Bloomington, IN: Indiana University Press.

Tabari, A. (1982a) 'Islam and the Struggle for Emancipation of Iranian Women', in A. Tabari and N. Yeganeh (eds) *In the Shadow of Islam*, London: Zed.

Tabari, A. (1982b) 'The Enigma of the Veiled Iranian Women', *Middle East Research and Information Project Reports* 12(2): 22–7.

Tabari, A. (1986) 'The Women's Movement in Iran: A Hopeful Prognosis', *Feminist Studies* 12(2): 342–60.

Tabari, A. and Yeganeh, N. (eds) (1982) *In the Shadow of Islam*, London: Zed.

Taleqani, A. (1370/1991) 'Fa'aliatha-ye Dah Saleh-ye Mo'assaseh-ye Islami-ye Zanan-e Iran' (Ten Years of Activities of the Islamic Organization of Iranian Women), in *Daftar-e Dowom: Masa'el-e Zanan (Second Volume: Women's Issues)*, Tehran: 1–10.

Torab, A. (1994) 'Piety as Gendered Agency', seminar paper, Department of Anthropology, School of Oriental and African Studies, University of London.

Wright, R. (1995) 'An Iranian Luther Shakes the Foundations of Islam', *Guardian* 1 February.

FURTHER READING

Fariba Adelkhah's (1991) *La Révolution sous le voile: femmes islamiques d'Iran*, is an anthropologist's account of life in post-revolutionary Iran, seen from the perspective of Islamic/Islamist women. Based on sixteen months' fieldwork in Tehran (between 1985 and 1987) and on interviews with seventy-two women of varied backgrounds – though all with a strong religious commitment – the book discusses aspects of religious practice, marriage, Islamic dress, and general participation in the life of the capital. The author avoids (or rather exposes the inadequacy of) stereotypes of women in Islam, arguing that far from being mute and passive in the face of an imposed Islamic ideology, these women see themselves, in their very varied ways, as articulate agents with some control of the conditions of their life. The book is rich in insights and a welcome contrast to the usual feminist writings on Iranian women, with which the author is thoroughly familiar.

Leila Ahmed's (1992) *Women and Gender in Islam: Historical Roots of a Modern Debate*, explores the historical roots and development of Islamic discourses on women and gender from the ancient Middle East to modern Arab societies. Its main thesis is that in conquering other civilisations early Islam came to adopt their gender systems, and that in its gradual evolution Islam lost its egalitarian gender vision and became hierarchical and sexist; its exposure to Western societies led to dramatic social change and the emergence of a new discourse on women. The book not only counters stereotypes of Islam but also poses a challenge to Muslim apologists.

Ziba Mir-Hosseini's (1993) *Marriage on Trial: A Study of Islamic Family Law* is about family law in theory and practice in two Muslim societies: Iran and Morocco. Based on fieldwork in the courts and outside, as well as on extensive analyses of both law books and court records, the book focuses on the dynamics of marriage and the consequences of its breakdown, as well as the way in which litigants manipulate the law in order to resolve marital difficulties. Taking an interdisciplinary approach which straddles law and anthropology, the book shows how women use the court system to renegotiate the terms of their Shari'a marriage contract, and how they can turn the very rules that give men power in marriage to contain that power and bring it in line with their personal marital aims.

Chapter 10

The women's movement, feminism and the national struggle in Palestine
Unresolved contradictions

Kathy Glavanis-Grantham

On 13 July 1992, a press conference organised by all four Palestinian women's committees was held in East Jerusalem under the title 'No To Intellectual Oppression'. The four speakers on the panel were, in typical Palestinian style, chosen with care to give representation to the spectrum of political and social forces that constitute the bulwark of the wider nationalist and women's movements: a leading activist from one of the women's committees, a well-known and nationally respected figure in a number of Nablus-based women's charitable societies, a university lecturer of English literature who has written on issues of feminism and national liberation, and most important of all, Faisal al-Hussaini, the only man, the leader of the Advisory Group to one of the first Palestinian peace delegation and the acknowledged figurehead of Fateh, the largest political organisation in the Occupied Territories. The immediate reason for the calling of the press conference was the receiving of a number of threatening letters from 'fundamentalist Islamic groups during the Women's Film Festival in Jerusalem in June' 1992,[1] an event organised by the Women's Studies Centre, the only women's organisation to my knowledge with an acknowledged commitment to a feminist agenda.[2] The speakers and audience affirmed that this was not an isolated incident, but was representative of a continuing assault on Palestinian women and their freedom of expression, which has primarily focused on the imposition of a dress code, where short sleeves, tights, and uncovered heads are equated with immoral behaviour. Analyses and suggested solutions varied, depending on gender and politics, ranging from al-Hussaini's focus on the lack of popular committees and a call for their reintroduction, to the lack of democracy within Palestinian society and institutions in general, and the specific call for a more active participation of women in these bodies.[3]

This event portrays in a microcosm the underlying dynamics and contradictions at play in the current Palestinian women's and nationalist movements within the Occupied Territories and the relationship between the two. First, it usually takes a crisis situation to address a 'social' issue within the Palestinian political context. The Ramallah venue of the Women's Film Festival had to be cancelled because of threats to the institution meant to host it, while members of the panel and audience admitted the widespread nature of the phenomenon. The main parameters of the organisation of the event and the discussion which ensued were nationalist and political, with a stress on the importance of unity. Both al-Hussaini and the women speakers, including members of the audience, stressed the necessity of a transformation in political organisation, with popular committees,[4] an essentially male domain, being the answer for al-Hussaini, while women participants stressed the need for greater democracy and the incorporation of larger numbers of women within the existing political structures. Within the women's movement in Palestine, democratisation essentially is used to refer to the inclusion of women in the political decision making process and remains an oblique but acceptable way of addressing gender inequality within Palestinian society. The composition of the panel ensured that the press conference was seen to be based on a consensus and represented a unified, nationalist position. A demographic, geographic and political cross-section of representatives was selected to give weight and legitimacy to the event and the issue at hand: women's oppression by Islamic 'fundamentalists'. Older, more traditional charitable society members, younger, more radical progressive women's committee activists, and professional, urban-based, middle-class independents were all represented. Finally, the inclusion of Faisal al-Hussaini is indicative of the women's committees' vulnerability in addressing publicly controversial social issues on their own and their need for political and male protection *vis à vis* the Islamic 'fundamentalists'. The presence of such a well-respected and mainstream political male personality is seen by the women's committees as one of the most effective means of counteracting charges of immoral and anti-nationalist behaviour by the more conservative elements in Palestinian society.

Although the Palestinian women's movement in the Occupied Territories has undergone considerable change and expansion since the late 1970s and early 1980s, when the four main women's committees affiliated to the four major political groups operating in the Occupied Territories were first established, much has remained the same.[5] At that time, women political activists from the main political parties came together to form specifically women's organisations in order to broaden the struggle for national liberation and to enhance women's role in this process.[6] Women's equality within the national movement and the political process was assumed to be gained primarily through education and women's integration into the workforce. It was thought that once women were educated and employed, their political consciousness would be raised to the necessary level for their participation on an equal footing with men in the political organisations and institutions within Palestinian society. Hence, all of the women's committees, despite their political differences, organised literacy programmes, established nurseries and kindergartens to facilitate working mother-members, and promoted income generation projects to lessen women's economic dependence and provide them with useful, remunerative skills.

Thus, from the very start, the contours, parameters and contradictions characterising the women's movement were set. The women's movement in general was inextricably part of the wider nationalist movement and in particular the women's committees were affiliated to separate political organisations and were organised by activist women from these organisations. This period of Palestinian history witnessed the proliferation of a whole variety of grass-roots committees, as the officially underground and illegal resistance organisations attempted to broaden their membership at a more popular level, especially after the 1982 Israeli invasion of Lebanon and the subsequent forced dispersal of PLO fighters from the area which made the option of armed struggle considerably more difficult. This was a crucial period in the development of a Palestinian national consciousness which gained its form and content through the daily acts of resistance and defiance against Israeli oppression and the denial of their national rights. As a result, regardless of the diversity among the political organisations and their affiliated committees as to ideology, the common and unifying agenda was national liberation and self-determination.[7] All other agendas, such as gender and class, were for the most part relegated as secondary and were seen essentially as relevant issues for post-independence society.

As women's organisations, the programmes of the committees were indistinguishable from those supported by the more traditional charitable societies. Income-generation projects were essentially an extension of women's domestic work, although some of the committees attempted to transform social relations through the establishment of small-scale co-operatives and to teach non-traditional female skills such as brasswork. As a movement, it gave expression to a female and not a feminist consciousness,[8] based on 'women's awareness of their rights within the prevailing division of labour and dominant ideology'.[9] That is, the contemporary Palestinian women's movement at its inception had no feminist agenda based on a feminist consciousness, i.e. 'women's awareness of their subordinate position within a cultural and power system and the articulation of a specifically female perspective on the social process'[10]

Thus, from its inception, the contemporary Palestinian women's movement in the Occupied Territories was built on inherent and objective contradictions and limitations. Although the women's committees focused their recruitment along gender lines, the primary content of their agenda was political and nationalistic. And as the focus was on the national struggle, the rhetoric of unity was predominant in spite of the underlying political differences and competition among the four committees and their parent political organisations.

This particular configuration of forces and conditions which shaped the formation of the contemporary Palestinian women's movement had long-term repercussions on its future development, making the transformation of the committees into a united, independent democratic women's movement, with a clearly defined 'social' agenda, the goal espoused by all of the four major women's committees to a varying degree, a seemingly impossible achievement.

Today, as indicated by the July press conference, the women's movement in particular and women's freedom and liberties in general are under attack by conservative social and political forces in Palestinian society. Although this opposition is expressed religiously and is spearheaded by *Hamas*[11] the Arabic acronym of the Islamic Resistance Movement founded in early 1988, it, like everything else in Palestinian society, represents primarily a contending political agenda which is vying for a larger constituency among Palestinians in the Occupied Territories.[12] At the same time, the women's movement is currently passing through a stage of self-criticism and re-evaluation. In May 1992, the Women's Research and Development Committee of the Bisan Research and Development Centre, Ramallah, organised a seminar under the title, 'Palestinian Women's Organisations and Democracy'.[13] The three seminar papers presented by female academics from Birzeit University, although one is also a committee activist, focused on the lack of democracy within Palestinian society at large and within the women's committees in particular. The activist and co-ordinator of the Bisan's Women's Committee, Eileen Kuttab, went so far as to say that 'the women's committees as they are currently constituted are elite groupings of women that do not represent the interests of the majority of Palestinian women, whom they have left as prey either to liberal western ideology or to Islamic fundamentalist ideology'.[14] She called for the expansion of leadership cadres 'and the base of Palestinian women's committees with new and different elements: these new elements must include young people and working class people and they must be incorporated into the decision-making process'.[15] A secondary criticism of both the women's committees and the nationalist movement was the continued absence of 'a complete social program which addresses the needs of Palestinian women',[16] the fifth out of six recommendations summarised at the close of the seminar. An even more scathing critique of the women's committees was expressed by Fadwa Labadi, a women's committee activist associated with the Jerusalem Women's Studies Centre, on the occasion of International Women's Day in March, 1992.[17]

> we have yet to witness a women's movement which has addressed the concrete and fundamental issues directly related to women. . . . What has our women's movement achieved for Palestinian women? Nothing. The women's movement has become paralysed, and disease has spread through its veins. The masses have left and the movement is not in a position to bring them back. . . . I think the most important demand women can raise on this day is that their leadership be put on trial. . . . The movement must demand a re-evaluation of its work. We must move from the reiteration of empty slogans to the implementation of our demands.[18]

This mood is a far cry from the heady and exuberant days of the first year and a half of the Intifada, at which time most women activists and commentators praised in near unequivocal fashion the social and political transformation occurring within Palestinian society in general and in women's role and position within it.[19] Women were seen to have broken the traditional patriarchal barriers to an activist role in the nationalist struggle, whereby they took to the streets in unprecedented numbers, physically fighting against heavily armed Israeli soldiers, thus challenging the predominant stereotype of the domesticated and repressed Arab woman.[20] How are we to understand and evaluate what has transpired during the nearly five years of the Palestinian Intifada as regards the women's movement? Are we to accept the devastating critique of Fadwa Labadi – that the women's committees have achieved nothing for their constituency and that the women's movement is back to square one of the pre-Intifada days?

During the Intifada, Palestinian society in the Occupied Territories has experienced far-reaching changes, but these changes have been neither unilinear nor geometric. While it is extremely difficult, if not impossible, to evaluate the precise nature of change during a period of flux, the collective and individual experiences of the Intifada have brought into serious question the hegemony of the Israeli Zionist state and its military rule over Palestinians and have contributed to the development of a revitalised national self confidence among Palestinians. As for women, while they too have been part of the above general process, their experiences of the Intifada have been gendered which has contributed to the development of a more feminist consciousness. As Peteet has argued for Palestinian women in Lebanon,

> A specifically Palestinian feminist perspective emerged in the context of a contradiction between women's national consciousness and a structurally grounded and culturally-sanctioned limit on female autonomy that prevented women from a practice of the former.[21]

Similar to their sisters in Lebanon, Palestinian women cadres and activists in the Occupied Territories through their participation in the nationalist struggle for self-determination have come increasingly to realise and acknowledge that participation in the struggle does not necessarily lead to greater political power and authority nor does it insure increased respect and prestige within society. From the consistent chorus of voices raised by women's committee activists in their publications and open forums since the latter half of 1990, it is possible to gauge the high level of their dissatisfaction with the extent of their representation within Palestinian political organisations and institutions in general.[22] On the level of the individual woman activist, it has come to be recognised that while the collectivity of women may have gained in social status as a result of women's participation in the struggle, the individual women involved often face considerable social stigma, especially if they have been in prison.[23]

Another expression of women activists' awareness of their current marginalisation *vis à vis* the wider nationalist struggle and their vulnerable position in post-independence society is their constant reference to the Algerian case as a foreboding of what is possibly in store for women in Palestine.[24] Palestinian women activists warn of the dangers of subordinating the social struggle to the national struggle to the extent that women may have the gains of the Intifada subverted and be forced to return to the domesticity of former years, as were women activists in post-liberation Algeria.

However, in spite of this emerging feminist consciousness among activists and cadres of the women's committees and a small number of 'independent' professional, middle-class women[25] who have been fighting for recognition and inclusion within the Palestinian women's movement in general, and specifically within the Unified Women's Council since 1989,[26] feminism remains on the whole a derogatory label which connotes unacceptable social and political behaviour for Palestinian women at this stage of the national struggle. In actuality, there is no word for feminism or feminist in the Arabic language. The adjectival form of the collective noun for women, *nisa'*, connotes feminine or women's. Thus, in order to connote the meaning of feminist, it is necessary to transliterate the word into Arabic.[27] Within Palestinian society, feminism is equated with sexual libertarianism which is thought to characterise women's social behaviour in the West and therefore to be antithetical to the family-oriented and gender-hierarchical Palestinian society. Within the women's committees who are sceptical of it, it is primarily identified with the political behaviour of the 'independents' and the committee members who have encouraged their inclusion in the Unified Women's Council.[28]

The extent of the general opposition to an explicit feminist agenda in Palestinian society is indicated by the difficulties faced by a group of women headed by Sahar Khalifa, a well-known Palestinian writer and considered avant-garde in her social behaviour, when they attempted to set up the Women's Resource and Training Centre in Nablus. During the year and a half it took for the centre to be established (1989–90), the founding group faced hostility and scepticism. They were confronted with questions such as:

> Do you plan on treating women as a separate category from men and encouraging women towards crime? Are you going to imitate American feminists, thereby distancing women from the problems and development of their country and their love of men?[29]

The founding group attributes their eventual success to the fact that [we] proved that we are with men, not against them, that we are for the development of women, without whom it makes talking about national liberation in its full sense difficult, . . . [we support] intellectual and political pluralism, differences of opinion and discussion, all liberation movements in all parts of the world and change contributing to progress. We are not partisan to any philosophy or particular ideology . . . and perhaps it is for this reason, [that we are open to all], that we were able to gain the confidence of a conservative city such as Nablus.[30]

Thus, in the general context of a society in the process of challenging the legitimacy of a colonial settler regime and its historical right to govern over that society, and in the specific context of the Zionist state and its unique relation to international Jewish organisations such as the Jewish National Fund, which claims legal ownership of all 'state' land occupied or purchased within the 1948 boundaries and likewise within those parts of historical Palestine occupied in 1967 (the West Bank, the Gaza Strip, and East Jerusalem), and in light of the recent historical phase of massive Jewish emigration from the former Soviet Union and the subsequent intensified settlement policy of the former Likud government within the Occupied Territories, it is not surprising that the national struggle for Palestinian self-determination has taken precedence over all other struggles and social issues within the Occupied Territories. In terms of the women's movement, 'social' or gender issues as they pertain to the cultural realm have come to the forefront of public debate only when the wider nationalist political struggle has been facing internal contradictions and in times of crisis when these issues have been forced upon it. And even then, the women's movement has been slow to act and challenge openly manifestations of gender inequality pertaining to women's social position within Palestinian society.

A clear example of this is the women's movement's handling of the attempt by *Hamas* and other conservative forces to impose a dress code among women in the Gaza Strip and, to a lesser degree, in the West Bank. The issue was not challenged publicly until the summer of 1989, following a particularly dramatic incident between two well-known activist women from the Gaza Strip and a group of youths in one of the main markets in Gaza City. Although the women were wearing headscarves, they were threatingly ordered to cover 'all' of their hair. When one of the women said she would defend herself with a knife which was in her bag and started to unzip it, the youths started shouting to the crowd that the women were collaborators and were carrying a tape recorder. They were then chased en masse by a crowd of men into a local shop, where they substantiated that they were not carrying any recording device. Subsequently, the youths were 'tried' by a popular committee and found guilty. They were made to apologise to the women and their families and to pay a considerable fine of 3,000 Jordanian dinars or approximately £1,100.[31]

It was only then that the Unified Women's Council pressurised the reticent Unified National Leadership of the Intifada to issue a statement in Leaflet 43, condemning the imposition of a dress code on Palestinian women. This occurred, however, only after the Unified Women's Council issued their own statement against the phenomenon.[32] But, by that time, it was virtually impossible for a woman in the Gaza Strip to walk on the street with her head uncovered, wearing short sleeves, or a skirt to the knees. Why had the women's committees waited so long to act concerning an issue which directly affected the personal freedom of thousands of Palestinian women and which had been going on for well over a year, especially since the summer of 1988?[33]

It was only in December 1990, one year and four months later, that the issue was addressed in a public forum. At that time, the Bisan Centre's Women's Studies Committee held a conference under the general and vague title of 'The Intifada and Some Women's Social Issues', where the issue of the dress code (*hijab*) and other negative phenomenon *vis à vis* women, e.g. the drop in the age of marriage for women and the increase in the dropout rate of female secondary and university students, were discussed.[34] However, it was not *the* issue discussed, as considerable attention was focused on Palestinian women's lack of political representation in this forum. The organisers had faced much trepidation in the actual holding of such an event, as fear of threats and reprisals were rampant. A well-known and nationally respected female head of a charitable society even declined to participate in the conference as part of one of the panels.[35] And, once again, Faisal al-Hussaini was needed to give legitimacy to the issue and protection to those organising the event by presenting one of the opening speeches which had little relevance to the subject of the conference. Nevertheless, the women's movement has been unsuccessful in reversing the imposition of a dress code in the Gaza Strip, in spite of official condemnation by *Hamas* and all nationalist political organisations, and has shifted its emphasis back again to the political arena and the issue of democracy within the women's committees.

In conclusion, I would argue that in the articulation of the women's movement's current slogans of *unity* and *democracy* and in its demand for the equal importance of the *social* and *political* agendas are inherent contradictions which emanate from the particular conjuncture of forces and circumstances which have given rise and helped to shape the contemporary Palestinian women's movement and which help to explain the current dilemma facing this movement in its struggle against gender inequality within Palestinian society. *Unity* is crucial in the struggle for Palestinian self-determination against Israeli occupation, while *democracy* provides the space needed for all marginal social and political forces to express themselves in the ongoing struggle over hegemony within Palestinian society, be they those arguing for gender issues or for a radical, non-capitalist alternative to the organisation of society. But these two things are in objective contradiction to one another. Likewise, a clear commitment to a *social agenda* by the women's movement is required if they are to justify their existence as a separate movement and if they are to address and give voice to the real gender inequalities characterising social and political relations within Palestinian society. On the other hand, the historical, ideological and pragmatic links between the women's committees, the vanguard of the Palestinian women's movement, and the political organisations and power structures cannot be denied. Similarly, the immediacy and the determinancy of the *political* within Palestinian society at its current juncture precludes the possibility of the withdrawal of the women's movement and its leaders from this arena. Not even the most critical of the women's committees' lack of a commitment to a social agenda would suggest that they abandon the nationalist struggle.[36]

In the end, the most serious dilemma facing the women's committees in my opinion is in the necessity to challenge that most basic and sacred unit of social organisation within Palestinian society, the family, and the gender inequalities on which it is built. For it is in the unequal gender division of labour within the household and in the lack of control over women's reproductive capabilities that lie the major objective factors which prohibit Palestinian women, at a theoretical or actual level, to participate as equal partners in the political process and the nationalist struggle. With extremely high birth rates,[37] and in conditions of inadequate infrastructure and poverty, especially in the refugee camps and villages where the majority of Palestinians live, and with social and kinship relations which increase the daily domestic chores for Palestinian women in an unequal gender division of labour, where men virtually do no domestic chores, most Palestinian women do not even have the option of participation in politics or in the women's committees. In spite of this, the women's committees have made only tangential remarks about these inequalities, with the most radical suggesting the need for communal, public laundromats, restaurants, etc., but not a reorganisation of the division of labour between the sexes.[38] Such an issue is seen as smacking of Western feminism and inappropriate for Palestinian society at this stage in its development.

But, perhaps the most problematic of all is the very pro-natalist attitude predominant within Palestinian society, with activists from the women's committees being no exception to the rule. While the size of their families may be small compared to the majority of those women living in refugee camps and villages, the majority see motherhood as a national duty. However, children and the work and responsibilities that they entail, most of which fall upon the shoulders of female family members, all act to limit women's freedom to participate in non-domestic and non-household activities.

These issues have yet to be confronted and addressed by the Palestinian women's committees in any serious way. For the majority of Palestinian women, most of whom have not even heard of the women's committees, let alone being members,[39] these underlying objective realities shape their everyday lives and limit the possibilities of their participation in the wider women's and nationalist movements. The real challenge to the Palestinian women's movement today is to what extent they can address the issues of gender inequality on the home front, while pursuing their political agenda of greater female participation in the decision-making process, while not alienating the bulk of ordinary women and without marginalising their movement even further. The Palestinian women's movement indeed has a difficult and an unenviable task in front of it.

NOTES

1 Habash (1992).
2 *News From Within* (1992), 8(5): 9.

3 Habash (1992).
4 Locally based popular committees (*lijan sha'biyya*) developed during the early days of the Intifada as an organisational basis to meet the new needs of the Palestinian national struggle: distribution of food and other aid to areas under long curfews, reproduction and distribution of the regular communiqués of the Unified National Leadership (UNL) of the Intifada, guarding against army and collaborator attacks and intrusions, etc. What al-Hussaini forgets is that the fundamentalist campaign to impose a dress code on women, mainly in the Gaza Strip, went unaddressed by the popular committees even in their heyday, as such a 'social' issue was considered at best, secondary, or unimportant relative to the nationalist agenda of the struggle, with some political forces actually agreeing to the dress code for tactical and ideological reasons.
5 The four main women's committees are: Federation of Palestinian Women's Action Committees (1978), formerly called the Women's Work Committees; Union of Palestinian Working Women's Committees (1979); Union of Palestinian Women's Committees (1981); and Union of Women's Committees for Social Work (1982).
6 See al-Barghuthi (1991) and Liftawi (1991).
7 The Popular Front for the Liberation of Palestine (PFLP) and the Democratic Front for the Liberation of Palestine (DFLP) and their affiliated committees proclaimed adherence to Marxism-Leninism and supported armed struggle. Fateh, the largest political organisation, focused exclusively on a nationalist agenda, the creation of a secular democratic state, and supported the armed struggle. The Palestine Communist Party (PCP), which in 1991 reorganised and renamed itself the Palestine People's Party (PPP), focused on the mobilization of the working class and trade union activity, was against armed struggle, and argued for a two-state solution. It was formally included in the PLO only in 1987.
8 Julie Peteet (1991) draws the distinction between female and feminist consciousness in her study on Palestinian women in Lebanon entitled *Gender in Crisis: Women and the Palestinian Resistance Movement* (p. 71), referring to the work of Temma Kaplan (1981) 'Female Consciousness and Collective Action: The Case of Barcelona, 1910–1918', in N. Keohane, M. Rosaldo and B. Gelpi (eds) *Feminist Theory: A Critique of Ideology*, Chicago: Chicago University Press.
9 Peteet (1991).
10 ibid.
11 *Hamas* is the political organ of the Muslim Brotherhood which was forced by the events of the Intifada to change its name and revitalise its organisation as the four main political groups expanded rapidly in the early days of the Uprising. It supports armed struggle and the establishment of an Islamic state.
12 For a more detailed discussion of *Hamas* and the women's movement in the Occupied Territories, see Hammami (1990).
13 For a summary of the seminar's proceedings, see *News From Within*, 8(6), 3 June 1992: 9–12 and *al-Fajr The Dawn 1992*, 13(626): 11. The full proceedings will be published by Bisan Research and Development Centre in Ramallah.
14 *News From Within 1992*, 8(6): 12.
15 ibid.
16 ibid.
17 For an adaptation and translation of the original article by Fadwa Labadi entitled 'On Women's Day: The Palestinian Women's Movement on Trial' in *al-Mar'a*, March 1992, 10, see *News From Within 1992*, 8(5): 8–11.
18 ibid., pp. 10–11.
19 For examples of this type of material, see the literature produced by the various women's committees during this period of the Intifada.

20 See for example Giacaman and Johnson (1989) and Kuttab (1990).
21 Peteet (1991: 72).
22 See Women's Studies Committee (1991) *The Intifada and Some Women's Social Issues*, 'Final Resolutions', pp. 23–9. See also the contributions of Kuttab, al-'Asali, and the four representatives of the Women's Committees' Workshop, Liftawi, Nassar, Qura, and al-Barghuthi. All but Qura, representing the Union of Women's Committees for Social Work, the mainstream women's committee, focus on the lack of female participation in political decision making.
23 ibid., p. 25. Peteet also mentions a similar phenomenon for Palestinian female resistance fighters in Lebanon, who are often considered to have loose morals, except if they are killed heroically in battle, and then they are catapulted to the status of hero. See Peteet (1991: 152–3).
24 Women's Studies Committee (1991) *The Intifada and Some Women's Social Issues*, p. 90 (Liftawi), p. 108 (al-Barghuthi) and p. 34 (Kuttab). See also Labadi (1992: 11).
25 The 'independents' (*al-mustaqilat*) emerged as a political and social force during the Intifada. They were, and remain, a disparate group of women academics and professionals who have had varying degrees of contact and relations with the four women's committees, but who have refused to join these organisations officially due primarily to the formers' political affiliation with illegal and underground organisations. They have tended to stress the need for a united women's movement, above 'factionalist' politics, which would focus on women's issues and not nationalist politics.
26 During the first year of the Intifada, the four women's committees formed the Higher Women's Council (HWC) primarily to enhance their political legitimacy and increase their weight *vis-à-vis* the Unified National Leadership of the Uprising. A co-ordinating committee for the women's committees had existed since 1984, but it was the political context that provided the main impetus for the formation of the HWC. It was later renamed the Unified Women's Council (UWC) and has been plagued by differences among the committee representatives emanating primarily from political differences. For a fuller discussion of the HWC and the UWC, see Hiltermann (1991). See also Liftawi (1991), Nassar (1991) and al-Barghuthi (1991) for a critique of the UWC from the point of view of the three progressive women's committees.
27 For an example, see 'Introduction' to *Women's Affairs*, May 1991: 2.
28 See Nassar (1991: 96) for a critique of the political role of the 'independents' and their supporters within the women's committees.
29 'Introduction', *Women's Affairs*, May 1991: 2. *Women's Affairs* is the first publication of the Nablus-based Women's Resource and Training Centre, which has also set up a branch in the Gaza Strip.
30 ibid.
31 For more details of this incident, see Hammami (1990).
32 See Nassar (1991: 97).
33 Part of the explanation is the fact that the women's political leadership resides predominantly in the central region of the West Bank, i.e. Jerusalem and Ramallah, and hence was basically unaffected by the phenomenon, which focused on Gazan women. Had it not been for the dramatic event involving the two well-known activists with strong links with the movement in the West Bank, the issue might have not gained the attention it did at that time.
34 In the discourse on the issue of the dress code within Palestine and the Arab world in general, the Arabic word for women's veiling (*hijab*) is used.
35 Personal communication with one of the organisers of the conference, December 1990.

36 See Labadi (1992: 11).
37 In 1990, the birth rate in Gaza was 54.6 per thousand population, and in the
    West Bank it was 44.1 per thousand. The annual population growth rate for
    the same year was 5.2 in Gaza, and 4.3 in the West Bank (*Israel Statistical Abstract
    1991*, Jerusalem: Central Bureau of Statistics).
38 See Nassar (1991).
39 See the summary of a research project on Shati', a refugee camp in the Gaza
    Strip, by Erica Lang and Itimad Mohanna (1991) 'Women and Work in One
    Refugee Camp of the Gaza Strip', where they state that 57.8 per cent of the
    sample of women had not even heard of the women's committees (p. 15). A study
    by Suha Hindiyyeh and Afaf Ghazauna (nd) shows that 93.1 per cent of the
    women interviewed were not active in the women's committees (p. 5).

REFERENCES

Abdo, N. (1991) 'Women of the Intifada: Gender, Class and National Liberation',
    Race and Class 32(4): 19–34.
Anon. (1991) 'Introduction', in S. Khalifa, R. Giacaman and I. Jad (eds) *Women's
    Affairs (Shu'un al-Mar'a)* May: 2–3 (in Arabic).
Anon. (1992) 'The Feminist Women's Studies Centre in East Jerusalem', *News From
    Within* 8(6): 9.
al-Barghuthi, A. (1991) 'The Challenges and Responsibilities of the Women's
    Committees', in Women's Studies Committee, *The Intifada and Some Women's Social
    Issues*, Ramallah: Bisan Centre (in Arabic).
Baumman, P. and Hammami, R. (1989) *Annotated Bibliography on Palestinian Women*,
    Jerusalem: Arab Thought Forum.
Central Bureau of Statistics (1991) *Statistical Abstract of Israel 1991*, Jeruzalem: Central
    Bureau of Statistics.
'Continued Struggle – New Agendas: The Future of the Palestinian Women's
    Movement' (1995) Roundtable Organised by the Women's Studies Centre of Birzeit
    University, *News from Within* 11(4): 3–12.
Dajani, S. (1993) 'Palestinian Women under Israeli Occupation: Implication for
    Development', in J. Tucker, (ed.) *Arab Women: Old Boundaries, New Frontiers*,
    Bloomington, IN: Indiana University Press.
Giacaman, R. and Johnson, P. (1989) 'Palestinian Women: Building Barricades and
    Breaking Barriers', in Z. Lockman and J. Beinin (eds) *Intifada: The Palestinian Uprising
    Against Israeli Occupation*, Boston, MA: South End Press.
Giacaman, R. and Johnson, P. (1994) 'Searching for Strategies: The Palestinian
    Women's Movement in the New Era', *Middle East Report* 186: 22–5.
Gluck, S. B. (1991) 'Advocacy Oral History: Palestinian Women in Resistance', in
    S. B. Gluck and D. Patai (eds.) *Women's Words: The Feminist Practice of Oral History*,
    New York and London: Routledge.
Gluck, S. B. (1995) *An American Feminist in Palestine: The Intifada Years*, Philadelphia, PA:
    Temple University Press.
Habash, D. (1992) 'Women Say Threats Will Not Deter their Struggle for
    Democratization', *al-Fajr The Dawn* 13(635): 3.
Hammami, R. (1990) 'Women, the Hijab, and the Intifada', *Middle East Report* 164–5:
    24–31.
Hasso, F. and Abdel Hadi. 'I. (1992a) 'Seminar Discusses Democracy and the Role
    of Palestinian Women', *al-Fajr The Dawn* 13(626): 11.
Hasso, F. and Abdul Hadi, 'I. (1992b), 'Palestinian Women's Organizations and
    Democracy', *News From Within* 8(6): 9–12.

Hiltermann, J. (1991), *Behind the Intifada: Labor and Women's Movements in the Occupied Territories*, Princeton, NJ: Princeton University Press.

Hindiyyeh, S. and Ghazauna, A. (nd) 'The Socio-Economic Conditions of Working Women in Palestinian Factories', Jerusalem: Women's Studies Centre.

Khalifa, S., Giacaman, R. and Jad, I. (eds) (1991) *Women's Affairs (Shu'un al-Mar'a)*, May, Nablus, Women's Affairs Society (in Arabic).

Kuttab, E. (1990) 'Women's Participation in the Intifada: The Important Element in a Movement of National Liberation', in A Group of Researchers, *The Intifada: A Popular Initiative*, Ramallah: Bisan Centre (in Arabic).

Kuttab, E. (1993) 'Palestinian Women in the Intifada: Fighting on Two Fronts', *Arab Studies Quarterly* 15(2): 69–85.

Labadi, F. (1992) 'On Women's Day: The Palestinian Women's Movement on Trial', *News From Within* 8(5): 8–11.

Lang, E. and Mohanna, I. (1991) 'Women and Work in One Refugee Camp of the Gaza Strip', *Shu'un Tanmawiyyeh* autumn: 12–15.

Liftawi, S. (1991) 'The Nature of the Relationship between the General National Struggle and the Democratic and Women's Struggle in Particular', in Women's Studies Committee, *The Intifada and Some Women's Social Issues*, Ramallah: Bisan Centre.

Mayer, T. (ed.) (1994) *Women and the Israeli Occupation: The Politics of Change*, London and New York: Routledge.

Nassar, M. (1991) 'The Political Role of the Palestinian Woman during the Intifada', in Women's Studies Committee, *The Intifada and Some Women's Social Issues*, Ramallah: Bisan Centre.

Peteet, J. (1991) *Gender in Crisis: Women and the Palestinian Resistance Movement*, New York: Columbia University Press.

Peteet, J. (1993) 'Authenticity and Gender', in J. Tucker (ed.) *Arab Women: Old Boundaries, New Frontiers*, Bloomington IN: Indiana University Press.

Sayigh, R. (1993) 'Palestinian Women and Politics in Lebanon', in J. Tucker (ed.), *Arab Women: Old Boundaries, New Frontiers*, Bloomington IN: Indiana University Press.

Sayigh, R. and Peteet, J. (1986) 'Between Two Fires: Palestinian Women in Lebanon', in R. Ridd and H. Callaway (eds) *Caught Up in Conflict: Women's Responses to Political Strife*, Basingstoke, Macmillan Education with Oxford University Women's Studies Committee.

Sharoni, S. (1995) *Gender and the Israeli–Palestinian Conflict*, New York: Syracuse University Press.

Strum, P. (1992) *The Women are Marching: The Second Sex and the Palestinian Revolution*, New York: Lawrence Hill.

Warnock, K. (1990) *Land Before Honour: Palestinian Women in the Occupied Territories*, Basingstoke: Macmillan.

Women's Studies Committee (1991) *The Intifada and Some Women's Social Issues*, Ramallah: Bisan Centre.

Women's Studies Committee, Bisan Centre for Research and Development (1993) *Directory of Palestinian Women's Organizations 1993*, Ramallah: Bisan Centre.

FURTHER READING

It is necessary to make a few general comments about the nature of the literature on Palestinian society under Israeli occupation. First, sociological and anthropological studies on Palestinian society in English and in Arabic are limited in number. Given the primacy of the political and military struggle, most works on Palestine have focused on these dimensions. Second, the ethics and sensitivity of undertaking research on a people under occupation need to be taken into consideration. The realities of Israeli occupation determine to a large extent what can and cannot be researched, both practically and politically. Finally, due to the highly politicised nature of Palestinian society, most researchers will tend to have a closer relationship with those in a particular political group. This political reality may affect the researcher's access to data and their interpretation.

In terms of studies on gender issues in Palestine, there is an even greater paucity. As the reader will have noticed from the sources used in this chapter, most of the literature is written in Arabic by local women's committees and organisations. Hence, it is not easily accessible, especially to the non-Arabic reader. Likewise, as it is mainly produced by politicised women's groups for mobilisation and recruitment purposes, this literature tends to be more journalistic than academic. Thus, there are very few detailed, empirically grounded and analytical texts on gender issues in Palestine. A useful bibliography of the literature is *Annotated Bibliography on Palestinian Women*, compiled by Pari Baumman and updated by Rema Hammami (1989, Jerusalem: Arab Thought Forum).

Nevertheless, there are a few texts available to the English reader which provide an overview of the women's question in Palestine. Perhaps the best introduction is Kitty Warnock's (1990) *Land Before Honour: Palestinian Women in the Occupied Territories* (Basingstoke: Macmillan). Warnock taught cultural studies at Birzeit University from 1981 until 1986 and hence developed a well-grounded understanding of Palestinian society. Her study is built upon a series of in-depth interviews with Palestinian women.

Another useful text is Joost Hiltermann's (1991) *Behind the Intifada: Labor and Women's Movements in the Occupied Territories*. Hiltermann carried out his research, which was originally for his doctorate in sociology, from 1984 until 1989 while he worked for al-Haq, a Palestinian human rights organisation in Ramallah. Hiltermann's study examines the processes of mass mobilisation under occupation, with a specific focus on the labour and the women's movements. By his own account, Hiltermann originally relied upon his close ties to 'one particular faction of the Palestinian national movement' (1991: x). Although he states that he has tried to rectify this bias in the final published text, I think that this tendency still remains. However, a more general comment is that his analysis of the women's movement relies heavily upon the textual analysis of women's committees' documents and interviews with their leadership. Hence, there are few data about or analysis of ordinary women in villages and refugee camps. The sex/gender of the researcher is relevant in this respect.

Another body of literature on Palestine grew considerably during the Intifada years, 1987–93. During this period, the Occupied Territories of Palestine were inundated with foreign journalists, activists and academics, many of whom had no previous expertise in the area, knew no Arabic, and usually stayed for brief periods. Some of them wrote autobiographical accounts of their experiences. Many of these accounts are written for women. Examples includes Helen Winternitz's (1991) *A Season of Stones: Living in a Palestinian Village* (New York: Atlantic Monthly), Janine Di Giovanni's (1993) *Against the Stranger: Lives in Occupied Territory* (London: Viking) and Sherna Berger Gluck's (1995) *An American Feminist in Palestine: The Intifada Years* (Philadelphia, PA: Temple University Press). One account which focuses specifically on women and gender issues is Philippa Strum's (1992) *The Women are Marching: The Second Sex and the Palestinian Revolution* (New York: Lawrence Hill). These works should be read with considerable caution.

Finally, particular mention should be made of Julie M. Peteet's (1991) *Gender in Crisis: Women and the Palestinian Resistance Movement*. Although this work focuses on Lebanon, it is well worth reading for those interested in gender issues in Palestine.

Peteet, an anthropologist, carried out her fieldwork from 1980 to 1982, but had previously lived in Lebanon. She brings to her data a highly nuanced analytical and critical perspective. This work represents, in my opinion, the best study to date of the complex relationship between nationalism and feminism within a Palestinian context.

Chapter 11

Palestinian women and the Intifada
An exploration of images and realities

Maria Holt

Palestinians in the Occupied Territories stand poised on the threshold of a new chapter in their history. Ever since the revelation of secret negotiations in Oslo between the Palestine Liberation Organisation (PLO) and the government of Israel, and the signing of a 'Declaration of Principles' on Interim Self-Government Arrangements on 13 September 1993, at the White House in Washington, there has been a feeling amongst the Palestinian population in the West Bank and Gaza Strip that a state of their own might at last be in sight.

Their optimism, however, defies both facts on the ground,[1] and also the increasing absence of unanimity among Palestinians themselves. There is no widely shared vision about how a future state might look. Women's place within such a state is even more uncertain. Indeed, one could go as far as to say that the Palestinian women's movement, far from advancing the concerns of women through the uprising (the Intifada) which began in 1987, has suffered a series of setbacks. For even while the Declaration of Principles – or 'Gaza-Jericho first' agreement – was being signed, a few women in the Gaza Strip were to be seen completely shrouded, including their faces and hands, in the type of Islamic costume previously associated with Iran or the Gulf states. This suggests, at the very least, a striking lack of consensus about goals and objectives. While no one would quarrel with the desirability of encouraging a multiplicity of modes of expression, many women of late have indicated a preference for the Islamic alternative and others have felt obliged to submit to this trend. This apparent narrowing of options suggests the encroachment of religious rigidity in Palestinian society, with all the limitations that this implies for women.

I would like to argue that Palestinian women, at this decisive moment in their history, are poorly positioned to take advantage of the changing political climate. Instead of benefiting from the rapid movement at national level, they find themselves trapped within a series of conflicts. The central dilemma pits 'tradition' against 'progress', but these are amorphous generalities and may be better understood in terms of women's rights, national rights, Islamism, nationalism, and the insoluble battle between human and political needs.

Hopes that were raised by the 1988 'Palestinian Declaration of Independence',[2] which laid down principles of equality and non-discrimination, have been disappointed. The Islamic movement, increasingly regarded as a force to be reckoned with, has distanced itself from the lofty pronouncements about equality and democracy enshrined in the Declaration of Independence. The Islamists' view of womanhood is considerably more restricted, and their blueprint for an ideal state, the Charter of the Islamic Resistance Movement (*Hamas*) of Palestine, confines the role of women to two short paragraphs.[3] Based on a particular interpretation of the Koran, the vision of *Hamas* requires women to embrace an existence centred around the maintenance of the household and the raising of children. When she leaves her home, a woman must ensure that she is modestly attired and that her head is covered.

This is a matter of concern in the Palestinian context suggesting as it does that modern Muslim society should be a faithful imitation of life in seventh-century Arabia, when the Koran was revealed to the Prophet Muhammad. Islamism, in other words,

> provides no innovative prospects for the future but solely a vision of the future as a restoration of the past, obtained from the 'good old' ways. . . . Political Islam may therefore . . . be interpreted as a backward-oriented utopia. . . . The Islamic past is perceived as the *primeval* democratic form of government of the people, to be regarded as a divine order and to be restored for precisely this reason.
>
> (Tibi 1991: 120)

In this utopian former state, men and women coexisted in harmony, each occupying a clearly defined and quite separate space. On the other hand, the vision of *Hamas* – in common with Islamist groups elsewhere – transforms women into trespassers in the public sphere. Although some Palestinian women welcome the imposition of a more 'Islamic' lifestyle, many others fear that, in general, the situation does not bode at all well for women in the sense that it removes the element of choice. It is important to appreciate precisely how this state of affairs came about. It stems only partly from the growing influence of militant Islam. In part, it can be attributed to the deteriorating economic situation for Palestinians in the Occupied Territories which has had a deleterious effect on women's lives. This conclusion raises a number of questions.

First, why is religion, in this context, assumed – by Western and other observers – to have such a negative impact on women? Second, are women more adversely affected than men by the present situation? Third, have women participated in the liberation struggle only because men and societal norms have permitted them to do so, because the desperation of the Palestinian plight compels them to act or because they believe that national rights and women's rights are entirely compatible? Finally, are the signs for the future, as far as they can be ascertained, any more promising?

In order to answer these questions, I propose to contrast Western images of Palestinian women with the actions and words of these women. The first image is the familiar one of women in Arab-Muslim societies: they are veiled, submissive and largely invisible, perceived by Orientalists as either the power-less occupants of harems or beguiling objects of illicit desire. The image of the Arab and Muslim woman in Western literature 'is that of a totally help-less, uneducated woman who uses her head to carry parcels of goods or jugs of water, rather than use it to think and create, like the Western woman does' (Al-Helo 1992). A second image, in contrast, presents the defiant and outspoken Palestinian woman in her traditional embroidered dress, boldly confronting the Israeli army. A familiar figure in television reports and news-paper articles, she is hailed by Western supporters of women's rights as an 'unlikely revolutionary'. But when she encourages her children to imitate her militant actions and is evidently proud, even when they become martyrs, she is denounced as an 'unnatural' mother. The fourth image, beloved of Western feminists, sees the Palestinian woman as triply powerless: a victim of her gender, of her restraining culture and of the Israeli occupation. Let us begin by examining the issue of powerlessness.

If we consider the position of women in terms of exclusion from political power, we can see that, on the one hand, they are almost entirely absent from formal positions of leadership[4] – and have been throughout Palestinian history – and, on the other, their organisational voice is usually merely one strand in the larger factional picture. But, in the Palestinian case, there is more than one way to exercise power – it may be formal or informal, subtle or more obvious – and one should not make the mistake of dismissing the Palestinian woman as 'powerless'. Nonetheless, although there was some optimism at the beginning of the Intifada that the movement for women's rights would inevitably progress alongside the nationalist movement, disillusion is slowly taking root.

It is useful to view contemporary developments within the framework of Palestinian history which, for convenience, may be divided into five phases. First, in 1917, Ottoman control of Palestine was ended and shortly afterwards the British Mandate period began. It coincided with and gave practical support to Zionist encroachment into Palestine. Palestinian resistance to both the British and the Zionists escalated during the period 1920–48 but ultimately suffered disastrous defeat. Women, too, participated in resistance activities. They did so in ways which were conditioned by class, gender and tradition.

Many of the early women's organisations fell into the category of 'good works', in the sense that they were charitable societies run by wealthy, urban women with the aim of assisting the less well-off. These women were influ-enced by three distinct factors: the predominant cultural values of the society, rooted in Islamic custom and tradition; the very vigorous women's movement in Egypt at that time; and the rapidly worsening situation in Palestine itself which demanded the response of all citizens.

During the British Mandate period (1917–48), education for females slowly began to increase, although it was mainly the urban, better-off families that benefited. Although the number of girls attending elementary schools rose, they never exceeded 23 per cent of the total Palestinian enrolment. At secondary level, the numbers were even lower, and in rural areas girls had few opportunities for education. In 1935, they comprised a mere 6 per cent of the total enrolment in village schools. Out of four hundred government schools established in villages towards the end of the Mandate period, only forty-six of these were for girls. The purpose of female education at this time was

> to reinforce in them their traditional role in Palestinian society . . . most educators agree that the quantity and quality of facilities in the girls' government schools was inferior to that in the boys' schools. Today, the exceedingly high rate of illiteracy among women over 50 years of age, especially women from villages, is a direct result of the combination of restrictive Palestinian social practices, insufficient educational opportunities, and the inferior quality of education offered in girls' government schools.
>
> (Anon. 1993: 2)[5]

In the late 1930s, matters took a decidedly violent turn as the Palestinian population rose up in revolt. But the uprising that erupted in 1936, now described as the 'first Intifada', was brutally suppressed by the British. By 1948, the British Mandate having collapsed in disarray, Jewish forces were able to prevail and thus the state of Israel was established, resulting in the forcible uprooting of over 700,000 Palestinians. Only 160,000 remained in what now became 'Israel', while the rest were transformed into stateless refugees, in the West Bank and Gaza Strip – which were all that remained of Mandate Palestine – as well as the neighbouring countries of Jordan, Lebanon, Syria and Egypt. Thus, a second phase was initiated.

After their traumatic upheaval, Palestinians who had fled from their country struggled to come to terms with their grim new reality. Having lost their homes and their land, most people concentrated on day-to-day survival in alien environments, and also the preservation of their national identity. In the wake of the exile,

> two opposing trends appeared. One, based on the belief that their own ignorance had contributed to the disaster, was a determination to acquire as much formal education as possible. The other was a nostalgic longing to preserve the old society's structures and habits, which led to the metaphysical resurrection of the destroyed villages and urban neighbourhoods within the chaos of the refugee camps and to a strict enforcement of the old mores.
>
> (Antonius 1979: 28)

Slowly, Palestinian determination to resist returned and social, political and military organisation began to take place. The PLO was established in 1964, together with its women's section, the General Union of Palestinian Women (GUPW). However, in 1967, as a result of the disastrous Six-Day War, the rest of Mandate Palestine – the West Bank, East Jerusalem and the narrow Gaza Strip – fell to Israel.

With the Israeli occupation, a third phase began in which new sorts of organisation were explored. In the 1970s a

> new generation of women, many of whom had been politicised in the student movements at the Palestinian universities, founded grassroots women's committees that, in contrast to the charitable society network of women's organisations, sought to involve the majority of women in the West Bank who lived in villages – along with women in camps, the urban poor, and women workers as well as intellectuals and urban middle-class women – in a united women's movement.
>
> (Giacaman and Johnson 1990: 133)

Over the years, Palestinians have responded to Israeli power in several ways. They have used resistance, both violent and non-violent. A handful of women have broken through traditional prejudices to become fighters. One of the best known of these is Leila Khaled who, as a member of the Popular Front for the Liberation of Palestine (PFLP), was responsible for a number of spectacular hijackings in the early 1970s. Her present life is taken up with trying to improve conditions for women and children in the Palestinian camps of Damascus. She admits, however, that her 'work as a freedom fighter has given me happiness; you identify yourself with the struggle. It is the difference between a freedom fighter and an ordinary person. As a Palestinian I wouldn't be happy with myself unless I was a freedom fighter. I am glad I have done so much' (MacDonald 1991: 132). Her experiences are unusual. On the whole, women's roles have conformed to more traditional patterns. They have looked after home and children while the men went away to fight; they have tended sick and wounded fighters, and provided support systems for resistance activities.

Another response has been political. Palestinians have formed organisations and parties in order to negotiate with the Israelis and also to present their case at the international level. The first women's political organisation, the Palestine Women's Union, was formed in 1921 during the British Mandate by a group of mainly upper-middle-class urban women whose interests 'were in welfare activities designed to improve the standard of living of the poor and to organise women around national activities' (Peteet 1991: 44).

The Palestinian Union of Women's Work Committee (PUWWC) was established in 1978 but the ideological divisions within the broader national movement soon caused the organisation to split along factional lines. It was succeeded by the Federation of Palestinian Women's Action Committees (FPWAC), which supports the aims of the Democratic Front for the Liberation of Palestine (DFLP); the Union of Palestinian Working Women's Committees

(UPWWC), which aligns itself with the former Palestinian Communist Party, now the People's Party; the Women's Committee for Social Work (WCSW), which is supportive of Fatah; and the Union of Palestinian Women's Committees (UPWC), which identifies with the Popular Front for the Liberation of Palestine (PFLP). The General Union of Palestinian Women (GUPW), which is a component of the PLO, represents the interests of women in the Palestinian camps outside the Occupied Territories and also in the international arena.

Another way in which Palestinians have responded to the Israeli occupation has been through the medium of Islam. This is by no means a new phenomenon. As long ago as the 1930s, when Palestinian Arabs were fighting the Zionist takeover of their land, Islam was used as an effective source for galvanising support. The 1936–9 revolt was described by Nels Johnson as 'Islamic populist', by which he means 'any movement which uses Islamic concepts to argue for, and in many cases to demand, the participation of a mass of people in social action' (Johnson 1982: 54). As such, it was able to provide women with an acceptable, religiously sanctioned way of participating in the resistance. With the loss of Palestine and the growth of Arab nationalism, the appeal of Islam faded and was replaced by more secular ideologies. As secular rhetoric has proved empty, however, Islam has once again entered the fray as a powerful and compelling alternative.

The Intifada, which began in December 1987, signalled a fourth phase in the Palestinian national struggle and one in which women have played an active and increasingly assertive role. To understand their position, it is necessary to examine the sorts of tasks they have performed in support of the Intifada; the historical precedents for their involvement, which have already been briefly described; and the institutional constraints preventing broader female participation. One should be aware, however, when discussing political action by women, that such comments apply to a very small percentage of the population. One should also bear in mind that 'political action' has different meanings for different women: while some women consider their day-to-day resistance against Israeli rule a political act, others have a more traditional understanding of politics.

Let us now investigate the obstacles to women's development and also some of the ways in which these obstacles have galvanised women into forms of action which might otherwise have remained unfamiliar or undesirable to them. These actions and reactions account for the creation of a unique situation for the Palestinians which cannot be precisely equated with change, repression or social protest elsewhere.

The first obstacle, clearly, is the twenty-seven-year Israeli occupation, which has been a source of massive repression and brutalisation. It has had the effect of reducing the opportunities available to women. When, for example, access to education and employment is restricted, women tend to be the first to suffer. As a result of the increasingly tight framework in which they are forced to operate, even their traditional support roles have been thrown into question. At the same time, threatened with a loss of national identity, Palestinians have responded by developing an usually strong determination to fight back through education and enlightenment. Women, too, have both contributed to and benefited from this.

For example, the attitude of Palestinian society, which tends towards conservatism and respect for traditional ways, towards female prisoners in Israeli detention has undergone dramatic changes, particularly since the beginning of the Intifada. Previously equated with loss of honour, imprisonment for women has slowly been accepted by society. Indeed, it is 'no longer shameful for a woman to be arrested for political reasons; instead, increasingly it is becoming a source of pride for their families' (Atwan 1993: 58). This change in attitudes has worked to the detriment of the Israeli occupation authorities who routinely employ sexual humiliation and make a practice of seeking to demoralise a female detainee 'by suggesting that the fact that she, a woman, has been in detention will make her a social outcast in her own society' (Thornhill 1992: 35). This policy is now less effective. Nonetheless, despite a relaxation of attitudes, families still prefer that young female members stay out of the political limelight, avoid confrontation and pursue a more traditionally respectable course of behaviour.

The second obstacle is that, in the absence of an independent state with its formal structures and processes, women have suffered both economically and politically. They have been unable to improve their standard of living, or their basic rights. They also face the ever-present threat of unjust treatment by husbands or other males in the society. Since there has been no competent authority to which they can turn, the marriage age for girls has fallen, men have the option of abandoning their wives or taking more than one wife, and the level of domestic violence against women is rising. According to lawyer Hanan Bakri, Islamic law, under which most marriages are performed, is unresponsive to women's needs. Secular laws, in contrast, would 'allow women to file for divorce when harmed'.[6] But until there is a properly constituted Palestinian government, the disturbing tendency towards ignoring or even abusing women's meagre rights is liable to continue.

But this, of course, is not the whole picture. Women, faced with insurmountable odds, have taken a variety of steps towards overcoming their disadvantages. They have attempted to construct alternative frameworks in which to organise their lives. The very young, the very old and the sick are particularly vulnerable and women's organisations have addressed some of the problems which arise when government protection is lacking. Especially since the Intifada began, women have been active in economic and welfare committees, educational facilities to fill the gap when schools and colleges are forcibly closed by the Israeli authorities, and community health projects.

Finally, since the early 1990s, there has been a growth in political Islam, an ideology which many in the West and in the Arab world too believe oppresses women. Three arguments are habitually raised to explain this phenomenon. The first pays homage to a Western stereotype which perceives the Arab-Muslim 'ideal woman' as 'a completely private creature, secluded in her home, hidden behind a veil' (Strum 1992: 25). This image is in no way compatible with the central issue of national liberation, of which the women's movement is an integral component, and has little relevance to the lives of contemporary Palestinian women. A second interpretation regards the development of this particular brand of Islam as threatening to the embryonic women's rights movement. In the words of teacher and researcher Najah Manasrah: 'The kind of women I fear most are women who defend their own enslavement' (Manasrah 1992: 66). A third view, in contrast, believes that a reversion to Islam will provide dignity and empowerment for women. Since secular movements have apparently failed and most of Palestine remains under alien control, according to this line of reasoning, it is time to return to a more 'authentic' mode of struggle. Islam is both culturally familiar and historically respectable.

A closer identification with Islamic practices certainly does not imply the clichéd Western image of the veiled and oppressed woman. By returning to the origin and true principles of Islam 'women [will] find their due status and proper role' (Warnock 1990: 66). Many Palestinian women claim that the adoption of 'Islamic dress', which refers to anything from a headscarf and modest clothing to a full-scale, Iranian-style *chador*, allows them to move around with greater ease outside their homes. It should be noted that this is in line with female responses to Islamic movements elsewhere in the Arab world (see, for example, MacLeod 1991).

There have been four distinct phases of the Intifada. When it began, women and girls of all ages joined in the spontaneous demonstrations against the Israeli army. It would certainly not be accurate to assert, as Israeli and other propagandists sometimes do, that Palestinian parents deliberately force their children into dangerous positions on the front-line. On the contrary, the Intifada, from the beginning, has been a genuinely popular uprising and mothers have been unable to prevent their children from confronting the occupation authorities. We should also take into account the generational argument, whereby older Palestinians – the parents and grandparents – have adopted an attitude of resignation, rooted in despair at the apparent hopelessness of combating Israeli hegemony, while young people and children display anger stemming from a determination to sacrifice anything, even their own lives, in the cause of self-respect and self-determination.

The next phase was organisational and involved the setting up of popular and neighbourhood committees, but women's role in these, it is generally acknowledged, 'became an extension of what it traditionally had been in the society: teaching and rendering services' (Hiltermann 1991: 51). Nonetheless, the committees succeeded in providing the initial impetus towards an embryonic infrastructure and women's contributions were both valuable and, for a time at least, innovative. This potentially exciting period, however, was tinged with exasperation as women experienced the fetters not just of the occupation but also of tradition, which many complained was 'suffocating'.

When the committees were declared illegal by the Israeli military authorities, in September 1988, a third phase began during which the women's committees started to think more concretely in terms of future state structures. In December of that year, an umbrella organisation, the Higher Women's Committee (HWC), was created, with the aim of uniting the four factional committees. However, during the first two years of the Intifada, the four women's committees changed the focus of their activities, which had previously concentrated on the provision of such basic services as nurseries, literacy classes and training centres,

> to accommodate the revolutionary upheaval. Their emphasis shifted from providing services to recruiting and organising the thousands of women who joined the popular uprising and swelled the ranks of the women's organisations. Women's organisations played a decisive role in organising demonstrations, marches, and sit-in strikes on a daily basis.
>
> (Rosenfeld 1993)

There has been a growth in assertiveness on the part of the factional women's committees. At the beginning of 1994, even the relatively conservative Fatah-affiliated Women's Committee for Social Work declared its insistence on some form of commitment to a women's agenda in the future Palestinian state. Even PLO leader Yasir Arafat has spoken in public about the importance of maintaining the principles of equality and non-discrimation contained in the 1988 Declaration of Independence.

In addition, in the latter part of the Intifada, other women's organisations, which claim to be non-factional, have been established, with the intention of educating women as to their basic rights, offering a series of training programmes, and developing a resource base. The Women's Studies Centre in East Jerusalem, for example, was set up with the intention that application of its research

> would lead to the crystallisation of a Palestinian feminist agenda and to the development of mechanisms at the grass-roots level to deal with women's issues. A feminist agenda and an awareness of women's issues are particularly important now during this nation-building period, namely in the drafting of legislation, in restructuring curricula and social services, and in developing our national economy
>
> (*News From Within* 1992)

Reference to a 'feminist agenda' is interesting given the long-standing resistance among members of the women's movement to notions of feminism, which tend to be linked to Western definitions and are usually regarded as negative or inappropriate.

Other groups and individual Palestinian women have engaged in dialogue and joint activities with Israeli women's groups. Such encounters have been judged the most successful contact between Palestinians and Israelis. One example occurred in September 1992, when forty Israeli and Palestinian women met in Brussels at a conference sponsored by the European Community. Here, a number of vital issues were addressed and agreement was reached on three central points.[7] Israeli peace groups, such as Women in Black, have been campaigning for years against the occupation of Palestinian lands.

As the initial optimism about a speedy and successful outcome to the Intifada was destroyed, a fourth phase got underway. It stemmed from a sense of the failure of the national parties, the ensuing feelings of frustration caused by this realisation, and a desire to find a more effective approach. For many Palestinians, including women, political action inspired by Islam was able to provide the answer. The Islamic groups *Hamas* and Islamic Jihad have enjoyed a substantial upsurge in popularity in the 1990s and particularly since the Madrid peace process (initiated in 1991) was perceived as having reached a stalemate.

Their effect on women, however, has not been altogether beneficial. Although some women support the wearing of more modest Islamic dress and a head-covering and, for them, the Islamic vision is empowering and exciting, it would probably be fair to say that the majority are alarmed by what they see as an intrusive imposition of outmoded and restrictive ideals. The element of choice, in other words, has been removed. One could argue, of course, that choice, under present conditions, is a luxury and not even particularly appropriate. Furthermore, most women in the Occupied Territories have never enjoyed much choice; on the contrary, they have responded to the Intifada in ways that are more or less spontaneous and usually practical.

One of the objectives of the Intifada, for example, has been to achieve a degree of economic independence from Israel. In order to do this, Palestinians have attempted to replace Israeli products with Palestinian alternatives. Women have contributed to this effort by the creation of a home economy, including growing vegetables, producing bread, preserves, pickles etc., and raising livestock. The United Nations Relief and Works Agency for Palestine Refugees in the Near East (UNRWA) runs training schemes in sewing, embroidery and other skills at some of its camps, which gives at least some refugee women the chance to earn an income. In 1991, UNRWA launched an income-generation programme, offering low-cost loans for Palestinian businesses; a small number of women have taken advantage of this and have prospered. An example is Um Adib, a resident of the Gaza Strip, who received a $5,000 loan to purchase a computerised electronic knitting machine. She reports that her production of woollen sweaters has almost doubled.[8]

When the Israelis responded to the Intifada by placing restrictions on education at all levels, including the prolonged closure of schools, women made an attempt to compensate for this by organising informal classes in homes, mosques and gardens. Though these were soon pronounced illegal by the military authorities, they continued in a clandestine and makeshift form. One of the inevitable outcomes of the Israeli decision to punish the Palestinian population by depriving it of education has been a significant drop in educational standards. Illiteracy rates have soared. Another side-effect is that women 'deprived of education are marrying earlier rather than waiting for schools to reopen. Women without education and training are moreover less able to work outside the home for remuneration' (Kamal 1992).

Lang and Mohanna's (1992) survey carried out in a Gaza Strip refugee camp reveals that almost half the women in the camp were unaware of the activities of the women's committees. A substantial number of women

> did not necessarily perceive of the women's committees in a localised sense at all. Instead they saw them as some high-up, detached and inaccessible body. . . . The feeling that the committees were not integral or relevant to their lives is one of the main barriers to their development.
>
> (Lang and Mohanna 1992: 169)

One may discern a conflict here between spontaneous resistance to the occupation (which takes the form of outrage, a woman's instinct to protect her home and children, traditional coping activities, and an underlying determination not to succumb to Israeli domination) and organised and carefully articulated programmes by committees and other women's groups, including some which are avowedly feminist. It is a fundamental dilemma.

> While the community approves of and encourages acts of national resistance, it categorically condemns a female's revolt against male authority. The one is called *patriotism*; the other, *unholy disobedience*. After all, an Israeli soldier or policeman is an *outsider* and an *enemy*, but a woman's father, brother or husband is an *insider* and a *kinsman* whom she must love or at least obey. While blessing the national Intifada, the community's 'mind and conscience' are not yet prepared to recognise the legitimacy of a gender Intifada.
>
> (Idris 1993)

The sentiment is revealing and gives some idea of the debate being waged in elite Palestinian circles.

With the signing of the 'Gaza-Jericho first' deal, it could be argued, a new phase of the Intifada has begun, although some might claim that the uprising has been all but extinguished by a mixture of battle fatigue and faith in a peaceful solution. But demographic realities indicate that the agreement is a far from adequate response to the desperate plight of the Palestinian people. There are now estimated to be about 5.4 million Palestinians dispersed around the world. Of these, approximately 2 million live in the West Bank and Gaza Strip, while 900,000, or 18 per cent of the total Israeli population, remain within Israel. In the West Bank, 39 per cent of the population are refugees, of whom 26 per cent reside in nineteen camps. In the densely populated Gaza Strip, 75 per cent out of roughly 800,000 inhabitants are refugees, of whom 55 per cent live in eight camps. Out of the total population in the Occupied Territories today, as many as 50 per cent are under the age of 15 (World University Service 1993: 3–6). In response to Israel's determination to remove Palestinians from their land and to erase their national identity, Palestinian parents feel under an obligation to produce large numbers of children and the image of the 'heroic mother' is a potent one.

While the shape of future Palestinian autonomy remains unclear, violence is continuing in the occupied areas and political support for the 'self-governing arrangements' is gradually slipping away. According to an opinion poll carried out in the West Bank and Gaza Strip in January 1994, only 18.6 per cent of Palestinians remain 'very optimistic' about their future in the coming year. Of the rest, 38.7 per cent are 'somewhat optimistic' and 37.7 per cent declare themselves 'pessimistic'. A startling 24.3 per cent admit that their support for the Declaration of Principles has decreased, while 22.6 per cent report an increase in opposition.[9] It should be added that neither responses to the agreement nor conditions on the ground are exactly the same throughout the Occupied Territories. The Gaza Strip is well known for both its conservatism and its activism. The Intifada of 1987 initially erupted in one of Gaza's teeming camps and some of the most intense and confrontational episodes since the late 1980s have taken place in this squalid and overcrowded strip of land.

Gaza was also the scene of the '*hijab* campaign' of the late 1980s, during which Islamist elements, led by *Hamas*, conducted a frequently intimidating crusade to force every woman in the Gaza Strip to wear some form of head-covering whenever she leaves her home (Hammami 1990). The fact that the Islamists, who represent a minority of public opinion in the area, were so successful is a sad testament to the priorities, or perhaps the courage, of the nationalist leadership of the uprising. National cohesion was evidently considered more important than freedom of choice or movement for women.

Hamas's *hijab* campaign has been less successful in the West Bank, however, although it has received support in more conservative centres such as Hebron. The population of the West Bank, including East Jerusalem, tends to be more urban and better educated. Yet, even here, the pressures on women to 'return' to a more traditional life-style have been great. These can be attributed to rapidly escalating unemployment resulting from the recent reluctance of Israelis to employ Palestinian workers, growing desperation caused by the lack of a meaningful peace agreement, an increase in poverty and disillusion, and a growth in conservatism, inspired by the Islamist trend and a perception of lawlessness and anarchy in Palestinian society.

Although the Intifada may have catapulted certain exceptional women, such as the Palestinian spokesperson at the Middle East peace talks, Hanan Ashrawi, into the limelight, it has had 'negative repercussions too: a rising tide of religious radicalism, male-dominated battles on the streets and economic hardship which often forced young women to abandon studies and seek menial work' (*Guardian*, 6 December 1993). So far, the male PLO leadership, in Tunis and the Occupied Territories, has been curiously reluctant to address women's concerns. This is thought to stem partly from the belief that nationalist issues must take priority over social ones and partly from a deeply ingrained conservatism. Some women even blame themselves. Said human rights worker Randa Siniora, for example:

> It's true that women have been excluded from key political bodies where major decisions are made, and that's a dangerous development. . . . But whose fault is it really? There's much talking and soul-searching on the need for equality and on our role in society. But what tangible steps have we women taken to fight this?
>
> (*Guardian*, 6 December 1993)

On 11 December 1993, at a press conference in East Jerusalem, a group of Palestinian women, who are members of the No to Violence Against Women Committee, called on the PLO 'to make a declaration affirming the right of women to a dignified life, employment and freedom of thought and to prohibit all kinds of violence against women, whether it is in the street, home, or in the ranks of nationalist factions'. Wife-beating, they reported, remains a feature of Palestinian society (*Al-Quds*, 12 December 1993).

Quite clearly, however, a very wide gap exists between the activities of women's committees and the lives of the mass of Palestinian women, which suggests that little has changed since the 1920s and 1930s when elite women formed charitable organisations to help the less well off. Most women are primarily concerned with the welfare of their children, with having enough money to survive and with the myriad insecurities of an aggressive occupation. Three of the four women's committees, which originated in the late 1970s and early 1980s,

> despite the political differences among them, as well as membership bases from different districts and social strata . . . have held to a similar social outlook and adopted the same pragmatic methods. They share the analysis that Palestinian women face triple oppression: as members of an oppressed nation, an oppressed class, and an oppressed gender. They also all provide a similar range of services for women of various age groups and various needs.
>
> (Rosenfeld 1993: 9)

As a result of the September 1993 agreement, two of the committees – the Union of Palestinian Working Women's Committees (UPWWC), which supports the PFLP, and the Federation of Palestinian Women's Action Committees (PFWAC), which is affiliated with the DFLP – decided to merge.

It should not surprise us that the majority of women do not participate in organised politics. This raises the question as to the likely impact of the women's movement on a future Palestinian state. A small number of women who describe themselves as Palestinian 'feminists' are of the opinion that, unless the 'women's agenda' is firmly maintained during the present period, any rights that women might have gained will not necessarily be sustained after independence. On 3 August 1994, the GUPW presented a declaration of women's rights to the Palestine National Authority (PNA). Basing itself on the Palestinian Declaration of Independence, the 1948 Universal Declaration of Human Rights and other international conventions, the document insists on the abolition of all discrimination against women and a commitment to equality between men and women in the future state.[10]

In conclusion, it would be fair to say that, although women are not substantially involved in either formal production or formal organisation, their informal activities have increased significantly since the beginning of the Intifada. As a result of the fact that many Palestinian men are either in Israeli prisons or, before the Gulf War at any rate, working in the oil-producing countries of the Arabian Gulf, women have had to assume responsibility for their families. Many also perform wage-earning tasks in their homes.

Women's involvement in the Palestinian national struggle, both at the grassroots level and in terms of formal political participation, has led to greater confidence among women. It is important, however, to distinguish between two current trends: empowerment through the secular political system and empowerment through Islam. Although it is popular for Western observers and secular Palestinians to argue that the effect of Islamic groups such as *Hamas* has, on the whole, been negative for women and that the success of these groups has thrown into question any notion of rights or progress, this analysis fails to take into account the genuinely enriching qualities of this type of participation for certain women. There is a heartfelt belief among a growing section of the population that 'Islam is the solution' to all the ills and tragedies that have befallen Palestinian society in the twentieth century, from Israeli occupation to the immorality of youth.[11]

On the other hand, it cannot be denied that the growth in popularity of Islamist groups has weakened the national movement, in which the women's committees have played a role. There is now some doubt as to the direction of a future Palestinian state and this, with its implied reduction of choice and room to manoeuvre, must serve as a source of anxiety to the majority of Palestinian women. At the same time, however, it may very well be true to assert that women have come a very long way since the 1920s and there is indeed no turning back.

NOTES

1 Facts on the ground include continuing Israeli settlement activities in the Occupied Territories, the expropriation of water and Israel's apparent reluctance to concede any more than the barest minimum of territory in return for peace and security.

2 In the words of the Palestinian Declaration of Independence, agreed by the Palestinian National Council (the Palestinians' parliament in exile) on 15 November 1988:

> The State of Palestine is the state of Palestinians wherever they may be. The state is for them to enjoy it in their collective national and cultural identity, theirs to pursue it in a complete equality of rights. In it will be safeguarded their political and religious convictions and their human dignity by means of a parliamentary democratic system of governance, itself based on freedom of expression and the freedom to form parties. ... Governance will be based on principles of social justice, equality and nondiscrimination in public rights on grounds of race, religion, color, or sex, under the aegis of a constitution which ensures the role of law and on independent judiciary. Thus shall these principles allow no departure from Palestine's age-old spiritual and civilizational heritage of tolerance and religious co-existence.
>
> (*Journal of Palestine Studies* 1989, 18(2): 215)

3 According to the Charter of the Islamic Resistance Movement (*Hamas*) of Palestine:

> The Muslim woman has a role in the battle for the liberation which is no less than the role of the man for she is the factory of men. Her role in directing generations and training them is a big role. The enemies have realized her role: they think that if they are able to direct and raise her the way they want, far from Islam then they have won the battle (Article 17).
>
> The women in the house of the Mujahid, (and the striving family), be she a mother or a sister, has the most important role in taking care of the home and raising children of ethical character and understanding that comes from Islam, and of training her children to perform the religious obligations to prepare them for the *Jihadic* role that awaits them. From this perspective it is necessary to take care of schools and the curricula that educate the Muslim girl to become a righteous mother aware of her role in the battle of liberation (Article 18).
>
> (*Journal of Palestine Studies* 1993, 22(4): 127–8)

4 The Palestine National Authority (PNA), established in the wake of May 1994 Cairo Agreement (the practical formalisation of the agreement between the PLO and the government of Israel about Palestinian 'self-rule' areas in the Gaza Strip and the West Bank town of Jericho) includes just one woman, Intisar Al-Wazir, Minister of Social Affairs, out of a total of nineteen (eventually to be increased to twenty-four).

5 In 1992, 90 per cent of women over the age of 60 in the Occupied Territories were illiterate (Anon. 1993: 7).

6 Personal interview with Palestinian lawyer Hanan Bakri of the Women's Centre for Legal Social Counselling, Ramallah, West Bank, May 1992. Also report in *Al-Quds* newspaper (Jerusalem), 12 December 1993.

7 The Palestinian and Israeli women agreed that (1) there must be a two-state solution; (2) the PLO is the representative of the Palestinian people; and (3) the peace process must be supported, from article 'Palestinian and Israeli women meet in Brussels', *Al-Fajr* newspaper (Jerusalem), 5 October 1992.

8 'Getting down to business', Palestine Refugees Today (UNWRA newsletter) 1993, 133 (January). Also, personal interview with Um Adib, May 1992.

9 Public Opinion Poll no. 4 on Palestinian Attitudes to PLO–Israeli Agreement, carried out by Jerusalem Media and Communication Centre (JMCC) in co-operation with CNN and MBC, *Palestine Report*, 13 January 1994.
10 'Principle of Women's Legal Status', declaration of women's rights submitted to PNA to be included in any state constitution. Text of document reproduced in *Palestine Report* (JMCC), 7 August 1994. Also reported in the *Jerusalem Times* ('Principles of Palestinian women's rights presented at Jerusalem conference'), 5 August 1994.
11 According to a public opinion poll carried out by the Survey and Polls Unit at the Center for Palestine Research and Studies in Nablus, in August 1994, 13.9 per cent of Palestinians (an average of West Bank and Gaza Strip responses) would vote for *Hamas* in a general election, 3 per cent for Islamic Jihad and 4.3 per cent for Islamic independents (*Jerusalem Times*, 2 September 1994). *Hamas* itself estimates its support at 40 per cent and a higher level of support is certainly indicated by the fact that *Hamas* won student council elections in Hebron and Jerusalem after the signing of the May 1994 Agreement. *Hamas* also won the majority of seats in Chamber of Commerce elections in Hebron and Ramallah in 1992.

REFERENCES

Al-Nelo, N. (1992) 'Palestinian Women More Productive than Many of their Counterparts', *Al-Fajr* 1 June.
Anon. (1993) 'Female Education in Palestine', *Education Network* 12 and 13 (June–September).
Antonius, S. (1979) 'Fighting on Two Fronts: Conversations with Palestinian Women', *Journal of Palestine Studies* 7(3).
Atwan, T. (pseudonym) (1993) 'Life is Struggle Inside and Outside the Green Line', in E. Augustin (ed.) *Palestinian Women: Identity and Experience*, London: Zed.
Giacaman, R. and Johnson, P. (1990) 'Palestinian Women: Building Barricades and Breaking Barriers', in L. Albrecht and R. M. Brewer (eds) *Bridges of Power: Women's Multicultural Alliances*, Philadelphia, PA: New Society.
Hammami, R. (1990) 'Women, the Hijab and the Intifada', *Middle East Report* 164–5: 24–31.
Hiltermann, R. J. (1990) 'The Women's Movement during the Uprising', *Journal of Palestine Studies* 20(3).
Idris, M. (1993) 'Of Walls and Women: Sahar Khalifeh's Babul Saha', *Democratic Palestine* 53.
Johnson, N. (1982) *Islam and the Politics of Meaning in Palestinian Nationalism*, London: Routledge & Kegan Paul.
Kamal, Z. (1992) 'The Federation of Palestinian Women's Action Committees', Paper given at UN Asian Seminar and NGO Symposium, Cyprus, January.
Lang, E. and Mohanna, I. (1992) *A Study of Women and Work in the Shatti' Refugee Camp of the Gaza Strip*, Jerusalem: Arab Thought Forum.
MacDonald, E. (1991) *Shoot the Women First*, London: Fourth Estate.
MacLeod, A. E. (1991) *Accommodating Protest: Working Women, the New Veiling and Change in Cairo*, New York: Columbia University Press.
Manasrah, N. (1992) 'Coping with the Loss of Palestine', in O. A. Najjar (ed.) *Portraits of Palestinian Women*, Salt Lake City, UT: University of Utah Press.
Peteet, J. M. (1991) *Gender in Crisis: Women and the Palestinian Resistance Movement*, New York: Columbia University Press.

Rosenfeld, M. (1993) 'Women of the Opposition Unite' (interview), *Challenge* 22 (November–December).

Strum, P. (1992) *The Women are Marching: The Second Sex and the Palestinian Revolution*, New York: Lawrence Hill.

Thornhill, T. (1992) *Making Women Talk: The Interrogation of Palestinian Women Detainees by the Israeli Security Services*, London: Lawyers for Palestinian Human Rights.

Tibi, B. (1991) *Islam and the Cultural Accommodation of Social Change*, trans. C. Krojzl, Boulder, CO: Westview (original publication in German 1985).

Warnock, K. (1990) *Land Before Honour: Palestinian Women in the Occupied Territories*, Basingstoke: Macmillan.

World University Service (1993) *Learning the Hard Way*, London: WUS.

FURTHER READING

Ebba Augustin (ed.) (1993) *Palestinian Women: Identity and Experience* is a collection of chapters mainly by Palestinian women. They include political activists, a trade unionist, an artist and an ex-prisoner. There are also two short stories by the woman who rose to fame as spokesperson for the Palestinian delegation to the Madrid peace talks, Hanan Ashrawi. Nels Johnson's (1982) *Islam and the Politics of Meaning in Palestinian Nationalism* is a fascinating anthropological account of the changing 'meanings' of Islam and the uses to which it has been put in the context of the Palestinian national struggle.

Erica Lang and Itimad Mohanna's (1992) *A Study of Women and Work in the Shatti' Refugee Camp of the Gaza Strip* is an interesting and scrupulously researched description of a single refugee camp, backed up by maps and tables. Small details of women's daily lives – and the comments that 'ordinary' women make about themselves – are often more revealing than panoramic generalisations.

Eileen MacDonald's (1991) *Shoot the Women First* is a book about 'terrorist' women, for which the author interviewed a wide range of females (German, Irish, Korean, Palestinian, etc.) who planned and carried out 'cold-blooded' acts of violence. Are these women freaks or simply prepared to sacrifice anything – even their own identities – for the larger national cause?

In Orayb Aref Najjar's (1992) *Portraits of Palestinian Women*, as the title implies, Palestinian women themselves describe aspects of their lives. The book takes the form of a series of interviews by the author with an extraordinarily wide range of women. It includes a few fascinating recollections of pre-1948 Palestine.

Julie Peteet's (1991) *Gender in Crisis: Women and the Palestinian Resistance Movement*, written by an American anthropologist, is mainly devoted to an examination of the activities of Palestinian women in the refugee camps of Lebanon. It covers the period 1968–82 and, although the language frequently assumes an air of social-science correctness, the author raises a number of important issues, such as the conflict between national liberation and women's rights and the acute tension between revolution and preservation. Peteet's Western feminist standpoint tends to support a particular notion of 'progress' at the expense of alternative models.

In Philippa Strum's (1992) *The Women are Marching: The Second Sex and the Palestinian Revolution*, a Jewish American writer tackles the issue of Palestinian women and their role in the Intifada from a political science perspective. Although she is clearly torn at times between her own identity and her obvious affection for the women she is studying, the author exposes some of the dilemmas and practical difficulties to which Palestinian women have been subjected as a result both of the Israeli occupation and their own traditions.

Teresa Thornhill's (1992) *Making Women Talk: the Interrogation of Palestinian Women Detainees by the Israeli Security Services*, although relatively short, is full of useful, concise and often shocking information about the frequently appalling experiences suffered by Palestinian women detainees, arrested for real or imagined crimes against the Israeli state. Despite the formidable body of international and human rights laws to protect Palestinians, prisoners have remarkably little recourse to the mechanisms of justice. Ill-treatment, the author maintains, is often used for purposes of control rather than punishment, and this is particularly true in the case of women.

Kitty Warnock's (1990) *Land Before Honour: Palestinian Women in the Occupied Territories* is a very accessible book that provides useful background information about Palestinian women and creates a framework (Arab, Islamic and tribal) in which to discuss their experiences in the twentieth century. It is also fascinating from the point of view of the personal anecdotes it includes; the author obviously developed a close and trusting relationship with her subjects.

World University Service (1993) *Learning the Hard Way* is a report of a study tour by a group of British educationalists to the Occupied Territories during the Intifada.

Index